The Rebirth of the Hero

The Rebirth of the Hero

Mythology as a Guide to Spiritual Transformation

KEIRON LE GRICE

Muswell Hill Press

First published by Muswell Hill Press, London, 2013

www.muswellhillpress.co.uk

British Library Cataloguing in Publication Data

A C.I.P. for this title is available from the British Library

ISBN-13: 9781908995056

Printed in Great Britain

To my son, Lukas Rafael Le Grice

Contents

PART I: The Context

Chapter 1: Joseph Campbell and the Place of Myth in Modern Culture 3

Chapter 2: Mythology: East and West................................**27**

Chapter 3: The Death of God and the *Übermensch* **51**

Table of Figures

And until you have experienced this: Die and become!
you are but a ghost-like visitor on the dark earth.
—Goethe,
"Selige Sehnsucht"

Preface

The process of psychospiritual transformation is among the deepest and most consequential of all human experiences. This book draws on a number of perspectives that I have found to be particularly helpful for illuminating and navigating this process, including the theories of C. G. Jung in depth psychology, the work of Joseph Campbell on the psychological significance of the myth of the hero's journey, the writings of German philosopher Friedrich Nietzsche, and the enigmatic logia in *The Gospel of Thomas*. In the personal reflections and testimonies of Jung and Nietzsche especially, I found accounts of psychological transformation that most closely parallel my own life experience. *The Rebirth of the Hero* is an attempt to situate the individual's personal journey of transformation within the larger narrative of the evolution of Western civilization, and to convey something of my understanding of this process in the hope that others might find it of value.

Much has been written in recent decades about the "evolution of consciousness" and the potential emergence of higher transpersonal or integral levels of conscious awareness and psychological functioning in our time. However, these accounts often fail to place adequate emphasis on the most crucial of processes for human psychospiritual development: the death of the old ego personality and the rebirth into a deeper, fuller mode of existence. The death-rebirth experience or "second birth," as it is also known, is fundamental to shamanism, the ancient mystery traditions of the Near East, the Christ myth with its symbolism of the crucifixion, the alchemical tradition, and hero myths the world over. These sources have informed modern depth psychology, especially the ideas of Jung and his followers, and the work of transpersonal psychologists such as Roberto Assagioli, John Weir Perry, Ralph Metzner, and Stanislav Grof, who have each helped to explain the relevance of mythic stories and religious symbolism for the death-rebirth experience and the process of psychological development that Jung called *individuation*. However, it was Joseph Campbell, more than anyone, who was responsible for bringing the value of myth as a guide to individuation and spiritual transformation to the attention of the wider culture. It is principally through the work of Jung and Campbell that I approach the topic in this book.

Campbell's *The Hero with a Thousand Faces*, published in 1949, remains his most influential work. This remarkable study of the archetypal pattern of the hero's adventure, illuminated with examples from world mythology and interpreted using the theories of Freud and Jung, resonated with a wide range of people on many levels, inspiring the storyteller, creative artist, and filmmaker as much as the mythologist, psychotherapist, and spiritual seeker. Selling over a million copies to date, *Hero*, as it is affectionately known, became something of a guidebook for psychological self-exploration in the 1960s. Campbell's ideas have since inspired a number of prominent film directors and authors, directly or indirectly influencing a range of mythically themed Hollywood movies—both in the retelling of classical myths and the creation of new ones, vividly portrayed through this most powerful of media.

Despite the popular appeal of Campbell's work, and audiences' passionate responses to mythic adventures portrayed in film, the individuation process—to which the hero myth refers—remains poorly understood. "We know nothing of man," Jung proclaimed in a television interview near the end of his life, bemoaning the alarming lack of knowledge in modern culture of the depths of the soul and the psyche.[1] Individuation—the process of transformation leading towards psychological wholeness and the realization of a greater identity—exposes us to the deepest mysteries of existence; it is a dark, uncertain, and extraordinarily difficult process, and for this reason it remains a rare occurrence. Yet, if news reports and mental health statistics are to be believed, the psychological experiences that might provide openings to the depths of the psyche and thus potentially initiate individuation—such as psychological breakdowns, existential crises, episodes of depression, spiritual awakenings, non-ordinary states of consciousness, psychotic states, and even schizophrenia—are increasingly widespread occurrences. Viewed in isolation these experiences are often perceived as wholly pathological, something to be prevented and medicated, rather than as potentially constructive phases within a larger process or journey of psychological transformation. One central aim of this book, therefore, is to provide a framework and context showing how, in some instances, these kinds of experiences might relate to individuation and map onto Campbell's model of the hero's journey, which, as we will see, is a mythic representation of the individuation process.

Using examples from modern films, classical myths, and the biographies of Nietzsche, Jung, and Campbell, the narrative set forth in the pages to follow takes the reader on a guided journey through the different phases of the hero's adventure, explaining how these phases relate to the spiritual life and to personal transformation. The analysis aims to make the significance of Jung's and Campbell's work accessible to readers who might be immersed in spiritual matters but perhaps do not readily see connections between their own experiences and themes conveyed in myths. It is also intended for individuals in the midst of periods of psychospiritual transformation who might be in critical need of guidance through this difficult and dangerous process. For the general reader, the book might provide insight into the deeper psychological dynamics informing the human imagination and portrayed in film and literature.

Like Campbell, I am primarily concerned not with the academic study of mythology for its own sake, but with helping people find orientation and meaning for their own life paths, both through individuation and through a deep engagement with the creative process. This emphasis is reflected in the style of this book. Part One introduces the theoretical framework, evolutionary perspective, and historical overview that are essential for understanding the transformative processes taking place in the human psyche. Part Two then explores the deeply personal, inner process of individuation. Given the nature of this material, I felt it appropriate, on occasion, to address the reader directly, in the second person, interweaving theoretical perspectives with examples and descriptions of how different phases of spiritual transformation are actually experienced.

I believe a clear, accessible understanding of individuation (and its connection with what Campbell calls the era of *creative mythology*) is becoming increasingly important as more and more individuals embark on their own spiritual paths. As Campbell emphasized, the renewal of our civilization depends on the spiritual renewal and the creative vitality of individuals. I hope the ideas in this book might serve these ends.

PART I

The Context

CHAPTER 1

Joseph Campbell and the Place of Myth in Modern Culture

Mythology is the womb of mankind's initiation to life and death.
— Joseph Campbell

We are living in a period of immense cultural and spiritual transition, a period in which the traditional religions and the dominant world views are in a state of decline and dissolution. Many of us recognize in our inner experience, as much as outside in the ecological crisis and the economic and political turmoil all around us, that we are approaching the end of the current form of Western civilization, and that we are experiencing the birth pangs accompanying the critical emergence of something new—new modes of consciousness, new ways of living and relating, new attitudes to the Earth and to nature, and perhaps even an altered understanding of the nature of the divine. What is to be our new world view or myth to replace the old? Where are we to turn today for spiritual and psychological guidance? How might we access the inner depths of spirit to creatively rejuvenate ourselves and give shape to our emerging global civilization?

Joseph Campbell's work provides one source of direction and guidance for our time. Campbell was one of the foremost authorities on mythology and without question its most successful advocate. Erudite and charismatic, with a wide breadth of knowledge of world mythology, religion, depth psychology, philosophy, and the arts, he was a great storyteller, able to communicate complex ideas and a wide range of mythological stories from different cultures in a way that drew out the relevance of myth for the modern individual's life. His work has been especially influential on those individuals seeking to find a deeper source of life meaning and spiritual orientation in the modern world.

The year of Campbell's birth, 1904, fell in the middle of a period of far-reaching transformation in Western civilization.[1] On many fronts, developments were taking place in the first decades of the twentieth century that were to have an immense impact on the modern sensibility and our understanding of the universe. Relativity theory and quantum mechanics in physics were utterly transforming our understanding of the nature of matter, space, time, and causality. Depth psychology was emerging, with Freud and Jung shining a light on the hidden recesses of the human psyche. The art world was changing dramatically with the emergence of modern art, influenced by figures such as Cezanne, Matisse, and Picasso. Of the many technological developments of this period, the invention of planes was among the most significant, with flights more rapidly connecting diverse and distant cultures. As we will see, Campbell's work is effectively a bridge between a number of these developments and the situation we are now in—connecting the ideas of Schopenhauer and Nietzsche, Freud and Jung, Joyce and Mann to the spiritual and psychological problems of modern life. His work also bridges European high culture and the American spiritual counterculture, Eastern and Western religion, and premodern mythologies and modern science. Campbell's teachings are a response to the problems, challenges, and opportunities of our age. The primary source of his teaching is the treasure-house of wisdom contained in world mythology.

In this chapter, we will look at Campbell's understanding of myth and its place in the rise of a new mythic sensibility and spiritual awareness in modern culture over the last few decades. What is the value of myth for the modern world view? How does Campbell's understanding of myth relate to depth psychology, religion, and Romanticism? How might Campbell's approach to myth help us on our individual life paths?

To begin, let us attempt to get a general sense of just what mythology is by exploring the accepted approaches to myth, the different theories to account for it, and its main functions. We can then look specifically at Campbell, to try to understand his views within this larger field.

Approaching Myths

The word *myth* refers to the stories and sets of symbolic images that have informed human lives across the ages, shaping tribal societies, local cultures, and the world's great civilizations alike.[2] Myths are stories that provide perspective and meaning to help individuals and cultures orient themselves to the requirements of living. They serve as a record of humanity's spiritual heritage, and they have inspired all the great religions and cultural world views.

Today, of course, this understanding of the word *myth* is secondary to its more common usage, in which it signifies a mere falsehood or superstitious belief. The term is used dismissively. Myths are now seen as illusions and deceptions to be exposed, debunked, and rejected. Even if myths were believed to be true at one time, we commonly assume—or are led to believe—that we now know better, that science has shown us otherwise. Myths are now seen as primitive, naïve ways of understanding the world that have been superseded by scientific explanations and rational philosophies.

In contrast to this view, Campbell saw myths in exalted, even grandiose, terms as symbolic narratives that communicate deep spiritual truths about human experience and the nature of the universe. For Campbell, myths are the living forces of society, providing guiding images and symbols "by which the energies of aspiration are evoked and gathered towards a focus."[3] His dramatic opening to *The Hero with a Thousand Faces* sets the tone for his study:

> Throughout the inhabited world, in all times and under every circumstance, the myths of man have flourished; and they have been the living inspiration of whatever else may have appeared out of the activities of the human body and mind. It would not be too much to say that myth is the secret opening through which the inexhaustible energies of the cosmos pour into human cultural manifestation. Religions, philosophies, arts, the social forms of primitive and historic man, prime discoveries in science and technology, the very dreams that blister sleep, boil up from the basic, magic ring of myth.
>
> The wonder is that the characteristic efficacy to touch and inspire deep creative centers dwells in the smallest nursery fairy tale—as the flavor of the ocean is contained in a droplet or

the whole mystery of life in the egg of a flea. For the symbols of mythology are not manufactured; they cannot be ordered, invented, or permanently suppressed. They are spontaneous productions of the psyche, and each bears within it, undamaged, the germ power of its source.[4]

How, then, are we to account for two such starkly contrasting perspectives as to the value and significance of myth?

Definitions of Myth

One answer lies in the definition of myth, in how we understand its meaning. Myth can be defined differently depending on whether one is concerned with its origin, purpose, or content. Generally speaking, myths can be distinguished from both legends and fairytales. A legend is usually about a real historical person, or a person that probably existed—such as the British legends of Robin Hood and King Arthur—in which the story is embellished as it is transmitted over time. In myth the characters are often both human beings and supernatural powers, such as gods and goddesses. Legends are typically set in the remote past, whereas myths seem to point to dimensions of reality outside of history, suggested by intentionally vague references to "once upon a time" or "in a galaxy far, far away," to give two well-known examples.[5] The setting of the mythic story is generally unknown, in no specific geographic location, at no specific historical moment. Understood in terms of its psychological import, myth, as we will see, refers to the timeless realm of the deep psyche—to what Jung called the *collective unconscious.*

A myth is also distinguished from a fairytale, which is usually told primarily for entertainment, whereas myths purport to be true in some fundamental sense; properly understood, they have a spiritual and cosmological or existential significance. A myth is *a sacred narrative*; it is a story with spiritual import that puts us in touch with the numinous—the "awesome mystery . . . within and beyond all things."[6] These sacred narratives can later take on the form of settled doctrines if they become established religions.

For Campbell, however, the distinctions between myths, legends, and fairytales, and between myths and religions, are less significant than their common basis. All of these, he thought, express the same basic *archetypes* or fundamental patterns in the mind and therefore convey psychological truths, telling us something important about the human psyche, and about the universal nature of human experience. The tale of *Beauty and the Beast*, for example, has an instructive value even if told for entertainment, exploring perennial themes of human life, such as the transforming power of love. Although certain myths or works of spiritual literature obviously penetrate further into the deeper dimensions of existence than fairytales, both myths and fairytales typically express the same core motifs.

A further distinction can be made between modern myths (exemplified by *Star Wars* and *The Lord of the Rings*, which we will later consider) and ancient myths. In the past, myths were seen as being true—perhaps not literally true in terms of recorded history and facts about the world, but conveying spiritual truth, a deep truth about the nature of existence. Modern myths, such as that told in George Lucas's *Star Wars*, are not seen as being true in any sense; however inspired we might feel by entering into the mythic world of film at the cinema, on leaving the theater we return to the "real world," leaving the mythic adventure behind. We smile at people who choose to give their official religion as "Jedi" on census surveys, but obviously few people would actually draw on the significance of a mythic film and carry that through to a world view or life philosophy. We live with a sharp division between the mythic world of the imagination and the real world of practical concerns.

Campbell's work helps us to understand how to interpret both ancient and modern forms of myth, and to take from them their spiritual, instructive value. This task has taken on particular urgency and importance today, in modern secular, consumerist society. If one visits the Metropolitan Museum in New York, or the Louvre in Paris, or the British Museum in London, it is immediately apparent that the art forms of the great cultures of the past served as vehicles for the revelation of spirit. Whether of China, Japan, India, Egypt, Greece, Rome, or elsewhere, the creative energy of these cultures was explicitly informed by the guiding myth or religion reflecting an encompassing spiritual vision. This situation contrasts starkly with our own era, in which spirituality is not at the core of the modern world view, the modern lifestyle; indeed, within the Western medical model spiritual experiences are often viewed as pathological abnormalities rather than numinous revelations. The rapid emergence of modern industrial civilization over the last three centuries has brought forth innumerable improvements to living conditions, furnishing us with a freedom of opportunity and access to technology undreamed of by earlier generations. But during that process, we seem to have experienced a diminishment in the depth of meaning of human experience—a consequence, to a large extent, of not having a coherent collective myth to inform our understanding of how our lives are related to the culture, the world, the cosmos, and to God (or whatever name we give to the spiritual dimension of reality).

We find ourselves living in the midst of a period of spiritual transformation in which, as Campbell stressed, the local cultures and enclosed mythologies pertaining to specific geographical regions have effectively dissolved as we have entered the global, planetary era. In response, we now need a global myth or narrative to provide life orientation. This has never happened before. Powerful religions have spread across the globe—Hinduism, Buddhism, Judaism, Christianity, Islam—but we are now searching for a new means of finding orientation in the cosmos, a myth or world view that draws upon but perhaps goes beyond these particular religions, a myth suited to the unique challenges of our time, one that complements and coheres with our scientific understanding and yet leads us beyond that too.

One purpose myth serves in human life, then, is to provide meaning. Such meaning, however, is deeper and more encompassing than merely intellectual understanding. It is, rather, a *living meaning*, relevant to the heart and to the spirit, as much as to the mind—to be conveyed through painting, dance, music, poetry, and literature, and not just through rational discourse and theories. As a culture, we are lacking a collective myth that can put us in touch with this deeper level of meaning, and we see the consequences reflected in all manner of social and psychological ills. "Meaninglessness," Jung wrote in his autobiography, "inhibits the fullness of life and is therefore equivalent to illness."[7] If you are not living a fully meaningful life, such that you feel vitally connected to the numinous wellsprings of the psyche, then in all likelihood you are not living out of your full power. In such a scenario, you could become psychologically or even physically sick, as the life power that you might be experiencing and expressing as a positive force instead finds expression unconsciously, or, if suppressed, manifests in destructive form. For this reason, it is important, perhaps even imperative, to have a guiding myth or life philosophy that helps you to draw upon and express everything you are, such that you can pour your full being into your life, affirming joy and suffering alike. To cultivate such an affirmative response to life is what Joseph Campbell's teaching helps people to do. As we will see, this affirmative, "yea-saying" attitude is also a central aim and requirement of the individuation process.

Theorists of myth are often more interested in the differences between myths than in their common themes. Many anthropologists, for example, want to understand any given myth within the culture, society, and environment in which it originated, and are less concerned with the possible universal wisdom the myth conveys. This approach, emphasizing the socio-cultural relevance and function of myth, is very much in vogue in our time, when, in the spirit of post-modernism, differences and plurality are championed at the expense of universal views and metaphysical frameworks. We live in a time of immense specialization, when the fields of human knowledge have been fragmented to an extraordinary degree, but what we lack is a perspective to draw together these specializations, to provide a unifying framework. Campbell took a "big picture" view of the field of mythology, trying to see comparative themes, common patterns, within different myths—comparing an Arthurian legend, perhaps, with the Buddha's journey of enlightenment or the life of Jesus with the adventures of Odysseus. Campbell was looking primarily for commonalities rather than differences, in so doing going against the grain of the dominant focus within academia.

Christianity and Science

Why, then, has the modern culture such a negative view of myth? Why are myths seen to be false? Partly, this negative view has to do with the rise of Christianity in the West, and its establishment as the official religion of the Roman Empire. The Greco-Roman myths were superseded by Christianity, which then became the dominant spiritual-religious perspective. The Judeo-Christian God was proclaimed as the one true god. The Greek and Roman gods and goddesses were forgotten. To recognize a mythic pantheon of many gods was seen as blasphemous, as decreed in the commandment inscribed in stone on Sinai: "Thou shalt have no other gods before me" (Exodus 20:3). And so it was that Judeo-Christian monotheism (the belief in one god) replaced the polytheism (the belief in many gods) of the nature religions and the Greco-Roman myths.

The ascendancy of Christianity is one factor in the process by which myths were rejected and forgotten, but more important, I would say, was the rise of the Enlightenment world view shaped by Cartesian dualism and the philosophy of mechanistic materialism, which reached its peak in nineteenth-century science. René Descartes, the seventeenth-century French philosopher, established a fundamental distinction between inner and outer, subject and object, mind and matter. The inner world is the world of thought, feeling, the subjective realm; the outer world is that which is extended in space and can be measured, and its workings understood in terms of the mechanistic interaction of forces—like a billiard ball chain of causation with each event triggered by a sequence of prior causes. Isaac Newton's mathematical model, including the three laws of motion and the theory of gravity, helped support Descartes's claim that the world could be explained in mechanistic terms. The Cartesian distinction enabled religion and science to coexist. An implicit compromise was achieved: the arts, religion, and myths, it was supposed, pertain to the inner world of subjective experience; science, cosmology, and history pertain to the outer world of objective experience and hard facts. Accordingly, religion and science each govern their own domains of relevance and influence, and need not therefore come into outright conflict—although this rather artificial division is increasingly challenged as science continues to gain in power.

Consequently, whereas an ancient creation myth might once have been seen as actually referring to the process of the creation of the universe, today it would be viewed as nothing but a story, a fantastic but false account of how the universe came into being. Although a good many people in the world still believe that God created the world in seven days and that the first human beings lived in the Garden of Eden, this view is obviously contested by science. If you accept science, you cannot, without outright contradiction, believe that the world was created by the actions and interventions of God or supernatural forces. Today, viewed through the scientific mindset of the modern era, no one would seriously believe that the Greek

creation myth describing the birth of the goddess Gaia from the primal Chaos is actually to do with cosmology. The same goes for the
biblical creation story in Genesis. These are obvious statements, but
it is important to point out that this incredulity towards mythic explanations is one of the reasons that the status of myth was relegated to
pertaining only to the inner world, or even rejected entirely. Science
demonstrated that myths are not literally, historically true—a fact
that impressed itself on Campbell as he sought to convey the deeper
meaning contained within them.

The Enlightenment and Romantic Views of Myth

The Enlightenment theory of myth, which is reflected in the work of
figures such as E. B. Tyler and James G. Frazer, author of the classic
The Golden Bough, sees myths as primitive forms of explanation. The
idea that Zeus or Thor or Yahweh might cause a thunderstorm as an
expression of anger or wrath would, in the view of these theorists, be
seen as a reflection of the pre-scientific mind trying to find an explanation for a particular phenomenon that was inexplicable in terms of
the knowledge at the time. Science, it is now supposed, renders such
fanciful accounts unnecessary; we now know that a thunderstorm
has nothing to do with the moods of a god, for it is to be explained
solely in terms of meteorological conditions. Myths are thus seen as
stories told by the less advanced people to account for something
they did not understand. This is the standard Enlightenment view of
myth, which became dominant in the late nineteenth century, at the
height of the mechanistic materialistic world view, and remains so
today.[8] The prevailing understanding of myth at the time was also
characterized by a European colonialism that viewed myths of non-
Western and premodern cultures as essentially inferior to modern
scientific understanding.

The Enlightenment tradition informed the work of Sigmund Freud
in the early decades of the twentieth century. Freud not only saw
myths as fallacies, however, but also as inherently pathological.
Myth and religion, for Freud, are infantile delusions, the dynamics
of parental psychology projected onto metaphysics. The religious
belief in God is the comforting delusion of the neurotic mind that
cannot accept reality as it really is—a situation that is akin, he

thought, to the childhood state in which the child needs to know there is a protective, loving father or mother watching over him or her. When one reaches psychological maturity, Freud believed, one should no longer need that kind of illusory prop.

Freud also provides an explanation of the origin of myth in terms of the psychology of the unconscious. Myths and religions appear to pertain to the cosmos, the outer world, but they only actually pertain, said Freud, to the inner world. What was happening in our inner, psychological world was projected out onto the external world—a projected psychology that became mythology and religion. If we understand the dynamics of the unconscious psyche, he proposed, we will see this process of projection at work; we will realize that mythology arises from psychology and is not to do with metaphysics or cosmology.

Despite this rather reductive explanation, Freud is also a key figure in the *Romantic* understanding of myth. He does not just claim that myth is nonsense, for it is rooted in a psychological reality. For Freud, although myth is not actually true in terms of its apparent, surface meaning, its hidden or latent meaning expresses a truth about the psyche. Myth is not merely primitive thinking; it comes from a deeper, unconscious source. This position marks an exceptionally important turn in the modern understanding of just what myth is, and how it originates.

The Enlightenment tradition holds that the "light of reason" can eradicate all primitive, childish, delusory, superstitious, magical explanations of the world, illuminating "the truth" in the light of day. The Enlightenment champions reason and science as the powers that can deliver humans to freedom from ignorance, even if this quest is itself sometimes fueled by an almost religious zeal. Romanticism, by contrast, is concerned with the irrational interior world of the human psyche, feelings and instincts, the imagination and poetry and art, nature and her hidden depths, and with mystery and that which transcends reason. The Romantic tradition goes back to poets such as Blake, Wordsworth, and Shelley in Britain and Hölderlin in Germany, as well as German idealist and Romantic philosophers Goethe, Schelling, Schopenhauer, and Nietzsche. This tradition continues with the depth psychology of Freud and Jung. Campbell's interpretation of myth, informed by depth psychology, also falls into this Romantic lineage.

A Romantic perspective on myth is concerned with trying to understand its deeper spiritual import. Romantics do not claim that myth is necessarily true in respect of its accounts of history or the creation of the world and so forth, but they do not claim either that myth is totally false. Romantics are actually proposing that myth can reveal something that reason and science cannot. Myth can help illuminate the irrational givens of existence and the spiritual dimension of human experience in a way that rationality cannot. Indeed, in some respects cultivating a mythic view of life can be seen as an advance on a purely rational view. "In the life of the human race," as Thomas Mann observed, "the mythical is an early and primitive stage, in the life of the individual it is a late and mature one."[9]

Mann gives an original and illuminating twist on the standard, accepted view that myth is a primitive stage of human development for both a culture and an individual. A number of evolution of consciousness theorists view mythic consciousness as developmentally prior to the emergence of rational consciousness, which is itself superseded by integral or spiritual modes of consciousness. Mann's insight suggests, however, that in individual experience mythic consciousness might actually be transrational. The mythic level of existence is not something that is outgrown once you develop conceptual thinking and rationality. For those few individuals who really comprehend myth at its deepest, most significant level of meaning, myth is transpersonal; it lies beyond rationality; it is higher, comes later in the developmental scheme, and has the potential to illuminate existence in a deeper, more profound way than reason can.

For the Romantic, myth is the revelation of mystery, and its meaning is not, therefore, readily apparent as it might be, say, in an academic paper, where one sentence leads logically to another, words are used clearly, concisely, and the meaning is plain. In the stories of myth, as in poetry, words are used to point beyond themselves to the ineffable mystery of experience, for the deeper mysteries of the soul, of the spiritual life, cannot be adequately conveyed through words. The myth is intended to put you in a state of mind in which you are receptive to the revelation of these mysteries. Myth, Campbell liked to say, is the penultimate truth, pointing beyond conceptualization to the ultimate mystery of existence.

The Enlightenment view of myth, which is reflected in the dominant modern scientific and rational world view, effects what is called a *total demythologization*, such that the world is stripped of all mythic elements; all myths are rejected outright as obsolete and as untruths.[10] The Romantic view engenders a *partial* or *interpretive demythologization* for although myth is no longer viewed as pertaining to the world, it is not dismissed as nonsense, but is interpreted in terms of its symbolic, metaphorical meaning for human experience; it is read in terms of its latent, rather than its manifest meaning. In so doing, myth is retrieved from the scrapheap; the value and meaning of myth for modern life is recovered.

Romanticism and Depth Psychology

The Romantic interpretation of myth was further developed in the field of depth psychology in the early twentieth century, which brought the Enlightenment emphasis on scientific empiricism and rational inquiry to bear on the inner depths of human experience. In so doing, depth psychology brought together major elements of the Romantic and Enlightenment traditions—confirming, on the one hand, insights into the unconscious basis of human motivations identified by the philosophies of Schopenhauer and Nietzsche, and, on the other, applying to human psychology the rationalism and causal determinism that informed natural science and medicine.

A key figure whose ideas prefigured the depth psychological interpretation of myth is Adolf Bastian, writing in the late nineteenth century. He put forward a theory of "elementary ideas," suggesting that the same core themes and motifs manifest in diverse myths from different parts of the world and different periods of history because they all express universal formative ideas that are intrinsic to the human mind. This concept was influential on C. G. Jung as he developed his theory of archetypes, a theory that is especially important for the perspective we are considering here.

Usually, if a myth in one culture is similar to a myth in another culture the similarity is explained in terms of a process of *diffusion*, based, that is, on the idea that the myth is geographically transmitted from one place to another, passed on through trade links or through the migration of people to different regions. Diffusion is the generally accepted explanation of how the myths of disparate cultures have common elements. Bastian's ideas of elementary ideas and

Jung's theory of archetypes and the collective unconscious, however, suggest another possibility: namely, that common elements and themes in myth might arise out of human psychology. In this view, myths are similar across cultures not necessarily because they have been geographically transmitted, but because they express a universally shared deep structure in the human psyche.

From this perspective, myths address common themes and have common structural forms because the human mind has a universal psychological structure—a *collective unconscious*, to use Jung's term. In any part of the world, and in any culture or period of history, the human imagination works in a certain consistent way to shape myths; it is informed by the same core principles or universal archetypal images in the psyche, such as the hero, the wise old man, the great mother, the child, the trickster, and the process of rebirth.

In many myths, for example, one finds the idea that the god or the hero dies and is resurrected, reborn into a different form. This theme is evident in myths of Osiris, Attis, Adonis, Persephone, Dionysus, Mithras, Christ, and more. It is intrinsic to shamanic mythology, too, in which the shaman, afflicted by a mysterious spiritual illness, embarks on an initiatory descent into underworld of the spirits (typically involving an encounter with death), and returns to the daylight world, transformed and transfigured as a result of the experience, able then to serve as guide and healer for the community. From a Jungian perspective, all these myths might be seen to stem from an archetypal image, that of rebirth—an archetypal experience that is evident in the natural world too. Indeed, James G. Frazer demonstrated that myths of dying and rising gods and heroes, such as those listed above, were variations on the agricultural myth of the corn spirit, which tells of the death of the corn spirit at the harvest and its resurrection the next spring with the sprouting forth of new life.

The archetypal process of change and transformation is inherent in life. Always we are dying to what we were, becoming something else, something more. We cannot escape this, however much we might like to. The human ego is the part of us that erects a wall to stop or halt this process, to attempt to keep things a certain way, to remain in control, to ensure it gets the life we believe we want. But, irrespective of our wishes, the greater being of which the ego is but a part is always participating in this process of transformation that entails a continual dying to the old life.

So too the motif of the journey is archetypal: The story of a hero who leaves behind his or her old life and goes on an adventure is almost ubiquitous, common to many myths the world over. Campbell would see parallels, for example, between the journey of the Buddha—encountering suffering, old age, and death in the world, then embarking on a quest for enlightenment before returning to proclaim the Four Noble Truths and the Eightfold Path to spiritual liberation—and Odysseus's long sea journey in which he overcame the Cyclops, encountered the goddesses Calypso and Circe, and passed through a sequence of transformative experiences before finally completing the cycle by returning home to his wife, Penelope. Although the specific content of these stories obviously differs markedly, they both express core motifs of transformation, realization, tests and trials, and of a journey—with a departure, an adventure consisting of a series of initiatory experiences, and then some form of return. While many theorists of myth are more concerned with differences, Campbell was a universalist in that he believed myth speaks from and to the depths of human nature and the depths of spirit, dealing with the universal themes and constants in human experience. However diverse their content and place of origin, myths express the same core archetypal motifs. Myths are not just applicable to the cultures that created them.

Jung discovered that archetypal themes are especially apparent in certain types of "big dreams," as he called them, those dreams possessing an uncanny numinous quality and populated with mythic figures and symbols, rather than images drawn solely from the familiar scenes of personal experience. Such dreams give insights into the activity of the archetypes and the collective unconscious, counterbalancing the individual's inevitably one-sided viewpoint and conscious attitude. Numinous dreams provide, as it were, a universal perspective on an individual life within a particular historical, cultural, and personal context, revealing the activity of the archetypes as creative ordering factors in the background of experience.

From a depth psychological perspective, interpreting myth follows similar principles to interpreting a dream. As Campbell stressed, the dream might be construed as an expression of the individual's own myth, just as the myth might be imagined as a shared dream of the culture. Unlike a dream, however, the content of a myth has been *amplified*, which is Jung's term for the process of consciously working with dream images to expand on them and to better understand their meaning by finding connections and associations in the world's mythic and religious traditions to themes presented within the dream. Because they have been amplified over the centuries, the symbols within a myth are generally more developed, more cultivated than those of dream. The spontaneous but often chaotic or confused production of symbolic images in the dream becomes part of a more coherent narrative and symbol system in myth. Myths are "spontaneous productions of the psyche," coming to consciousness through particular exceptional individuals, such as shamans and visionaries, who then give the myth form and communicate it on behalf of the entire culture.[11]

In Campbell's view, in the absence of a living collective mythology, we today might each perform this role for ourselves, and perhaps, in the process, bring forth insights of value to the wider culture. We might discover within ourselves our own myths, pieced together from dreams, fantasies, synchronicities, and our deepest intuitions about what life is about, yet guided by the wisdom of ancient myths, read and interpreted for their psychological significance and spiritual meaning. This endeavor, he believed, offers one way to counteract the collective loss of meaning we have experienced in the West.

The exploration of the content of dreams and fantasies in Jungian depth psychology demonstrates that myths, and the human capacity for mythmaking, are still very much active in the psyches of modern individuals, shaping our experiences whether or not we are aware of it. This idea, again, is in close agreement with the Romantic interpretation of myth, which, in contrast to the Enlightenment perspective, sees myth as something that is still being created, not as something pertaining only to the past. As Henry A. Murray observes, "no definitions of primitive and classic myths make room for any kinds of novel emanations from contemporary minds."[12] He points out that it was left to Romantics such as D. H. Lawrence and W. B. Yeats to reclaim the word *myth* for the contemporary artist. Campbell assimilated this perspective as his own, arguing to great effect that myth is something still evolving, that it remains a living, vital form of expression. Myth is not only to do with some historical past, either real or imagined, but is actively shaping our life experiences in the depths of each individual's psyche.

The Functions of Myth

From Campbell's study of world mythology, he identified four main functions of myth. The first is the *metaphysical* or *mystical* function, which, he proposes, should serve "to reconcile the waking consciousness to the *mysterium tremendum et fascinans* of this universe as it is."[13] In fulfilling this function, myth should put individuals or the cultural group as a whole into a mode of realization where they can experience the ultimate source or spiritual ground from whence they came. This function might refer to a Christian mystic's direct experience of God, for example, in which the divine is realized as the absolute creative source of the world or as the ultimate transcendent power outside of creation—an experience that supports a metaphysical understanding of the universe and informs human life within it. Or it might refer to a Buddhist experiencing *sunyata*, the clear light of the Void, or to a Hindu's experience of *Brahman*, the ultimate ground of reality. This function of myth describes a core realization; it relates to what Rudolf Otto called the experience of the numinous—the tremendous and fascinating spiritual power of the mystery of the divine. The mystical experience breaks through all concepts to the direct realization of the nature of things, to the divine source underlying all of existence.

This mystical function of myth has also been recognized by other theorists. The French anthropologist Levi-Bruhl, for example, proposed that the purpose of myth was to help civilized human beings reconnect to a quasi-mystical state of being—a *participation mystique* with nature. For Campbell, however, such mystical experience is also a revelation of an actual metaphysical reality. Myth is the penultimate truth surpassed only by direct spiritual experience. Myth can put you into a mindset where you can be more open to spiritual realization. It can take you to the edge of the mystery.

This metaphysical-mystical realization supports the second function of myth, the *cosmological function*, which is that of "formulating and rendering an image of the universe, a cosmological image in keeping with the science of our time."[14] If the mystical function relates to a spiritual realization of the numinous ground of existence, the cosmological function portrays the spiritual ground as manifest throughout the cosmos, in all forms; this function of myth enables us to see the world and everything in it as "as parts of a single great holy picture" in which everything expresses divinity, from the most prosaic thing to the most sublime.[15] In this holy picture, we might, as William Blake put it, "see the universe in a grain of sand."[16] Collectively, we have totally lost the awareness that everything expresses divinity, that there is a divine radiance shining through all things. An individual might have a mystical experience of his or her own, of course, but often this is interpreted in entirely inner terms, as something unconnected to the outer world.

The cosmological function is also concerned with helping to orient individuals as to where they are in relation to the cosmos, to help them understand their place in the scheme of things. Jung recounts an episode from his travels in America when he encountered the Pueblo Indians, who believed that their role in the universe was, every day, to help the sun move across the sky. Imagine knowing this to be your life purpose! There can be no question then of doubting your life meaning. Obviously, today we have nothing like this. In our time the meaning of life has become more of an individual matter and in no way connected to a cosmological event of this kind. We have to find our own meanings, and this is both a great challenge and a great opportunity, as we will see in later chapters.

In Campbell's definition, the cosmological function has to reflect the science of the time. Modern science is obviously very developed and advanced but, fundamentally, it is materialistic; it only recognizes the existence of matter. We do not have a science that is open to different dimensions of experience, by and large, so the spiritual dimension and deeper levels of interiority are excluded. Indeed, mind is often conceived as a mere epiphenomenon of the brain, a spurious derivative of firing neurons.

Campbell suggests that myth in its cosmological function should bring forth the "revelation to waking consciousness of the powers of its own sustaining source."[17] Whereas the mystical function of myth is to point consciousness to the experience of a unitary spiritual ground, the cosmological function portrays this ground as manifest through a number of distinct powers of the universe. In many mythologies, such as Olympian pantheon of ancient Greece or the rich assemblage of figures in the Hindu tradition, the different powers are represented by deities, whether as gods and goddesses with quasi-human personalities or as animal figures or elemental forces. The unitary ground becomes manifest as a multiplicity of deities, which are associated with different aspects of the cosmos, different faces and features of the divine—the masks of God, to use Campbell's term.[18]

A third function identified by Campbell is *sociological*. This aspect of myth is to do with the "enforcement of a moral order" and "shaping the individual to the requirements of his geographically and historically conditioned social group."[19] In other words, the laws of a society, in a functioning myth, appear to have a deeper spiritual basis such that the members of a society do not challenge and question the laws and rules of conduct. The Pueblo Indian doesn't ask, "why should I be concerned with helping the sun move across the sky each day?" The law, the directive, comes from the divine, from spirit, and has cosmological significance, so it is not questioned. To question the sustaining myth of a culture is a hallmark of the modern era. The emergence of the individual, possessed of the power of reason and freedom of will, has contributed to and facilitated the challenging and rational scrutiny of the dominant myth of modern Western culture, which is Christianity. In a functioning living myth, the cosmological and the sociological flow out of the metaphysical-mystical insight and are sustained by it.

Some theorists place primary emphasis on the sociological aspect of myth, to the virtual exclusion of all else. Branislav Malinowski, for example, saw myths not as factually true, but as instruments to establish and sanctify the laws and rules of a society. Myths, he believed, support the culture by justifying social rules through the appeal to a greater mythic authority. Myths can help sanction certain ways of living in a society that are essential to the society's vital functioning.

In Campbell's view, society should function as a kind of second womb, effecting a person's transition from the natural, instinctive state of being to that of a civilized functioning member of the community.[20] In the higher stages of psychological development, however, the womb of society is itself to be left behind. Individuation, or the process of psychospiritual development leading to a "second birth," necessitates an emergence from the womb of culture as surely as biological birth brings a severance from the mother's womb. Because they represent archetypal processes that manifest at different levels, myths can serve as guides for both these transitions. Our primary concern here, however, is on the process of death-rebirth that leads the individual beyond the culture to his or her own "original experience" and a direct encounter with depths of the psyche.

Finally, the fourth function of mythology identified by Campbell is *psychological* or, as he sometimes called it, *pedagogical*, serving to instruct and educate on the reality of the psyche and the mysteries of life. The psychological function of myth was normally transmitted or exercised through rites of passage designed to effect a transition from one life stage to another, which was especially important to aid the passage from adolescence to adult maturity, to help the individual leave behind the childhood world and become a fully participating member of the tribe or social group. These rites often involved a high degree of suffering, which to us can seem brutal and horrific. The suffering involved is almost a prerequisite, however, for the rite has to be a defining, intense event to mark the transition to a new life phase; it has to effect an emotional maturation. Again, this kind of rite is obviously something we do not have today. The modern substitutes for rites of passage are often pleasurable or even hedonistic experiences that do not really effect a psychological transition of any lasting significance—think of a bachelor or bachelorette party, for instance, or a graduation celebration. Campbell was particularly concerned that, with no or very few meaningful rites of passage available to us, the individual can remain emotionally stuck at an early life stage. A life that is not structured by mythic rituals and religious dogma can be very liberating in some sense, part of the freedom of the modern world, but without a guiding mythic narrative the individual can also be thrown into confusion. As we will see, the challenge of dealing with these new circumstances lies at the heart of what Campbell calls *individual mythology*.

The psychological function of myth is "to initiate the individual into the order and realities of his own psyche guiding him to his own spiritual enrichment and realization."[21] Campbell therefore connects the psychological function of myth to spiritual realization. If you are passing through an initiatory experience of some kind, you will most likely enter altered states of consciousness in which you receive insights into the nature of reality that are not available to your normal waking consciousness. Mystical experience demands and initiates deep psychological transformation just as, conversely, a sustained process of psychological transformation can lead to enduring spiritual realization.

In Campbell's view, the gods and goddesses of myth are metaphors for powers at work in human experience. They do not exist as actual quasi-physical entities inhabiting Mount Olympus, of course, but the significance of this mythic vision of a pantheon of gods is still very much relevant, reflecting a reality that is alive within us. In this sense, a myth that recognizes the existence of gods is healthier and more accurate than a world view that utterly denies the existence of gods. If we do not recognize the gods, or the forces these gods represent, they move us unconsciously; we might then remain the victims or the puppets of unseen powers operating behind the scenes of conscious awareness. Without a living myth we are impoverished; we lack a certain deeper level of life meaning; we are unable to adequately relate to the powerful forces of the psyche. In this condition, we are inclined to assume that we are able to determine the course of our own lives solely through our own will pitted against chance and circumstance, which is the hubris of ego-consciousness. For, as depth psychology shows, the ego is not the controlling power of the psyche; it is not the "master of its own house," but exists alongside a number of other archetypes, centers, and powers. If our lives are informed by a myth populated by a pantheon of gods and goddesses, we have a means of recognizing the different principles in life and in the psyche that these gods represent. If, however, we conceive of the world in terms of a materialistic cosmology in which, as we are taught, everything has evolved by chance, the Earth is just a meaningless tiny speck in a vast impersonal cosmos, and the human mind is just an epiphenomenon of the brain, then in all likelihood we might well become closed off to deeper dimensions of experience, closed off to the enrichment potentially provided by a mythically informed world view that recognizes the reality of the spirit. This, of course, is precisely the situation in which we now find ourselves. Our age, for all its technological sophistication, has become for many people what Campbell describes as a spiritual "wasteland"—a theme to which we will later return.

Addressing the needs of the modern individual for spiritual and psychological orientation, Campbell's primary focus is on the psychological function of myth. Today, as never before, we are each on our own spiritually. Because our lives are not informed by a myth that recognizes the existence of different gods and goddesses, we have to come to terms with the powers of the psyche for ourselves; because we do not have effective rites of passage, we have to navigate major life transitions and transformations alone. Campbell's claim for mythology is therefore this: If we study the myths of different cultures, we can gather insights from these myths (if we learn how to read them psychologically) to find orientation for our own lives. Campbell believed that, because we are living in an increasingly secular, disenchanted world with no intrinsic spiritual-mythological orientation built into the culture, and as we need to get this orientation from somewhere, we could instead look to the core truths contained within myths—the *perennial mythology*, as he called it—and use these myths to guide us.

Because the circumstances of the modern world have changed so much, and so quickly, to many people the traditional religions no longer seem relevant; and because even the notion of objective scientific truth—the belief that science can provide an objectively valid description of reality—has been undermined by quantum indeterminacy and relativity, there seems to be nothing certain to hold onto in the modern world. Psychologically and existentially this presents an immense challenge: What and where is your center? What is your support? What is the spiritual, religious, and philosophical ground on which you stand? How do you find orientation for your life? The approach advocated by Campbell is to draw on the accumulated spiritual wisdom of the past, represented in myths, to guide us on our own life journeys, rather than reject myth as outmoded and irrelevant to modern life. In this way, the unique individual character of one's life journey can be brought into relationship with the timeless, archetypal wisdom of myth.

According to the perennial philosophy, so named by Aldous Huxley, the mystics within any given religion receive insights into a single spiritual truth, clothed in the language of different religious traditions. The Hindu mystic and the Christian mystic, in this view, experience the same divine ground, though called by different names and interpreted in different ways. From a perennialist perspective, all religions, in their esoteric forms, are concerned with the certain core truths, which remain the same forever, for everyone. Campbell advances the related idea of a perennial mythology: All myths are clothed in different forms, have different cultural inflections, are written in different languages, and so on, but ultimately they describe a single, unchanging eternal truth. The forms by which this truth is expressed change culture to culture, individual to individual, but the core patterns and motifs remain the same. Our challenge is to discern the perennial, archetypal, and universal aspects within any particular myth.

Religion, Spirituality, and Belief

For Campbell, religion is mythology that has become doctrine, such that the message of the myth has assumed a fixed and literal meaning. The Christ *myth* refers to the Virgin Birth, the Crucifixion, the Resurrection, the Ascension, and so on, which are core mythic motifs that have been woven around the few known details of the life of the historical person Jesus of Nazareth. When the life and teachings of Jesus were recounted in the Gospels (perhaps as much as one hundred years after his death), the Christ myth became dominant, reflecting the influence of the biblical mythmaker Paul. The details of Jesus's life were woven into a mythic form, that of the pattern of the dying and rising god. Later still, the Christ myth was concretized into religious doctrine by the Church. Christian worship and faith are thus built around a mythologized account of someone else's mystical transcendent experience, literalized as historical fact.

When it became religious doctrine, the Christ myth was thereafter held to be factually and historically true. As Campbell stresses, the metaphor that is inherent in the myth—that each of us can die to our old life and be spiritually reborn, that each is a son or daughter of the divine—is lost in the literal doctrine, which maintains that Jesus is the only Son of God, that his resurrection was an actual physical event, and that he will come again to save the pious, who will be taken up to Heaven, while unbelieving sinners will perish in an eternal damnation in Hell. In contrast to this literal interpretation, now maintained even in the face of reason and science, myth retains a mysterious, metaphorical element: the meaning of a religion becomes fixed, set in stone; the meaning of myth remains alive, ever open to interpretation at different levels and in different contexts.[22] As such, it might be applied to the unique circumstances of each individual life.

There is a crucial difference, too, between the myth that informs religion, on the one hand, and the spiritual wisdom and psychological insight that are contained in the teachings of that religion, on the other. The Christ myth is to be distinguished from the teachings of Jesus; the myth of the Buddha is different from the teachings of the Buddha. Thus, if you read the Gnostic *Gospel of Thomas*, which is believed to contain the teachings of Jesus, you will find that it is an immensely profound and insightful guide to psychospiritual transformation, expressed in parable and enigmatic logia. The majority of people respond to the Christ myth as it is interpreted through religious doctrine, based on the meaning attributed to it by the Church. Other people will have the awareness and imaginative capacity to respond to the deeper symbolism of the myth and understand its import for their own lives. And some people are able to respond directly to the psychospiritual insight contained in the teachings of Jesus, which in the Gospels are intermixed with the myth and religious doctrine. Of course, these three responses are not mutually exclusive. Campbell emphasizes the second (especially) and third approaches.[23]

Myths can also be distinguished from beliefs and world views. Belief—by which we usually mean religious belief—is expressed in questions such as "do you believe in God?" and "do you believe in an afterlife?" Belief, in this sense, is closely connected to acts of faith. However, for a growing number of people the quest for knowledge and direct personal experience has now displaced belief as the primary guiding principle in human life, even in spiritual matters. "I do not need to believe. I know" was Carl Jung's memorable reply to the question as to whether he believed in God, and this sentiment epitomizes this new spiritual attitude of our time.[24] For religion, Campbell was keen to point out, is often a defense against genuine religious experience. To move beyond the patterns of one's culture, beyond the womb of society, is also to leave behind the accepted religious truths in the quest for one's own spiritual experience. This quest, leading one beyond the protective shield of the Christian religious world view, exposes one to a primal experience of the unconscious psyche where the archetypes, the living dynamisms of life, are to be found. Such an experience can initiate profound psychospiritual transformation. In the chapters to come, we will consider just how the individual might navigate this process.

CHAPTER 2

Mythology: East and West

The West is the best. Get here and we'll do the rest.
—Jim Morrison

The sun sinks down in the west, where it dies and enters into the womb of the underworld that devours it. For this reason the west is the place of death.
—Erich Neumann

This chapter focuses on the background mythic context that has shaped the spiritual situation in which we find ourselves today and from which we can trace the origins of what Campbell calls the era of *creative* or *individual mythology*. This new mythological epoch is the result of the emergence of an eclectic, pluralistic cultural milieu, centered on the Western world, in which there is no single settled form of myth to which all members of a society subscribe. Rather, the last few centuries, Campbell observes, have seen the dissolution of the established mythic and religious traditions, and in their place the progressive emergence of individual forms of mythic expression characterized by a tremendous creative diversity in the arts and in forms of spirituality. To help understand the spiritual challenges facing us today, therefore, let us consider next Campbell's assessment of how myth has changed over time since its beginning in so-called primitive cultures.

In his four-volume *The Masks of God* series, Campbell classifies myth prior to the modern era into three "grandiose unitary stages": primitive, Oriental, and Occidental. *Primitive mythology* refers to the relatively long period of human existence before the invention of writing, from the dawn of consciousness in proto-humans to the emergence, around 3400 BCE to 2500 BCE, of the first civilization in the city-states of Mesopotamia, the "cradle of civilization," as the area around the Tigris and the Euphrates is known. It was here that not only writing, but also celestial mathematics were developed, supporting the first forms of astronomy and astrology. It was here, too, that scholars place the beginning of recorded religious history— although forms of worship and religious experience existed long before that time.

Out of primitive mythology came forth the two great traditions of *Oriental mythology*, primarily in India, China, and Japan; and *Occidental mythology* in the Levant, Greece, and Rome. There are two main branches of Occidental mythology: Zoroastrianism, Judaism, Islam, and Christianity—the major monotheistic traditions—comprise the first branch; and the Greco-Roman lineage, from the Homeric myths through the Pre-Socratics, Platonism, and later philosophical speculation, comprises the second branch. In the Eastern world, we find the major religions of Hinduism, Buddhism, and Jainism in India; Taoism and Confucianism in China; and Buddhism and Shinto in Japan.

For all the important differences between these religions, certain observations can be made regarding the general character of Eastern and Western traditions, reflected in the type of civilization and the prevailing attitudes towards existence that emerged in each. In particular, Campbell was interested in looking, in the broadest terms, at the distinctions that can be drawn between East and West— distinctions that have roots, he believed, in the two sources of primitive mythology: planting cultures and hunting cultures.

According to Campbell, planting cultures based their myths on observations of the recurring natural cycles in the life of plants, and on reverence for the sacred power of Mother Nature. These cultures were *matriarchal* in character. In such planting societies, there was an acceptance of life as it is, with no real attempt to change it. Unconsciously participating in nature, there was little concern for the value of individual life—indeed matriarchal societies, as Campbell points out, were often astonishingly brutal, showing little regard for personal suffering. In hunting cultures, by contrast, although the natural world was seen as sacred, the mythology reflected more aggressive, dominating, and individualistic qualities necessary for hunting or herding animals. These hunting societies thus assumed a more "masculine" character, in which the individual human will was imposed on the natural environment, set against the natural order. Accordingly, Campbell suggests, such cultures were also *patriarchal* in that men, as hunters and herders, occupied dominant positions within the community.

From these roots in primitive mythology, Campbell maintains that Occidental traditions took on an essentially patriarchal cast (in which the dominant gods were male) and the Oriental traditions a matriarchal one, a distinction that shaped the way the respective traditions subsequently developed.

Distinctions Between Eastern and Western Mythology

In mythic terms, matriarchal cultures are connected to the recognition of the Great Mother goddess as the containing womb of all existence. "The Great Goddess," Campbell notes,

> was already, as she is now in the Orient, a metaphysical symbol, the arch personification of the power of space, time, and matter, within whose bounds all beings arise and die: the substance of their bodies, configurator of their lives and thoughts, and receiver of their dead. And everything having form or name, including God, personified as good or evil, merciful or wrathful, was her child within her womb.[1]

Here, in the primitive and Oriental matriarchal mythic traditions, the eternal aspect of reality and divine ground, symbolized by the womb of the Great Mother, is of principal importance. The maternal womb of being embraces the pairs of opposites inherent in existence—life and death, existence and non-existence, male and female, good and evil, light and dark. Duality is recognized, but always as part of a greater encompassing oneness, as depicted by the well-known yin-yang symbol of Taoist thought, with the light and dark sections forming interlocking and interpenetrating halves of a circle. Such a perspective, as we will see, sharply contrasts with the absolute dualism of Judeo-Christianity in the West.

In many Eastern traditions, especially Hinduism, the ground of being is the source not only of all forms and all of existence, but of all personified expressions of the divine, as Campbell explains:

> Throughout the orient, the idea prevails that the ultimate ground of being transcends thought, imaging, and definition. It cannot be qualified. Hence to argue that God, man, nature is good, just, merciful, or benign is to fall short of the question. One could just as appropriately, or inappropriately, have argued evil, unjust, merciless, or malignant. All such anthropomorphic predications screen or mask the actual enigma, which is absolutely beyond rational consideration, and yet, according to this view, precisely that enigma is the ultimate ground of being of each and every one of us and of all things.[2]

From the perspective of the East, even the traditional Western figure of God would be situated within this more encompassing divine ground, imagined as the womb of the Great Mother. This idea represents a key distinction between the Western tradition and the Eastern perspectives. In the Western world, the Christian Father God is the ultimate reference—there is no mystery or encompassing spiritual ground beyond God. In Hinduism and Buddhism, the gods and goddesses (such as Shiva, Brahma, and Kali) are all seen as personifications of particular aspects of the divine. These deities are, as Campbell liked to say, "transparent to transcendence"; they are metaphors that point beyond themselves to the unlimited, unqualified divine mystery they represent.[3]

A further general distinction between Eastern and Western traditions may be drawn with regard to the understanding of time. The Oriental mythic cultures recognize time to be cyclical and therefore ultimately static, rather than linear-historical and progressive, as it generally came to be conceived in the West. In Hinduism, for example, change is seen in the context of a cyclical conception of existence mapped by *yugas*, *mayahugas*, and *kalpas*—immense eons of time, ever cycling, ever repeating. Campbell sees all these characteristics and themes—the eternal, the ground, oneness, harmony with nature, cyclical time, and an emphasis on eternal *being* rather than the process of *becoming* in history—as originating in and pertaining to a matriarchal mythic conception of life.

The primary emphasis in Oriental traditions, accordingly, is not on individual self-actualization in the world, as it has become in the West; rather, it is to bring oneself through some kind of mystical realization into relationship with, or absorption into, the divine ground.[4] The claims of the individual personality are to be relinquished, for against the eternal nature of the ground of being, or the vastness of the great eons of time, the significance of the personal self and the deeds of an individual life in the world of space and time are radically diminished.

According to Campbell's summary, Indian religions, generally speaking, seek to purge away individuality by a combination of three strategies: (1) adherence to the laws of caste (as in Hinduism), which determine a person's behavior based on position in society (*dharma*); (2) following a way of liberation (*marga*); and (3) the attainment of *nirvana* bringing release (*moksa*) from the delusion of individual self-existence (*maya*) and the twin entrapments of desiring/craving (*kama*) and fear (*mara*), which bind the individual to a self-perpetuating series of incarnations in the world of suffering and delusion (*samsara*).[5] In the Far East, too, Confucianism, emphasizes the fulfillment of one's social and familial duties, and Taoism describes an approach to life that de-emphasizes the personal will in favor of aligning oneself with the mysterious flow of the *Tao*, the inherent spiritual way of nature. The spiritual emphasis of the East is not on the fulfillment or realization of the self, but on liberation from the self and the limitations of egoic existence.

The notion of seeking to gratify one's personal desires by exercising one's own individual will—the ideal of modern life in the West—has been largely alien to the Eastern traditions. For it is the essence of the Western attitude to life, emerging particularly out of the Greek ideal of the rational self-determining individual, to place high value on individual choice, and to affirm the validity of the individual's own impulses and desires to live life as he or she sees fit.

It seems to have been the particular destiny of the West alone, therefore, to bring forth the modern individual self, as we know it today, possessed of the power of free will and self-determination. According to Campbell, by promoting the principle of assertive, heroic individualism, Occidental cultures broke away from the eternal womb of the timeless, perennial ground of being, emphasizing instead "the warrior principle of the great deed of the individual who matters."[6] This development, he claims, is the distinguishing characteristic of Western mythology:

> In the West, on the other hand, the principle of indeterminacy represented by the freely willing, historically effective hero not only gained but held the field and has retained it to the present. Moreover, this victory of the principle of free will, together with its moral corollary of individual responsibility, establishes the first distinguishing characteristic of specifically occidental myth.[7]

From the initial roots in primitive mythology, then, there was a branching out into two different directions: one direction emphasizing the human being's identity with the ground of being, the eternal womb of the Great Mother, and therefore de-emphasizing the significance of the individual life and even of the world itself; the other emphasizing the emergence of the individual self, in a movement away from the ground, establishing the self's independence and autonomy, affirming the reality of the world of space and time as God's Creation, even if this reality was, as in Christianity, sometimes conceived as secondary to a heavenly afterlife.

Accordingly, given the emphasis on the development of the individual self, characteristics that prevail in the Western world include self-determination, free will, democratic individualism, reason and rationality, the freedom to live life as one sees fit, a recognition of the sanctity of the individual life, and an insistence on the value of the individual's unique experience—all these attributes are reflected in the modern democratic rights and individual freedoms we often take for granted. The primary emphasis in modern Western civilization is on extraverted action and achievement in the world, a reflection, perhaps, of the initial character of a mythology shaped by the experience of the hunt. The main distinctions between the mythic and religious traditions of East and West are summarized in figure 1.

One might, of course, take issue with a number of aspects of Campbell's analysis of the historical development of mythology; his views are far from uncontroversial and they are sometimes inconsistent.[8] Indeed, Campbell vacillated between praising and critiquing both Eastern and Western myths and religions, as if he were struggling to bring together the different emphases of East and West

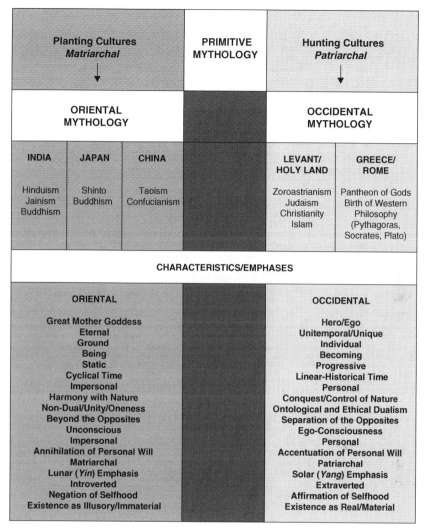

Planting Cultures *Matriarchal*			PRIMITIVE MYTHOLOGY	Hunting Cultures *Patriarchal*	
↓				↓	
ORIENTAL MYTHOLOGY				OCCIDENTAL MYTHOLOGY	
INDIA	JAPAN	CHINA		LEVANT/ HOLY LAND	GREECE/ ROME
Hinduism Jainism Buddhism	Shinto Buddhism	Taoism Confucianism		Zoroastrianism Judaism Christianity Islam	Pantheon of Gods Birth of Western Philosophy (Pythagoras, Socrates, Plato)
CHARACTERISTICS/EMPHASES					
ORIENTAL				OCCIDENTAL	
Great Mother Goddess Eternal Ground Being Static Cyclical Time Impersonal Harmony with Nature Non-Dual/Unity/Oneness Beyond the Opposites Unconscious Impersonal Annihilation of Personal Will Matriarchal Lunar (*Yin*) Emphasis Introverted Negation of Selfhood Existence as Illusory/Immaterial				Hero/Ego Unitemporal/Unique Individual Becoming Progressive Linear-Historical Time Personal Conquest/Control of Nature Ontological and Ethical Dualism Separation of the Opposites Ego-Consciousness Personal Accentuation of Personal Will Patriarchal Solar (*Yang*) Emphasis Extraverted Affirmation of Selfhood Existence as Real/Material	

Figure 1: Branches of Mythology

within his own life experience. On the one hand, he placed high value on the spiritual wisdom of the East. He held in high esteem the Eastern emphasis on the introverted path of spiritual realization, prominent especially in Hindu yoga and Buddhism, which has generally been neglected amidst the extraverted focus and world-redeeming zeal of the West. On the other hand, he was a champion of the Western ideal of the individual with a unique life path and potentiality to be willed, created, and realized—a notion that, as we have seen, is

..argely alien to the East. Despite these ambiguities, Campbell's analysis draws our attention to what is, without question, a fundamental distinction between life orientations and world views of East and West, one that has important implications, as we will later consider, for understanding the course of human psychological development and the evolutionary challenges we now face.

Mythic Dissociation

A further key distinction between Oriental and Occidental traditions is that the major religions in the West—Judaism, Islam, and Christianity—espouse an ethical dualism based on an absolute division of good and evil into separate ontological categories. In Christianity, this dualism establishes a clear mythological and moral separation of an all-loving, beneficent God and His Son, Jesus, from the Devil and the forces of evil. One is asked to choose good over evil, right over wrong, and the individual soul is held ethically accountable to God for its choices. In the East, as we have seen, although good and evil are recognized, the divine is not exclusively identified with the good; rather, the divine is "beyond good and evil" (to borrow Nietzsche's term), beyond all opposites, beyond all categories of thought. The divine ground encompasses both male and female, good and evil, being and non-being. There is an awareness in the East, that is, of the ground of being as greater than any human ethical standard or conceptual distinction.

In the Bible, by contrast, the opposites are thrust apart. The myth of the Fall of Man, describing the expulsion of Adam and Eve from the Garden of Eden, depicts the radical separation of God, nature, and humanity. The eating of the fruit of the Tree of the Knowledge of Good and Evil symbolizes a process by which human beings became aware of the opposites—male and female, good and evil, God and nature, and so on—and aware too of their separate existence, apart from God and apart from nature.[9]

According to Campbell, it is this threefold ontological separation of spirit, nature, and humanity that is the root of "an essential psychological problem of the Christianized Western world."[10] That is to say, it is because God is conceived as wholly transcendent, as wholly "other," that, according to popular Christian orthodoxy, the divine cannot be experienced either within (in the human soul) or without (in nature). Campbell calls this *mythic dissociation*, since it is through myth that humankind and nature are dissociated from God.[11] According to the teachings of the Church orthodoxy, we can only know God through a relationship with Jesus Christ and this relationship, in turn, is only possible through participation in the Church (*social identification*, as Campbell calls it). The increasing secularization of society and the rejection of Christian beliefs in recent years have created a spiritual problem because, Campbell notes, "There has now spread throughout the Christian world a desolating sense not only of no divinity within but also of no participation in divinity without."[12] Campbell therefore generally interprets the Fall of Man in negative terms, although, as we will later see, this event seems to reflect an essential development in the evolution of human consciousness.

In the Oriental as well as the primal "nature religions," Campbell observes, mythic dissociation does not arise because there is no corresponding literal reading of the mythological story of the Fall of Man.[13] Nature is seen not as fallen, but as a manifestation of spirit. Nature and spirit are one. The separation of the Fall thus represents a fundamental point of distinction between these mythologies of East and West.

In *The Power of Myth* interviews with Bill Moyers in the 1980s, Campbell tells of an encounter with D. T. Suzuki, who was very influential in introducing Eastern ideas to the West. Addressing an audience in Switzerland, Suzuki confessed that he could find very little religion in the Bible. "God against man," Suzuki remarked, "Man against God. Man against nature. Nature against man. Nature against God. God against nature. Very funny religion!"[14]

In the same series of interviews, Campbell recounts with enthusiasm his experience in Japan, spending time in Japanese gardens, where it was impossible, he reflected, to determine where "nature begins and art ends," such was the harmony of the human interaction with the natural environment.[15] In those civilizations in which there is no mythic dissociation—no radical separation of humanity, spirit, and nature—the natural world and the cosmos are more likely to be seen to reflect an immanent divinity. The divine is not, in the primal and oriental "nature religions," outside of nature and absolutely transcendent; rather, spirit is immanent, present within and throughout the natural world. In the Greco-Persian Hellenistic age too, Campbell contends, there prevailed a "mystical, world-loving . . . type of optimistic affirmation."[16] This was in contrast, he thought, to the moral, world-reforming character of orthodox Judaism and Christianity, which, spreading far beyond their place of origin in the Levant, established the doctrine of the Fall as the mythic bedrock that shaped attitudes to the natural world across the expanse of the entire Roman Empire.

Again, while Campbell's analysis of world myth and religion sometimes fails to adequately reflect the innumerable important distinctions between, and the diversity within, specific religious traditions (which sometimes contradict his general characterizations), his general assessment of the prevailing character of East and West holds good. For our purposes, his delineation of the main characteristics of the Occidental stream of myth and religion provides a basis for understanding the emergence of creative mythology out of the matrix of the Western tradition.

The Withdrawal of the Gods

A major consequence of the Judeo-Christian belief in a wholly transcendent spiritual power, existing outside of creation, is the so-called disenchantment of the universe—the now widely held, often uncritically accepted, assumption that the world is devoid of intrinsic spiritual meaning. In the modern view, the nature of the universe is no longer recognized to be or experienced as sacred in essence. In the primal world views of the Paleolithic and Neolithic eras, in the early civilizations, and in certain indigenous cultures today, the whole universe is understood to be ensouled, pervaded with spiritual meaning. In the West, too, in the sixth century BCE ancient Greek philosophers posited that "the All is alive," in the words of Thales, and that the entire universe "has soul in it."[17] However, in the Christian era, as Richard Tarnas observes, the locus of spiritual meaning increasingly shifted from the phenomenal world to a transcendent godhead.[18] Ultimately, by the modern era, all spiritual meaning was withdrawn from the world and was conceived as residing entirely in a divine Creator outside of this world whose aims and purposes for human beings were distinct from the natural order and seemingly set against nature. Spiritual meaning was no longer to be found in the cosmos itself, only in the transcendent divine.

This type of development was not unique to the Judaic tradition but had been prefigured in ancient Greece, as F. M. Cornford notes, by the process he called *Olympianization*, in which the gods of the mystery religions, immanent powers of natural transformation, became in time the Olympian deities who were far more remote from human affairs than their forerunners had been.[19] By the time of the Alexandrian conquests in 336–328 BCE, in the mythic imagination of the folk culture, the Olympian deities, although imbued with quasi-human temperaments, had migrated from their habitation on Mount Olympus to the celestial sphere, thereby losing their former proximity to the daily lives and deeds of humans. This trend continued with the transition from myth to philosophy in ancient Greece as the Olympian gods were eventually succeeded by the Platonic Forms, a shift emphasizing the transcendent metaphysical realm over and against the immanent reality of the natural world. Platonism also established a dualism between the human spirit and the body that both reflected and gave philosophical support to the growing separation of human consciousness and reason from the instinctual sphere of the bodily passions.

Metaphysical dualisms in Platonism and especially Judeo-Christianity spawned corresponding ethical or moral dualisms. Spirit, associated with the "good" and the principle of light, was set against nature, matter, and flesh, which came to be associated with darkness and "evil." The emphasis upon a heavenly afterlife in a transcendent realm that was not of this world fostered negative attitudes to nature and the material world, especially in later Western Christianity and in certain Gnostic and Neoplatonic schools of thought, which conceived of the world as a prison from which the human spirit or soul had to struggle to attain liberation.

In religious terminology, one might say that Christianity brought about an attunement to the transcendent spiritual father principle, neglecting, however, the maternal ground of existence and the inherent spirituality of the natural world. Our challenge now, as we will see, seems to be to bring these two aspects of the divine—the transcendent and immanent—into closer relationship within our own experience.

Myth and Monotheism: The Emergence of Linear Time

The establishment of the Judaic world view in place of the primal nature religions and the classical myths was also significant for two other closely related reasons, both of which had a significant impact on the modern world view. First, it signaled a radical transformation in the human experience of time. Whereas in the earlier primal and archaic world views time was experienced as cyclical, the Judaic religion was the first mythology to represent and interpret time in linear-historical terms as an irreversible linear progression. As Mircea Eliade notes:

> Compared with the archaic and paleo-oriental religions, as well as the mythic-philosophical conceptions of the eternal return, as they were elaborated in India and Greece, Judaism represents an innovation of the first importance. For Judaism, time has a beginning and will have an end. The idea of cyclic time is left behind. Yahweh no longer manifests himself in cosmic time (like the gods of the other religions) but in historical time, which is irreversible.[20]

In the primal, archaic world views human life was defined by the cycles of nature and, through participation in rituals mirroring these natural cycles, a harmony between the human and the natural order was maintained. At the end of each year, the ritual enactment of death-rebirth processes ensured the regeneration and unbroken continuation of cyclical time on which the archaic world views depended.[21] Year upon year was effectively the same, ever repeating, a cyclical, perpetual recurrence. The archaic and primal condition was characterized by what Eliade calls the "eternal return" in which all experiences were interpreted as conforming to endlessly repeating archetypes.[22] There was no genuine novelty as all events were thought to be merely a reenactment of timeless mythic patterns, replicating the deeds of gods "in the beginning."

The transition from a cyclical to a linear sense of time further contributed to the increasing separation of the human from the natural order. For with the ascendancy of Judaism and the worship of the creator-god Yahweh, the cyclical patterns of the natural world were no longer seen to reflect an inherent divinity. Henceforth, rather than harmonize their lives with the natural order, the Jewish people felt compelled to obey a divine principle outside of nature. They were compelled to break the cyclical patterns of nature, to defy the nature gods of the primal mythologies, and to adhere instead to the moralistic yet seemingly arbitrary will of Yahweh, whose ends and intentions for the Jews were to be fulfilled in some future time with the coming of the day of salvation and the delivery of the Jewish people into the Promised Land. With Judaism, then, the emphasis had dramatically shifted: human beings no longer played a part in maintaining the natural cosmic order and preserving the cycles of unchanging archetypal repetition, but they were now responsible for actualizing the will of the divine in history.

While these considerations seem rather remote to us today, we should keep in mind that the modern ideology of progress and development, now conceived in entirely material rather than spiritual terms, has its origins in the Judaic emphasis on linear time. Gradually, with the rise of secular society, the notion of a divine Father-God intervening in the course of history receded from view, but the idea of progress towards some future condition of utopia on Earth still remains today as a pervasive ideology, as a residual yet potent unconscious myth that has been maintained until now by the absence of a cogent alternative. By the modern era, human beings were concerned no more with harmonizing their lives with cosmic rhythms and natural cycles, but progress, ever more progress, became the guiding ideology as people aspired to the technological and material advancement that could make possible a utopian existence built solely by human intelligence and endeavor. The consequences of the Judaic myth of the Fall are particularly evident in the pervasive attempt to control, manipulate, and often exploit the resources of the natural world for human ends, an endeavor seemingly ordained in the biblical declaration of humanity's dominion over land and beast, and one that would eventually give rise to the modern scientific and technological world.

In addition to the transformation of the human experience of time, the ascendancy of the Judaic mythology was significant for a second reason, as it also marked a major transition from polytheism (as exemplified by the Greek pantheon) to monotheism. Most mythic traditions are polytheistic, recognizing a plurality of gods and goddesses or elemental or celestial deities, even if these powers are themselves expressions of a single divine ground. The Judaic worship of Yahweh, the "jealous god," maintained by the fear of his stern reproach and wrath for any transgression of his will, was the foundation behind the subsequent monotheism of the Christianized world, a monotheism that still profoundly conditions not only contemporary religious thinking, but also the popular understanding of human nature.[23] For as people in the West came to believe in only one God, so they came to believe in a singular human soul or self with its own moral autonomy and volition, possessing the power to choose right over wrong, good over evil, and directly accountable, therefore, to the divine creator.

The Psychological Significance of Christianity

Campbell points out that when a mythic tradition achieves domi-nance over an earlier one it tends to depict the deities of the old tradition as demonic. The values of the earlier religion or mythol-ogy are denigrated and rejected, deemed to be evil, and therefore eventually fall into the unconscious. Thus, when Judaism was becoming established, with Yahweh as the god to be appeased, the Jewish people were compelled, by fear of Yahweh's vengeance, to abandon the old nature religions of Babylonia. Any return to the ways of the old fertility gods, the Baales and the Astortes, was held responsible for subsequent catastrophes that befell the Jewish peo-ple. "Among the Hebrews," as Mircea Eliade explains, "every new historical calamity was regarded as punishment inflicted by Yahweh, angered by the orgy of sin to which the chosen people had aban-doned themselves."[24] So it was, then, that natural impulses were increasingly seen as sinful and evil, opposed to the moral order laid down by Yahweh. Increasingly, the Jewish people cleaved to a life governed by Yahweh's commandments, turning away from a more natural, instinctive mode of being—a shift which obviously had a significant impact on the way Judaism and later Christianity devel-oped. For in the Christian mythological imagination, in which nature is portrayed as fallen, the natural passions and appetites—for power, conquest, sex, food, pleasure, and the like—are seen as corrupting and threatening demonic forces. Such impulses are typically asso-ciated with the Devil or symbolized by the figure of the serpent. Repressed and rendered taboo by Christian morality, these impulses became powerful subterranean forces in human experience.

Given the promulgation of Christianity around the globe, the psy-chological consequences of the shift from the nature gods to Yahweh transcended its merely local and cultural significance for the Judaic tradition. Indeed, this development was to have a defining influence on the destiny of the entire human race, leaving its mark today in the basic Western attitude towards life.

I do not want to give the impression, however, that these developments were wholly undesirable—something that should never have happened. On the contrary, in Christian theological speculation, the Fall of Man has been interpreted as a "blessed fault," a "happy sin," (*o felix culpa*). Humanity's alienation from God and fall into sin, on this view, serves a constructive and "blessed" end, making possible the redemption of humanity and, indeed, the divine itself. Without the fall into separation and sin, there could be no redemption. In this context, the Fall of Man might be conceived a necessary phase in the evolution of consciousness.

As Jung argues in *Answer to Job*, human self-reflective awareness might be seen as the medium through which God becomes conscious—with the human ego serving as the divine organ of self-reflective consciousness. The development of a separate ego is essential, Jung maintains, for there to be self-reflective knowledge, to know the world as a subject to an object. This insight into the fundamental value of human consciousness impressed itself on him during his visit to the Athai Plains in Africa in 1925. Observing the timeless scene of herds of grazing animals moving slowly, almost silently, across a great expanse, Jung reflected,

> This was the stillness of the eternal beginning, the world as it had always been, in the state of non-being; for until then no one had been present to know that it was this world. . . . There I was now, the first human being to recognise that this was the world, but who did not know that in this moment he had first really created it.[25]

To illuminate nature in its depths of meaning—to effectively bring the world into being through an act of consciousness—the human ego has to become separate from nature, to perceive it as subject to object. For Jung, the act of self-reflected knowing of the world is tantamount, as the quote indicates, to an act of world creation.

The subject-object, self-world, human-nature separation is a defining feature of the modern individual's psychological experience. As the individual personality develops from childhood to adulthood, the conscious will, directed by rational thought, is increasingly set against the natural, instinctive way of being: reason stands in opposition to desires, morality to natural impulses. The instinctive spontaneity of the child is opposed by rules and regulations from without, a conflict that is reflected in the basic dynamics of Freudian psychology between the *ego* (the I), the *superego* (the internalized moral authority) and the *id* (the instinctual drives). With these psychodynamics in mind, we can appreciate the crucial role played by Judeo-Christian morality in the development of consciousness over the centuries. The separation of good from evil, and with it the Christian moral aspiration to avoid sin, forces human beings to become more conscious of their thoughts, feelings, and actions. Christian morality thus serves the end of increasing consciousness and preventing the unconscious expression of the natural instincts. Rational self-control and instinctual expression become opposed to each other; ethical standards and natural human desires become opposed. Every natural act is to be questioned, checked, curtailed, amended, or repressed so as not to allow oneself to fall into sin.

Consequently, many of our natural impulses, if they are incompatible with our moral values, are rendered taboo, pushed down into the unconscious, with the individual superego playing the role of Yahweh, censoring and repressing the natural drives and instincts of the id. Through this process, the natural state of psychological wholeness is brought to an end, and ego-consciousness is strengthened. In Jung's view, Christianity has thus provided a kind of protective buttress, serving, through its rituals and moral codes, to fortify human ego-consciousness against any relapse to the natural state of preconscious instinctive life. Christianity has been instrumental in helping Western civilization leave behind the unconsciousness of the "primitive" world.

Evolution and the Ego

The ethical duality in Christianity helped bring to an end patterns of instinctive living, and in the process ruptured the natural wholeness of the psyche. It therefore provided the necessary conditions for collective psychospiritual development, drawing forth independent self-reflective consciousness in opposition to the instincts. In this respect, Christianity seems to have an expressed an evolutionary need on the part of the psyche, or on the part of nature, to bring forth ego-consciousness as a psychological center existing separate from and often opposed to its instinctual unconscious roots. Indeed, in retrospect it might be observed that the entire course of development of the Western mythic, philosophical, religious, and even the scientific traditions has been directed to this end, informed by a kind of implicit *telos*—a hidden evolutionary purpose working itself out through human experience.

Such a purpose was already evident in ancient creation myths, which, according to Erich Neumann, symbolically describe the primal separation of human consciousness from nature, and the struggle of the nascent human self for independence and autonomy. Subsequent myths, and later religious and philosophical conceptions, reflect further developments of this evolutionary process.

According to Neumann, in *The Origins and History of Consciousness*, the primal differentiation of the unity of existence into opposite principles was portrayed through myths recounting the separation of Father Sky from Mother Earth, just as myths of the birth of light or fire in the darkness represented the birth of self-reflective conscious awareness illuminating the hitherto unconscious darkness of existence. As the centuries passed, human consciousness gradually became increasingly distinct from nature; the ego (symbolized in myth by the figure of the hero) emerged as a distinct, autonomous principle. In myth, this process of separation from nature culminates in the hero's fight with the dragon, which symbolizes the light of consciousness doing battle with the dark instinctual power of nature, as ego-consciousness struggled to be free from its prior state of unconsciousness and domination by the instincts. The emergence of the light of consciousness and the separation into opposites—sky and earth, male and female, light and dark—brought to an end the self-perpetuating unconscious cycle of existence, symbolized, Neumann suggests, by the uroborus, the self-consuming serpent, which eats its own tail.

As Campbell sought to understand the transformation of myth over time and the factors behind the emergence of creative mythology over the last few centuries, he too was analyzing myths in terms of their psychological and evolutionary significance. Campbell proposed that the course of development of Western myth gives a symbolic indication of the evolution of the Western psyche and its relationship to nature and to the divine. Episodes such as Yahweh's victory in battle over the sea monster Leviathan, for example, or Zeus, king of the Greek gods, defeating Typhon, child of the Earth goddess Gaia, portray the victory of a patriarchal god over nature, reflecting the attempt to conquer, control, and dominate nature that has characterized the Western world, particularly in the modern era. Such myths are indicative of the dominant character of the Western cultural traditions, out of which the modern individual self emerged, and with it the sense of personhood that we take for granted today.[26]

The Greco-Roman lineage fostered another decisive separation between human awareness and its containing existential context, one more subtle but no less dramatic in its consequences. Whereas the *mythic* Fall of Man was rooted in the Judaic tradition, the Greek philosophical tradition brought forth a parallel *ontological* fall. As Martin Heidegger recognized, during the rise of civilization and the emergence of the modern self in the West, there occurred a "fall of Being," as he called it, such that human awareness of the containing ground of our existence was gradually lost. William Barrett explains:

> The fall of Being, for Heidegger, occurred when the Greek thinkers detached things as clear and distinct forms from their encompassing background, in order that they might reckon clearly with them. The terms used in Gestalt psychology—figure and ground—may be helpful here: By detaching the figure from the ground the object could be made to emerge into the daylight of human consciousness; but the sense of the ground, the environing background, could also be lost. The figure comes into sharper focus, that is, but the ground recedes, becomes invisible, is forgotten. The Greeks detached beings from the vast environing ground of Being.[27]

This emphasis on the figure at the expense of the ground, on separate individual beings and individual things rather than Being itself, determined the future course of the Western philosophical tradition and ultimately brought forth the modern world as we know it today. In that long variegated process, the individual human ego was progressively differentiated, and in certain cases painfully alienated, from its own deeper ground as Being was forgotten, repressed, and became "invisible." It took the singular insight of Heidegger, centuries later, to turn his philosophical focus towards this concealed ground and to effectively think his way back to Being. In so doing, he was able to suggest a counterbalancing shift away from the foreground emphasis on individual things and individual beings, such that the neglected background started to return into focus.

Deepening separations of human consciousness from nature, and individual beings from Being-at-large, were increasingly apparent in later Western religious and philosophical developments. Indeed, an unconscious preference for those philosophical perspectives that accentuated the autonomy of the individual and screened out the background context to reality seems to have been essential to the process by which human civilization and the individual self could develop. According to Richard Tarnas, major shifts and revolutions in scientific paradigms and in philosophical theories and world views are not merely arbitrary transitions, nor do they reflect a straightforward incremental accretion of knowledge; rather, paradigmatic shifts are to a certain extent unconsciously dictated by the needs of human psychological development at the time:

> The emergence of a new philosophical paradigm, whether that of a Plato or Aquinas, Kant or Heidegger, is never simply the result of improved logical reasoning from the observed data. Rather, each philosophy, each metaphysical perspective and epistemology, reflects the emergence of a global experiential gestalt that informs the philosopher's vision, that governs his or her reasoning and observations, and that ultimately affects the entire cultural and sociological context within which the philosopher's vision is taking form. . . . A paradigm appears to account for more data, and for more important data, it seems more relevant, more cogent, more attractive, fundamentally because it has become more archetypally appropriate to that culture or individual at that moment of its evolution.[28]

What came to pass both with the emergence of Judaism and the birth of Greek philosophical speculation, therefore, seems to have met the needs of the reality of the evolving universe at that time, pressing the human mind to conceive of the universe and human nature in such a way as to foster its own differentiation from the cosmological matrix within which it is embedded.

Christianity placed emphasis on the cultivation of individual faith in God and, in Protestantism especially, the soul's accountability to God and the development of an independent moral conscience. The Greco-Roman tradition emphasized the ideal of the rational self-determining individual, the Socratic ideal. The thrust of Socratic and Platonic philosophical speculation was to subject experience and the world to rational scrutiny: "the unexamined life," as Socrates declared, "is not worth living."[29] For Socrates and Plato, a rationally inspired spiritual illumination rather than the animal passions should direct human life. By reflecting on one's experience, one can choose the right course of action and attune to the divine through one's own rational intelligence; to achieve illumination one must think for oneself, not simply accept and follow what one has been told or live according to an unreflective faith, or blindly follow one's natural impulses. This rational ideal, which later flourished in the Enlightenment tradition, is evident in the work of Freud too, in his notion that the I-principle, attuned to an objective outer reality, should replace the instinctive, unreflective activity of the psyche with the reasoned consideration of the ego. "Where id was, there ego shall be," according to Freud's well-known dictum.[30]

In the modern era, a number of other critical developments helped to effect a further separation of individual human consciousness from nature: the Renaissance marked a re-emergence in the Medieval world of the spirit of European individualism and the Enlightenment championed rationality, reason, and the democratic ideal of individual rights and freedoms—"liberty, equality, fraternity" in France; the individual's unalienable right to the pursuit of happiness in America. In philosophy, the Cartesian distinction between mind and matter, subject and object, was pivotal, decisively accentuating the separation of the inner world of human consciousness from the external world of nature, and establishing philosophical foundations for the new age of science. Descartes articulated the common human intuition of being an independent thinking being—a mind or consciousness—inhabiting a material body. According to Tarnas, the Cartesian distinction was "the prototypical declaration of the modern self, established as a fully separate defining entity, for whom its own rational awareness was absolutely primary."[31]

The movement towards autonomy, individualism, and freedom of choice was evident in Western myth and literature too. Campbell saw an anticipation of this trend towards individual self-determination, or an early form of it, in the Troubadours of the twelfth century, who, in affairs of the heart, made their own choices as to whom they would give their love. Romantic matters were directed by the individual's own wishes, not by social convention and duty, as was usual in that period. Campbell interpreted this romantic rebellion as a decisive affirmation of the individual, a prefiguration of the freedom most of us now take for granted. It was based on trusting one's own individual value judgment, not simply doing what should be done.

A similar attitude was also to be found among the Knights of the Round Table. On the quest for the Holy Grail, Campbell observed, each knight embarked on his own path into the dark forest, to embark on his own adventure, believing that it would be a disgrace to follow the path of another. The Holy Grail, a symbol of the culmination of spiritual realization, can only be attained, Campbell stressed, by the person who has lived his or her own life, not one who has followed the life path of another. To attain the Grail, that is, you must become who you are, realize your unique potentiality, become a type unto yourself. For no one else exactly like you has ever lived before, and no one exactly like you will ever live in the future.

Each of these transformations, then, reinforces the sense that what was occurring in the course of development of the Western world was shaped by the evolutionary imperatives of the time. Unwittingly, it seems, although perhaps inevitably, the human mind formulated, became attracted to, and became convinced of the rightness of those mythic and philosophic conceptions of the nature of reality that enabled its own self-development and that permitted the increasing separation of human consciousness and civilization from the natural world and from being at large.

The major developments contributing to the process of separation of human consciousness from nature are summarized in the diagram on page 48. The idea conveyed in figure 2 is that as self-awareness and the sense of individual self-determination increase, human consciousness becomes progressively more distant from its instinctual foundations. The "evolution of consciousness" does not mean human beings have necessarily become wiser, more enlightened, or more moral—there is plenty of evidence to the contrary on these counts. Rather, the evolution refers to a transformation in the interior dynamics of the human psyche, bringing a radical shift in the relationship

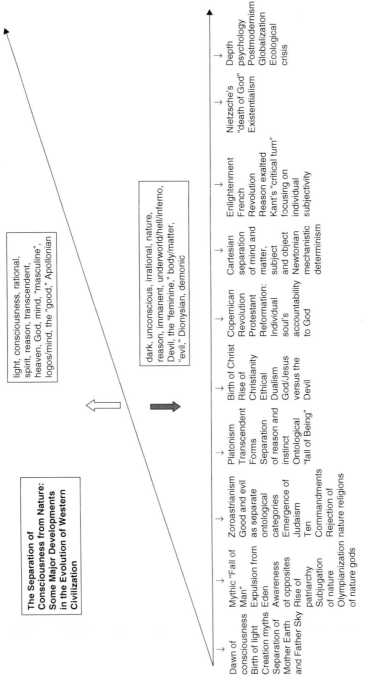

Figure 2: The Separation of Consciousness from Nature

between ego-consciousness and the larger psyche. Fundamentally, as we have seen, it refers to the continuing development of consciousness and the overcoming of instinctive unconscious modes of living. The former wholeness of the psyche—a natural, instinctive preconscious wholeness—is progressively destroyed through the development of self-reflective consciousness.

"Every step towards fuller consciousness," Jung wrote of the modern individual,

> removes him from his original, purely animal *participation mystique* with the herd, from submersion in a common unconsciousness. Every step forward means tearing oneself loose from the maternal womb of unconsciousness in which the mass of man dwells.[32]

Each time one has to go against one's natural tendency, to resist the way one instinctively wants to be and to act, the resulting tension potentially generates an increase in consciousness. One takes a step towards bringing into reality a new mode of being. Each step is experienced as a painful denial of instinct; it is a dying to the old life, which, in response to its violation, rises up against us. One feels that consciousness is literally being torn away from nature, ripped out of its former unconscious identity with desires and passions. Participation in this process is the essence of the Western spiritual odyssey and the way of individuation.

ſ

CHAPTER 3

The Death of God and the *Übermensch*

Man is not by any means of fixed and enduring form....
He is much more an experiment and a transition.
He is nothing else than the narrow and perilous
bridge between nature and spirit. His innermost destiny
drives him on to the spirit and to God. His inmost
longing draws him back to nature, the mother. Between
the two forces his life hangs tremulous and irresolute.
          —Hermann Hesse

Jung proposed that the various transformations of myth and religion, of the kind described above, might reflect the fact that the divine itself—to which, in the West, we commonly give the name *God*—is participating in a continual evolution through the medium of human experience. "The gods," Jung observes, "first lived in superhuman power and beauty on the top of snow-clad mountains or in the darkness of caves, woods and seas. Later on they drew together into one god, and then that god became man."[1] Here Jung is basically charting the transition we outlined from Greco-Roman *polytheism* (the Olympian pantheon of gods and goddesses) to the *monotheism* of Judaism (the one God) and on to the Incarnation of God in human form as Jesus Christ. As we will see in this chapter, in the last century or so a further transformation appears to be taking place, with the proclaimed "death of God" and, shortly thereafter, the rediscovery of the "gods" and the archetypal "God-image" within the depths of individual psychological experience—a development to which Jung's own work has made a major contribution.

Disenchantment and the Death of God

There comes a point in human psychological evolution at which it appears to be necessary to even deny the existence of God, to reject any notion that life is shaped by a transcendent power. Mircea Eliade describes this well:

> Modern nonreligious man assumes a new existential situation. He regards himself solely as the subject and agent of history, and he refuses all appeal to transcendence. . . . Man makes himself, and he only makes himself completely in proportion as he desacralizes himself with the whole. The sacred is the prime obstacle to his freedom.[2]

The human ego thus claims for itself the power previously attributed to nature, the gods, or God, and in so doing furthers its own autonomy and freedom of self-determination. Eliade calls this process *desacralization*, which is similar to Max Weber's notion of *disenchantment*, a process that has shaped modernity after the rise of science.

Disenchantment is the term employed by Weber to describe the world view of modern secular society in which, as he puts it, "no mysterious incalculable forces come into play"—a world view in which recourse to mysticism, supernatural powers, gods and goddesses, spirits, and magical explanations is considered both unnecessary and invalid.[3] This disenchanted vision, which gained ascendancy in Western civilization after the Enlightenment and especially during the nineteenth century, was created, Weber observes, by processes of "rationalization" according to which life was to be explained in terms of observable and measurable natural forces. Scientific knowledge increasingly replaced religious belief such that the world, no longer related to a spiritual principle of any kind, was stripped of intrinsic meaning; it was no longer seen as sacred.

Richard Tarnas connects disenchantment to the process of *objectification*, by which the external world was viewed no longer as a meaningful subject, possessing intentionality, interiority, and *telos*, but as an object—as unconscious, lifeless matter moved mechanistically by material forces, that could be measured, controlled, and manipulated. During the modern era, Tarnas points out, the locus of all meaning in the world shifted exclusively to the interior realm of human consciousness. The world itself was conceived as possessing no meaning save for that projected onto it by the human psyche. As we have seen, the term *demythologization* has similar connotations, referring explicitly to the process by which mythic elements were removed from explanations of the origin, purpose, and functioning of the world.

This disenchanting trajectory culminated in Friedrich Nietzsche's epochal proclamation of the "death of God" in the late nineteenth century. The conception of the Judeo-Christian God that has sustained Western civilization for thousands of years, Nietzsche believed, was no longer relevant and had been irrevocably eroded by the discoveries of science—a revelation that had a host of moral, cosmological, and metaphysical implications. God had been "killed," unwittingly, by modern individuals who were unconsciously complicit in this act both through the development of science and through an inner transformation of human consciousness that rendered obsolete the need for the traditional concept of God. With the act of divine patricide, the support that Christian morality provided for the culture was increasingly eroded too.

Nietzsche felt he was the first to fully experience and realize what was taking place. He had deeply assimilated the implications of science for modern life. He grasped the momentous consequences for psychology and spirituality of the scientific world view in which the Earth was just an insignificant planet adrift in a vast universe (no longer center of the cosmic scheme, as had been thought before Copernicus) and in which life was a chance and meaningless occurrence, the human being a "haphazard creature without meaning" as Jung later put it—a creature evolved from the apes rather than made in the image of God.[4]

Nietzsche's philosophy was centered upon the insight that the established religious teachings and morality, as far as he was concerned, had become impediments to a vital life; they made the human spirit "decadent" and sick, even if at a collective level the wider culture was yet to realize it. The doctrinal interpretation of biblical scripture propounded by the Church advocated a way of living that was inherently opposed to the expression of the instincts, often to the detriment of human wellbeing. Nietzsche believed that Christianity had elevated and promulgated values that were injurious to the development of the individual personality, injurious even to the healthy expression of human nature. In his challenge to Christian morality, he called into question the ethical division between good and evil, arguing that the modern, Christianized meaning of the word *good* had become inverted from its original meaning. If one looks back to the pre-Christian era, to the ancient Greeks and Romans, the term *good* was originally reserved for the person of excellence, nobility, authority, and power; goodness was not associated with charitable works, concern for others, acts of kindness, and so forth—such traits, Nietzsche argued, would have been connected with ineffectual weakness, and would thus have been deemed bad and undesirable.[5] What is the original and correct meaning of the word *good*, he asks? Is the good person the one who just follows the rules, is well liked, and never does anything wrong, never offends anyone, and is always kind to people, as in the Christian view? Or is the good person the one who dares to stand alone, be disliked if necessary, and perhaps even upset people in the pursuit of truth and in the commitment to authenticity and excellence? The life of Jesus, it should be pointed out, appears to embrace both these possibilities.

Nietzsche realized that the greatest good and the highest achievements are only possible through struggle and suffering, by engaging the instincts, affirming the life will. To live a vital existence, one cannot just deny the instincts and desires, and follow the prescribed rules of a moral code. Under the influence of Christian morality, people became so intent on trying to do good deeds and to not commit sins in order to get into Heaven and to avoid the terrible fate of sinners in Hell, they adopted a restrictive moral code that excessively suppressed the natural instincts and stifled individuality. "The person who does essentially nothing with his or her life but has avoided 'sin' might merit heaven, on the Christian view, while a creative person may be deemed 'immoral' for refusing to follow 'the herd'."[6] This summary, by Robert Solomon and Kathleen Higgins, captures well the essence of Nietzsche's insight.

Nietzsche pointed out that without a healthy relationship to the instinctual power of life our attempts to attain to humility and modesty have produced only a shallow mediocrity; the ideal of the love of our fellow human beings has often become merely an escape from the painful necessity of truly facing ourselves; our preoccupation with an afterlife in Heaven has devalued the importance of our embodied life here and now; and our emphasis on spirit has denigrated the body and alienated us from our natural instincts that might bring to our lives an authenticity, intensity, and spontaneity otherwise lacking.

Nietzsche affirmed individual experience; he affirmed instinct, biology, and the earth. He was not only anti-Christian, but anti-religious, although deeply spiritual in his own way. He sought to destroy all the old idols, the old myths, the old metaphysical beliefs and morals, in a radical overthrow of the entire religious and moral trajectory of the West. He wanted to wipe the metaphysical horizon clean, to begin again in a new direction.[7]

The Will to Power and the *Übermensch*

Nietzsche's philosophy can be understood in part as a reaction against his philosophical predecessor, Arthur Schopenhauer. Schopenhauer is generally considered to be a pessimistic philosopher in that life, as he saw it, consists of endless suffering and strife resulting from the inexorable activity of the Will. "Life is something that should never have been," is Schopenhauer's well-known summation of our existential condition in which we can never reside for more than a fleeting moment in a state of peace because the Will, which drives us all, is ceaseless in its desiring. Schopenhauer was resigned to this, and argues the best one can do is to attempt to endure this situation, developing compassion for other beings who also suffer. For him, the only respite can be achieved through aesthetic contemplation of the world of representation or perhaps through Eastern contemplative practices—a philosophical tradition which was of great solace for Schopenhauer personally.

Nietzsche, by contrast, sees the Will in far more positive terms, espousing a fundamentally different life philosophy. Rather than seek refuge from the Will, Nietzsche advocates that we affirm it, affirm the suffering that comes from the expression of the Will, and that we cultivate an attitude of *amor fati*—the love of one's fate. In this respect, in his affirmation of life and the world with all its passions and struggles, Nietzsche is most quintessentially Western in his approach, eschewing and condemning what he saw as Schopenhauer's—and later, Richard Wagner's—philosophy and art of "decadence."[8]

While it is true that the Will produces suffering, Nietzsche argues, the suffering can be used a stimulus to growth and evolution.[9] The Will, for Nietzsche, is not merely a will to exist and to propagate, but a *Will to power*, seeking ever to surpass itself, destroying and creating, impelling the individual to the self-overcoming and psychological metamorphosis that might bring forth the *Übermensch*—a form of being far beyond the normal human condition, existing as a distant possibility for the future of the human spirit. The *Übermensch*, or Superman, as it is often translated, is a being of greater power, greater courage, forged and molded by the Will, a being that is its own moral and spiritual authority, a god-like being "beyond good and evil"—the fashioner of values and maker of meaning within what is, for Nietzsche, an otherwise meaningless world.

For Nietzsche, the human exists as a bridge between the animal level and this god-like condition: "Man is a rope, fastened between animal and Superman—a rope over an abyss. A dangerous going-across, a dangerous wayfaring, a dangerous looking-back, a dangerous shuddering and staying-still."[10] The coming of the *Übermensch* heralds a momentous point in human evolution:

> And this is the great noontide: it is when man stands at the middle of his course between animal and Superman and celebrates his journey to the evening as the highest hope: for it is the journey to a new morning. Then man, going under, will bless himself; for he will be going over to Superman; and the sun of his knowledge will stand at noontide.[11]

Only through suffering can we become more than we are, growing beyond our existing limits. The whole purpose of the life struggle, the *telos* of the Will, is to give birth to the *Übermensch*, which for Nietzsche was the true "meaning of the Earth," the ideal that could lead humanity beyond the decaying and "decadent" Christian religion.[12]

In the affirmation of nature, the earth, and the body, the *Übermensch* would embrace and assimilate the repressed instinctual power in the unconscious that had been created by the separation of consciousness from nature—a development that, as we have seen, had characterized Occidental mythology in general and Christianity in particular. The exaltation of the light of consciousness, spirit, reason, and rationality, and the extraverted "masculine" and patriarchal emphasis of Western culture, were supported and sustained by the exclusion and repression of other, opposite qualities: the instinctual power of nature, the life energy residing in what is deemed evil, the feminine principle, the soul, biology, matter, sexuality, uncivilized urges, irrational feelings, desires, and drives. Because of their repression, these factors had become dark, demonic, unconscious, and had not been integrated into human experience. They existed in the background to civilized life as subterranean forces residing beneath the orderly world of everyday concerns, behind the supposed autonomy and freedom of the self-willing rational ego, behind the veneer of human culture, yet periodically erupting as episodes of violence and barbarism, wars and conflicts, collective manias and psychopathology. Set against reason and morality, the repressed instincts can assume gargantuan proportions and can irrupt into consciousness or take possession of us. Indeed, in large part, depth psychology has arisen because of this schism between human rational consciousness and its instinctual basis, in an attempt to bring the two into a more constructive and balanced relationship.

As Jung argued in *Answer to Job*, and recalling our earlier diagram (figure 2), the absolute separation of good and evil into the metaphysical principles personified by God/Christ and the Devil, has produced or reflected a corresponding schism in the human psyche between ego-consciousness, which invariably identifies itself with the "good," and the unconscious, which contains our "evil" or undesirable shadow qualities. This development is reflected in our religious and mythic symbolism, in which the Christ image in the modern era has lost much of its original power and dynamism. It has effectively become a two-dimensional image of pure goodness and light, lacking darkness and shadow, and as such it needs to be brought into relationship with its complementary opposite, which, Jung thought, is well-represented by the darker, chthonic, morally ambivalent *Mercurius* of the alchemical tradition.[13] For Nietzsche, it was the pre-Christian, Greek god Dionysus who best embodied this lost dynamism and life-affirming Will to power, and who is consequently the mythic inspiration behind the superman Zarathustra.

Nihilism and Mythology

What happens when, as a culture, we break out of the traditional
Christian world view into a period of history shaped by the dawn-
ing realization that "God is dead"? What happens when the primary
source of life meaning passes away? The answers and consequences
are plainly evident all around us: Secular and political ideologies
assume quasi-religious status; materialism, economics, and consum-
erism are pursued with a religious fervor; science, in the service of
the state, becomes the new moral authority; higher purposes and
aspirations are lost as many people live for exclusively secular values. Meanwhile, others—the creative spiritual minority—are forced
to confront the reality of nihilism. For when the old belief systems
and the old collective mythology that gave meaning to experience
are taken away, the metaphysical and cosmological frameworks that
supported human life are shaken to their foundations and begin to
crumble.

Recalling the four functions of myth—metaphysical, cosmological, sociological, and psychological—what, we might ask, is the
metaphysical basis for a myth or a religion at a time when science
discloses a meaningless, arbitrary, material, and mechanistic universe? There is none. Metaphysics has effectively been wiped away.
Regarding the cosmological function, a disenchanted, desacralized
vision of things has taken hold in which there is apparently no spiritual meaning in anything, and in which we are adrift, without purpose or design, on a miniscule planet in the infinite nothingness of
outer space. The cosmos is anything but a holy picture. The human
is seen as nothing more than an evolved animal moved by biological
drives. Sociologically, as Campbell realized, all the local cultures,
formerly bound in their own regions, separate from the wider world,
have been swept together in an emerging global civilization. All
boundaries between cultures are dissolving. All cultures have become
exposed to each other, transformed by science and the industrial and
technological revolutions it gave rise to, and infiltrated by the modern Western consumer society and its values. Psychologically, without valid cultural myths, there are no longer forms of guidance for
the individual to help navigate the stages of life or to come to terms
with the deeper psyche. The destruction of the Christian metaphysical foundations of the West has also shaken to the core the

psychological foundations of the human identity. The security of living in a meaningful universe created and overseen by a loving personal God has gone. The Christian moral code and prescription for living are thus no longer valid. The result, as we have seen, is that one now has to navigate one's life transformations for oneself; there are no effective rites of passage to help us, no valid collective myths to guide and instruct. For the self-aware individual, all this creates an unavoidable problem: an existential crisis.

As we leave behind the supporting structures of collective religion and mythology that have been discredited by the rational-scientific world view of our time, it is thus the fate of many of people, as it was for Nietzsche, to confront this nihilistic world—a world in which there appears to be no meaning outside of one's own being, and a world from which one feels oneself to be radically separate and perhaps even alienated. One often has to go through such an experience of meaninglessness, through an existential crisis, to come to a fuller realization of a more encompassing living meaning. In so doing, one transcends secondhand beliefs, inherited from one's culture, and one transcends too the purely conceptual sense of life meaning or the experience of meaninglessness. Part of our challenge now is to develop a new world view and new forms of spirituality that can lead us beyond the nihilism and absolute relativism that define the post-modern understanding of the world. An encounter with nihilism might ultimately prefigure the emergence of a new deeper mode of spiritual realization.

Obviously, the collective majority of people remain professed believers of one faith or another. If you can live comfortably within the bounds of an old mythic-religious tradition, then all well and good. But if for you the old religious signs and symbols no longer have the authentic credibility they used to have, you are forced to find your own way through life, to find your own life meanings, your own personal myth. This is the person the work of Jung and Campbell addresses.

Depth Psychology and the Archetypal Hero

"By my love and hope I conjure thee, cast not away the hero in thy soul."[14] With these words from Nietzsche's Zarathustra, Campbell ends his survey of Occidental mythology, making a forward glance

to the modern era. It is the potential in the soul for the heroic affirmation of life and for self-overcoming that is to become important
to the future destiny of the human spirit. It is the archetypal pattern
of the hero that might serve as our guide in the era of individual
creative mythology now upon us. The hero myth carries the individualism of the West to its logical conclusion, fulfilling the Western
spiritual ideal, leading the individual self to its own transformation
through the inner encounter with the depths of the psyche and spirit.
In effect, the hero myth leads to the death and transfiguration of the
ego. It can guide the individual through the experience of psychospiritual death-rebirth occurring during individuation.

In the past, when people lived within a world described and made
comprehensible by already established and unquestioned myths or
religious teachings, it was perhaps only the mystic having a personal
experience of God and the shaman making an inner descent into the
spirit world who were able to experience for themselves the numinous depths of the psyche. Now, however, this experience is happening to many, many more of us. The problematic consequences of the
increasing autonomy of the individual self, coupled with the modern
rejection of myth, are the psychological difficulties inherent in modern ego-consciousness: neurosis, psychotic breaks, schizophrenia—
the whole field of psychopathology as well as the less defined,
pervasive sense of angst or panic or meaninglessness that is often
experienced in modern life. It is through such pathology, however,
that depth psychology has helped to connect people to spiritual meaning. A person consulting a therapist with a crippling neurosis or on the
verge of a psychological breakdown can, by affirming the experience
and searching for its deeper significance, be introduced to the "reality
of the psyche," with its hidden depths of meaning. Psychopathology
can be the gateway to a new type of individual spirituality.

In this context, Jung and Campbell were both concerned with preserving and enhancing the integrity of individual consciousness,
safeguarding the spark of authentic individual selfhood amidst the
often suffocating or disorienting pressures of modern life, which
could easily result in self-loss, loss of soul, and even spiritual death.
According to Jung, individuation has therefore become an absolute
imperative.[15] The dissolution of the old myths, the incredulity
towards the doctrines of the orthodox religious traditions, the rise of
the disenchanted scientific world view, the alienation experienced by

the modern self: these unprecedented circumstances present an opportunity to the modern individual. For they demand that the individual undertake the pursuit of his or her own individual spiritual path; they draw forth individuation as a response to the current phase of our collective psychospiritual evolution.

Individuation is, in effect, Jung's answer to Nietzsche. It is a response, that is, to the fate that befell Nietzsche, who found himself cast into the role of sacrificial prophet of an unconscious transformation process that had significance for the entire culture. For it is almost as if the whole religious-metaphysical past and the cultural history that had shaped the modern self converged in Nietzsche, and imploded, breaking open the realization of the unconscious. Trying to wipe this history away, he became rootless—an isolated individual consciousness contemplating nihilism. Yet out of this nihilism, as a compensatory response, burst forth the new conception of the *Übermensch* and the empirical discovery of the unconscious, with the emergence of depth psychology. Thereafter, everything that had previously seemed external to us—God above in Heaven, the Greek gods on Olympus, celestial planetary deities, exalted metaphysical systems such as the Platonic Forms, religious ideals, moral codes of conduct, the world soul and world spirit—were effectively rediscovered within. All metaphysical and mythical frameworks collapsed, as it were, falling into the depths of the unconscious psyche, to be discovered afresh, and understood in a new way.

The rejected and long-forgotten gods, and the repressed powers of the instincts, have welled up in the unconscious psyche, demanding conscious recognition. The ego, having established its volitional autonomy, now finds itself in a new position within the trajectory of Western spiritual and cultural history, having to confront the powers that have been repressed and forgotten en route to this point. For it is not, of course, that God, mythology, religion, and spirituality actually came to an end; rather, they were transformed, appearing thereafter in a different guise, to be encountered directly within the individual's own psyche.

All these changes obviously amount to a momentous transformation in human experience, and one that is yet really to fully unfold, especially at the collective level. Jung, perhaps better than anyone, understood what was happening. He described the modern self-aware human being as standing "upon a peak, or at the very edge of

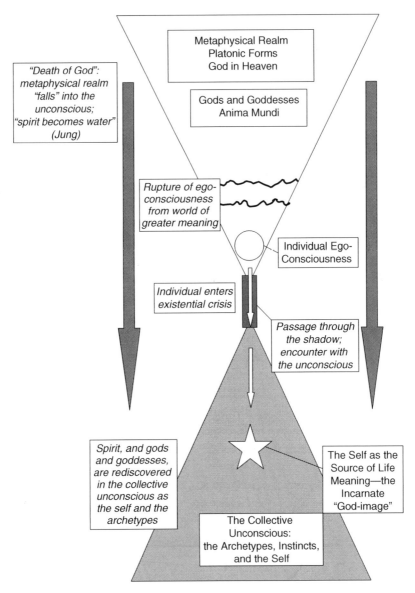

**Figure 3: The Collapse of Metaphysical Meaning
and the Discovery of the Unconscious**

the world, the abyss of the future before him, above him the heavens, and below him the whole of mankind with a history that disappears in primeval mists."[16] This is a powerful image of where the modern individual self currently stands.

The Coming Together of East and West,
Ancient and Modern

In the modern era, we are also experiencing a cross-fertilization of the Oriental and Occidental streams. These two streams represent, as it were, the two halves of the psyche. As we have seen, the Western stream emphasizes the heroic individual, the ascent of individual consciousness, extraverted activity, and conquest and domination; in all these respects, it is fundamentally "solar." The Eastern stream has a "lunar" or yin type character, emphasizing the matrix of being, the unconscious, more receptive, "feminine" qualities. As soon as the path of Western development glimpsed its apex, which is acutely evident in Nietzsche, it is as if the alienated ego reached out to its other half, unconsciously attempting to find a new relationship to its ground, its containing matrix. And so it was that Eastern philosophy and religion increasingly infiltrated Western thought around this time. Later, Eastern ideas began to reach a far wider audience through the work of figures such as D. T. Suzuki, Alan Watts, Paramahansa Yogananda, and Campbell himself. As the limits of the rational ego were approached, more and more people in the West began to contemplate the Eastern notions of the spiritual ground of being and quest for enlightenment through an introspective path of spiritual realization. The encounter with the East therefore suggested a possibility for a future spiritual direction in the West.

Conversely, Eastern scholars, most notably Sri Aurobindo and later Haridas Chauduri, began to assimilate the Western notion of evolution and apply this idea to the timeless spiritual philosophy of the East. The Hindu concept of an eternal spiritual ground was brought into relationship with the Western idea of an evolving cosmos. Aurobindo formulated a vision of reality in which an involution of a divine Supermind into matter gives rise to a subsequent evolution of the nascent consciousness in matter back towards the divine ground. Alongside this, of course, Western democratic ideals and scientific knowledge have been disseminated throughout much of the world, creating greater freedom for many people. Individual mythology emerges from the individualism of the West, yet it is informed too by a global spiritual perspective and the perennial mythology.

A further development of our age has seen the reemergence of premodern and suppressed occult perspectives from within the Western tradition. Indeed, a later influence on Campbell's own thought was *The Gospel of Thomas*, one of the so-called Gnostic Gospels that were unearthed in the Middle East in the 1940s, forming part of the Nag Hammadi library. These ancient Coptic scrolls, dating from the fourth century CE, which appear to be translations of earlier Greek documents, throw a fascinating new light on early Christianity. Among these texts, *The Gospel of Thomas*, believed to be based on the teachings of Jesus, is especially significant, containing profound psychospiritual insights and illuminating parables. Campbell saw Gnosticism, as exemplified in this text, as a Western equivalent to Buddhism. Like Buddhism and Hindu Yoga, Gnosticism held out the promise of individual spiritual enlightenment, attained through one's own efforts, something traditional Christian religion did not offer. Campbell was especially fond of quoting the following two logia from *The Gospel of Thomas*, passages which directly contradict the doctrines of Church orthodoxy and appear to put the teachings of Christ more in accord with Eastern thought:

> Jesus said: "He who drinks from my mouth shall become as me; and I myself will become him."[17]

Campbell points out that this idea—the notion that anyone can become like Christ, and thus like God—would be considered blasphemous in orthodox Christianity. It is more like the Buddhist idea, he noted, that everyone has "Buddha nature" and that you can, through your own efforts, realize this nature and achieve spiritual liberation.[18]

The second passage also challenges the orthodox Christian view of God:

> Jesus said: "I am the All. The All comes forth from me. . . . Cleave the wood, I am there; lift up the stone and you shall find me there."[19]

This logion points to Christ's spiritual identity with all things; it is the revelation that God pervades everything, the whole of nature—a view which is, of course, a radical deviation from the view of a Father God in Heaven, standing above and beyond His creation. According to this teaching, God is not wholly transcendent, wholly other, but also immanent in the world, in nature, present in each of us.

These influences—ancient, premodern, esoteric, and Eastern, as well as shamanic and indigenous—have significantly shaped the nature of contemporary spirituality.[20] Indeed, one could argue that we seem to have experienced a globalization of the psyche in step with the globalization of culture. Campbell once remarked that he had yet to learn of a Christian mystic who had been surprised by a vision of the Buddha, or vice versa.[21] Spiritual experiences, he noted, always appear clothed in the language of one's own tradition. Over the last fifty years, however, the research of transpersonal psychologist Stanislav Grof has revealed that in non-ordinary states of consciousness our collective spiritual history in its entirety seems to be potentially accessible to any individual. One can just as readily have an experience of a South American shaman as of Christ or Krishna, or an experience of Shiva as of Allah or the Great Spirit, no matter what tradition one originally belonged to. Contemporary creative mythology, in short, has access to and is informed by the whole spiritual-religious-mythic cultural heritage of the human species—an unprecedented development that marks our age as unique.

CHAPTER 4

Creative Mythology and Individuation

New wine should not be put into old bottles . . . like a snake changing its skin, the old myth needs to be clothed anew in every renewed age if it is not to lose its therapeutic effect.

The urge and compulsion to self-realization is a law of nature and thus of invincible power.

—C. G. Jung

To understand the emergence of the era of creative mythology, we need to keep in mind the narrative perspective on our spiritual history and the entire trajectory of the evolution of consciousness described above. As we have seen, creative mythology comes out of the individualism and individuation of the West; it is an expression of a differentiated, autonomous ego-consciousness that experiences itself as a self-willing, self-determining subject facing the world and separate from nature. The modern self, in claiming its autonomy and freedom, has rejected all forms of external spiritual authority, rejected the previously dominant myths and religions; the culture itself, as we have seen, provides no vital living myths or intrinsic spiritual orientation for its people. Consequently, new forms of mythic expression and individual spirituality have arisen, compensating, to an extent, for the cultural decline of myth.

There are two main aspects to what Campbell calls *creative mythology* or *individual mythology*: first, giving creative expression to the insights arising from one's own life experiences, creating one's own myth, as it were; and, second, reading existing myths metaphorically to find guidance for one's individual life journey. Let us now consider each of these in turn.

The Creative Artist and Modern Myths

According to Campbell, it is the role of creative artists, giving form to their own insights and perceptions, to articulate and communicate their own individual myths to the wider culture. This marks a key distinction from earlier forms of myth:

> In the context of a traditional mythology, the symbols are presented in socially maintained rites, through which the individual is required to experience . . . certain insights, sentiments, and commitments. In what I am calling "creative" mythology, on the other hand, this order is reversed: the individual has an experience of his or her own—of order, horror, beauty, or even mere exhilaration—which he or she needs to communicate through signs; and if this realization has been of a certain depth or import, his or her communication will have the value or force of a living myth. . .[1]

Campbell argues that myths in the modern world are no longer tied to particular places and particular cultures. The originating source of myths—the *mythogenetic zone*, as he calls it—has shifted to the inner world of the creative individual, which has brought forth an eclectic diversity of myths in our time:

> In the fields of literature, secular philosophy, and the arts, a totally new type of non-theological revelation, of great scope, great depth, and infinite variety, has become the actual spiritual guide and structuring force of the society. . .[2]

> [T]he released creative powers of a great company of towering individuals have broken forth: so that not one, or even two or three, but a galaxy of mythologies . . . must be taken into account in any study of our own titanic age.[3]

In the absence of a functioning collective mythology adequate to our age, it is the vocation of creative artists, says Campbell, to bring forth out of their own experiences modern forms of myth. Examples abound of artists whose work fulfils this function. So Jack Kerouac, for instance, writes *On the Road*, which portrays for every young person afterwards what it is like to throw off societal expectations and conventions in favor of the freedom and experimentation of one's own life adventure on the margins of society. And Georgia O'Keeffe's paintings mythologize the landscape of New Mexico, as Frida Kahlo's self-portraits give striking visual form to her experiences of extreme physical pain. And Jim Morrison and The Doors celebrate a reawakening of the Dionysian spirit in the 1960s, as The Beatles portray for a generation the life changes occurring through romantic relationships and through the spiritual seeking and idealism that characterized their later work. Throughout the arts, we now have unprecedented access to the creative products of millions of people around the world. Such creativity constitutes an eclectic, currently incoherent, mythological tapestry, reflecting the major cultural transformation of myth over the last few centuries.

Myths, for Campbell, give us clues and instruction as to how to live in the world, putting us in touch with energies and ways of being we might have forgotten or ignored, and connecting us to forces emerging from the unconscious into the cultural zeitgeist. Great works of art and literature and music do this too. The creative artist, if he or she has penetrated to sufficient depth, can direct our conscious awareness to universal truths, expressing these truths in new ways relevant to the culture at that time.

Modern mythology might thus be seen as the collection of stories and symbols and works of art that have been, and that continue to be, created by individuals around the world. Whether conveyed through painting, music, literature, film, or dance, or through philosophy and science, these creative emanations are each contributing to new narratives that address the unique challenges facing the individual, civilization, and our planet in the postmodern world, and yet addressing universally human concerns.

It is the mythic function of modern art, then, to give new forms of expression to the universal truths of myth—a function admirably fulfilled, Campbell believed, by George Lucas's *Star Wars*, which presents a new inflection, a new telling, of the archetypal themes of the myth of the hero. These themes appear relevant to the modern individual, Campbell claims, because the myth is futuristic and technological in its setting, and it cannot be historically located and thus literalized as historical fact. One is not watching fishermen living two-thousand years ago in the Holy Land, which one could write off as being outdated and thus perhaps irrelevant to modern life. The great value of modern artists, such as those listed above, is that they were communicating in the language and ideas of their time, often dealing with universal problems but in a language specific to their time or their own experiences.

Clearly, though, artistic expression is of many different kinds, and those art forms that penetrate to the deeper dimensions of the psyche are, perforce, exceptions rather than the norm. Jung drew a distinction between two modes of artistic creation, which he called *psychological* and *visionary*. The former encompasses almost every type of artistic, poetic, and literary work, whose content, according to Jung, is drawn from the typical core experiences of human life—from "eternally repeated joys and sorrows," and from "passion and its fated outcome, human destiny and its sufferings, eternal nature with its beauty and horror."[4] In psychological art such experiences are "raised from the commonplace to the level of poetic experience."[5] There is nothing strange or uncanny about the content of such creative works. Their subject matter is well known to us.

Visionary creation, by contrast, describes only the rarest of artworks: the second part of Goethe's *Faust*, Hölderlin's poetry, Nietzsche's *Thus Spoke Zarathustra*, and Wagner's *Ring Cycle*, for instance. Such works are based on the experience of a primordial revelation, and their character strikes one as strange, numinous, perhaps disturbing, as Jung explains:

> It is something strange that derives its existence from the hinterland of man's mind, as if it had emerged from the abyss of pre-human ages, or from a superhuman world of contrasting light and darkness. . . . Sublime, pregnant with meaning, yet chilling the blood with its strangeness, it arises from the timeless depths: glamorous, daemonic and grotesque, it bursts asunder our human standards of value and aesthetic form, a terrifying tangle of eternal chaos.[6]

Jung's own *Red Book*, with its revelations of the terrifying numinous power of the dark side of the divine, would clearly fall into this category. More generally, visionary experiences of this kind seem to constitute the very stuff of myth, which is born from revelation, from an original experience of the depths of the unconscious psyche.

For his own part, Campbell was careful to distinguish between great art, which can touch upon the deepest of truths, and merely commercial art, which is often alarmingly superficial. For Campbell, creative mythology emerges from *visionary*, rather than merely *descriptive*, art—although the meaning he attaches to the word *visionary* is rather different from Jung's usage, above.[7] It is the purpose of great artists, according to Campbell, to inspire the individual journey by illuminating the universal "elementary ideas" in human experience, revealing how they manifest in contemporary life. Visionary art, for Campbell, is therefore essentially archetypal, portraying the perennial themes of human experience.

One of Campbell's own heroes and guides, the German novelist Thomas Mann, had this to say about the influence of mythic insight on artistic creation:

> There is no doubt about it, the moment when the story-teller acquires the mythical way of looking at things, the gift of seeing the typical features of characteristics and events, that moment marks a beginning in his life. It means a particular intensification of his artistic mood, a new serenity in his powers of perception and creation.[8]

Campbell thought that the painters Picasso and Paul Klee, as well as Joyce and Mann, were prime examples of contemporary mythmakers.[9] Indeed, Picasso was perhaps the best example of Nietzsche's *Übermensch*: he was a self-determining and ruthlessly creative, often amoral, individual, who did not seem to be bound by any external moral code or social expectation or the normal sensitivities of human feeling, but was just able to be as he was, without apology, spontaneously expressing himself in a stream of playful creativity.

Discussing the mythically inspired paintings from Picasso's work in Antibes, such as "Night Fishing at Antibes," "Triumph of Pan," "The Rape of Europa," and "La Joie De Vivre," Boeck, a prominent writer on Picasso, notes:

> The importance of this work . . . lies in the fact that these mythological themes [in the paintings] are not intended as some kind of classical revival, but are Picasso's intuitions, through which the Mediterranean spirit speaks to our age. Or, to use psychological terms, Picasso's art succeeds in transforming archetypes of the collective unconscious into visible and understandable symbols.[10]

.his analysis closely accords with Campbell's view of the significance of the creative artist as mythmaker. However, perhaps reflecting the influence of Jung, Campbell's work is concerned not merely
with portraying the archetypes, but also with the process of psychospiritual transformation—a further expression of his essentially
Romantic life philosophy.

As M. H. Abrams's classic study of Romanticism has shown, the
deepest forms of artistic expression are often inextricably connected
with psychospiritual transformation. Surveying the work of Blake,
Wordsworth, Hölderlin, Shelley, and others, Abrams shows that
these visionary artists were concerned with a transformative movement from a natural state of innocence and wholeness to a condition
of alienated separation and then, ideally, towards the recovery of a
higher spiritual wholeness. This process is also symbolically
described in biblical terms as a threefold movement from: (1) the
blissful paradise of the Garden of Eden representing the undivided
unity of God, nature, and human beings; (2) the Fall and the expulsion from Eden, indicative of the alienation of human beings from
God and nature; and (3) the long, tortuous journey towards the attainment of the Kingdom of Heaven by which the original unity might
be restored. The parable of the Prodigal Son would suggest that this
process, even the state of alienation, has divine sanction.[11]

The Three Metamorphoses of the Spirit

Nietzsche's parable, "On the Three Metamorphoses of the Spirit" in
Thus Spoke Zarathustra (which Campbell discusses in *The Power
of Myth* interviews) is especially relevant for understanding the process of psychological transformation informing creative mythology. In describing the movement of the human spirit through three
forms—camel, lion, and child—the parable essentially conforms to
the Romantic pattern, culminating in the realization of what might
be described as a condition of *higher naturalness*.

In the first metamorphosis, Nietzsche depicts the human spirit
assuming the form of a camel, stooping to take on the heavy load of
the knowledge, experience, and values that one's socio-cultural
background can provide. The camel relates to that stage of life when
we learn from those who have gone before us, master the skills that

enable us to function and prosper in the world, and assimilate the accumulated wisdom of the culture. The more that can be absorbed, the heavier the burden assumed, the more power of influence one will subsequently be able to wield in life.

To remain at this life stage, however, is to stay within the bounds of the culture, and the possibilities it provides for individual fulfil-ment—an unhappy prospect for the creative individual for whom such limitation can be severely injurious. By adhering to the accepted patterns of life in society, such people would be forced to live at a level far beneath their potential. The creative individual often finds it difficult to function within the confines of conventional experience simply because the roles presented as valid life patterns and possi-bilities by the culture are too restrictive and limiting, focused pri-marily upon economic and wholly personal matters rather than the deeper concerns of life. Obviously, if you belong to this creative minority, it is imperative to become more than a mere reflection of what has been learned; you must be willing to follow your own path and to dedicate yourself to the expression of your own creative impulses—a challenge addressed by the second and third metamor-phoses in Nietzsche's parable.

Having taken upon itself the burden of knowledge from the cul-ture, the human spirit must next, Nietzsche instructs, use this knowl-edge to achieve self-mastery and win through to individual freedom. The spirit, no longer satisfied with merely reflecting and espousing what has been learned, thus assumes the form of a lion. Roaring the proclamation "I will," the lion confronts that which stands in the way of its freedom to create anew; it confronts a fearsome dragon whose name, "Thou Shalt," is inscribed across each of its many scales. Signifying the authority of the established order, the dragon repre-sents the force of history and tradition, of accepted values ("the val-ues of a thousand years"), all the moral imperatives and expectations placed on us by society and culture—that one must live a certain way, behave a certain way. The dragon here represents the judging, censoring authority of something like a Freudian superego. Some of these moral imperatives and "thou shalts" can be traced far back in human history; others are derived from the attitudes and fashions of the day. The function of the lion is that of liberator: It has to over-come the dragon and throw off all external pressures and expectations.

Over the course of the last century, for a number of prominent artists and thinkers the struggle for spiritual and psychological freedom was primarily directed against the orthodox Christian church, which formed the major component of the religious and philosophical conditioning of their youth. In *A Portrait of the Artist as a Young Man*, for example, James Joyce explores the process of the awakening of an independent aesthetic sensibility in early-twentieth-century Catholic Dublin. Joyce paints an exceptionally vivid picture of the nightmarish tortures of Hell, described by Catholic priests as the inescapable fate of all sinners, a vision that was instilled into the impressionable young minds of schoolboys in Joyce's novel, constituting a fearsome and formidable barrier to individual psychological and spiritual unfolding. Part of Campbell's own life journey was the rebellion against and rejection of certain aspects of Roman Catholicism.[12] In time, he seems to have reconciled himself to his Catholic background by distinguishing the Christian myth and teachings of Jesus from the doctrine espoused by the Church, enabling him to take from the religion its deeper psychospiritual import.

The development of an independent spiritual perspective and judgment are crucial, Campbell realized, to enable the modern individual to withstand the pressures to conform—from mass society, from cultural and religious conditioning, and from the individual's own internalized moral code. As an antidote, Campbell's teaching encourages individuals to do what it is they really want to do in life, to cultivate a form of spirituality that affirms nature and the instincts, a form of spirituality that arises from natural life rather than negates it—in accord with a Romantic philosophy of life.

We can see something of this attitude in Joyce's character Stephen Dedalus, who affirms an impassioned commitment to authentic individual experience, whatever the cost. In *The Masks of God, Volume 4: Creative Mythology,* Campbell champions Joyce's summation of an unswerving determination to be true to one's self even if this means transgressing the moral imperatives and laws of one's society and religion, even if it means facing the prospect of an eternity in Hell: "Better Hell in one's own character than Heaven as somebody else," Joyce declares, "for that would be exactly to make of Hell, Heaven, and of Heaven, Hell"—a sentiment with which Nietzsche, ever the fierce individualist, would surely have concurred.[13]

The human spirit, to return to Nietzsche's parable, is thus transformed from camel to lion that it might "capture freedom and be lord in its own desert" to "create itself freedom for new creation," to proclaim a "sacred No even to duty."[14] Symbolizing instinctually empowered individualism, the lion's purpose is to reject and repudiate everything that stands in the way of creative individual freedom, even if this means, as it did for Nietzsche, rejecting the religious morality of his age in its entirety.

In the final transformation, according to Nietzsche, the human spirit assumes the form of a child who represents "innocence and forgetfulness, a new beginning, a sport, a self-propelling wheel, a first motion, a sacred Yes."[15] Nietzsche's image of a "self-propelling wheel," moving out of its own center, points to a state of being in which one lives and acts not out of a sense of duty, convention, or social expectation, but from one's own inner, creative depths, as a self-generating, self-determining being. It alludes to the transformation of individuation in which the existential center of gravity shifts from the thinking rational ego to what Jung calls the Self—the point of organic interconnection with the whole of existence, reflecting the wholeness of individual experience.[16] With this transition, the "sacred No" roared by the lion in anger and defiance against the conformist pressure of socio-cultural conditioning, becomes a "'sacred Yes," a wholehearted acceptance of life as it is by the child for whom life has become creative play. The inner nature—the creative child within—previously submerged by layer upon layer of conditioning, becomes free to live and create anew.

A process of this kind may be observed in the lives of many great artists, particularly those who became pioneers in their fields. To be proficient in any field of endeavor, it is first necessary to learn the rules and techniques of one's craft, whatever that might be. To remain at this stage, however, one would simply be a craftsman, skilled perhaps at replicating and implementing established styles or regurgitating knowledge secondhand, but not yet able to bring forth anything original. To be genuinely creative, one must be willing to set aside a rigid adherence to learned techniques and the knowledge one has assimilated to allow the emergence of one's own unique style of expression. Picasso was a master of his craft at a young age, but obviously Picasso only set himself apart after he developed his own new approaches to forms of representation in painting. To do this, he had to dare to leave behind more traditional styles, of which he was a master. In time, his painting exhibited a quality of childlike freedom of creative expression. He created as if he were a child, living out of the spontaneity of his own center, unhindered by what was expected, without concern for what others thought. "It took me four years to paint like Raphael," Picasso remarked, "but a lifetime to paint like a child."[17]

In an altogether different field, the great martial arts practitioner and pioneer Bruce Lee recognized a similar process, describing martial arts training as comprising three stages: the primitive stage, the stage of art, and the stage of artlessness.[18] Prior to any kind of training, combat, in its *natural* or primitive condition, is just instinctive fighting. Then, during the years of practice of set routines or *kata*, the combatant no longer fights instinctively but in a controlled, trained, and therefore a rather mechanical and *unnatural* way, employing learned techniques in combat. Finally, for the adept, according to Lee, a state of artlessness or *conscious naturalness* might arise, characterized by a creative freedom and controlled spontaneity emerging out of a total mastery of technique and corresponding, therefore, to the spirit as child in Nietzsche's model. Lee also describes this condition as one in which the individual is "consciously unconscious" or "unconsciously conscious."[19]

In the New Testament, Jesus's exhortation to "become as little children" (Matthew 18:3) points to just this kind of developmental trajectory. This teaching does not, of course, imply that we should return to a condition of childlike dependency or infantilism. Rather, it seems to refer to the attainment, in conscious self-awareness, of the spiritual freedom, playfulness, and spontaneity that result from deep psychological transformation. For all his critical judgments of the morality of orthodox Christianity, Nietzsche's parable points to a remarkably similar goal. As we will see, this aim finds fuller articulation in Jung's model of individuation and its mythic portrayal in the hero's journey. The insights of Nietzsche and Jung suggest that if the old god is indeed dead, a new god—the deeper Self, in Jungian terms, born as a "child" in the psyche of each of us—is emerging as

a living center within. It is the individual's challenge to consciousl
participate in this unfolding spiritual transformation, a process that is
symbolically illuminated by the motifs of the mythic hero's
journey.

Reading Myth as Metaphor

The second aspect of individual mythology, the one to which we will
be giving our attention in the chapters to follow, is concerned with
the interpretation of myths, old and new, to illuminate the themes,
challenges, and transformations of human psychological and spiritual experience. For those people who can no longer find meaning
within established religious traditions, a metaphorical reading of
myth, Campbell proposes, can disclose the deeper truth contained
within it and provide guidance for the individual's life journey. To
this end, myths are to be read as metaphorical of psychospiritual
processes.

From a depth psychological perspective, myths generally do not
mean what they appear to mean; their true meaning is not always
readily apparent, but often can only be discerned by considering the
symbolic implications of the stories within them—reading them, as
Campbell put it, in terms of their *connotation* rather than their *deno-
tation*. This point is absolutely crucial. Descriptions of an impending
apocalypse in myth or religious literature, for example, do not mean
that the end of the world is literally coming. For Campbell, these
accounts describe the psychological experience of the death of the
old ego, which, for the person experiencing it, always feels like it is
indeed the end of the world. The myth expresses, through a metaphorical description of a physical event, a psychospiritual experience. A metaphor is written in such a way that it appears to be a
statement of fact, which makes it susceptible to a concretized misin-
terpretation by the more literal minded. Thus, the myth of the hero's
adventure, which is Campbell's primary focus in his early work,
does not literally pertain to heroic deeds performed in the world, but
with facing and battling the inner demons of one's psyche in the
form of drives and complexes, resistances and blockages, archetypes
and instincts.[20] The adventure is one of spiritual transformation
through the overcoming of the forces and powers of one's own

psyche; it is not to do with domination and conquest of the outer world.

The significance of the hero myth as a guide to psychospiritual transformation was explored in Jung's *Symbols of Transformation* and further elaborated in Neumann's *The Origins and History of Consciousness*. Both works address the struggle of ego-consciousness to differentiate itself from, and then overcome, the instinctual power of the unconscious, symbolized by the hero's confrontation with the dark powers of nature (as in the dragon fight) and encounter with the maternal ground of being (symbolized by the Great Mother). Campbell puts forward a similar, if less technical, approach to interpreting the hero myth in *The Hero with a Thousand Faces*, drawing on both Freudian and Jungian psychology, and informed too by mysticism, literature, and classical mythology.

It is essential to the metaphorical approach that one try to discern the universal themes within myths. To this end, Campbell calls upon Jung's understanding of the dynamics of the unconscious psyche. From analyzing myths and dreams, especially numinous "big dreams," Jung discovered that certain core themes tend to occur over and over again, such as an encounter with a dark figure, fighting a ferocious beast, going off into a dark forest, encountering a wise guide or hearing a "voice" that announces with absolute authority what is to occur. He therefore concluded that there is a universal dimension or collective region of the human psyche that gives rise to these core themes. Such themes are all related, he suggests, to archetypes in the collective unconscious.

Archetypes, for Jung, are predispositions to think, imagine, and experience in certain ways. They are numinous creative centers that can seize hold of the conscious mind or impress themselves on us in dreams and fantasies, shaping both our inner and outer experiences. They are relatively autonomous centers of energy, drive, and purpose in the background of the psyche that give to human experience an a priori structure. The content of consciousness and our experience of the world are continually shaped by the archetypes.

We ordinarily think of ourselves as singular in character: one person with one will that is the overriding determining power in our life. But this conception is something of a delusion, Jung says. It comes out of the nineteenth-century belief that "man" is the master of nature and master of himself. Following Freud's exploration of the unconscious through psychoanalysis, Jung's discovery of the archetypes further undermined the assumption that we can control the psyche through rationality and acts of willpower alone. Jung's work advanced a psychological equivalent of a polytheistic view of the world, not unlike the Greco-Roman pantheon of gods and goddesses—except, in Jung's view, the gods exist within us, as psychological forces. They are not physical beings controlling human affairs from on high. Rather, the gods symbolize archetypes, instincts, and complexes in the depths of the human mind.

Campbell drew on the ideas of Freud and especially Jung to show that, read psychologically, myths contain great wisdom, providing clues as to how we can orient ourselves to the archetypes and find guidance for the individuation process:

> The bold and truly epoch-making writings of the psychoanalysts are indispensable to the student of mythology; for, whatever might be thought of the detailed and sometimes contradictory interpretations of specific causes and problems, Freud, Jung, and their followers have demonstrated irrefutably that the logic, the heroes, and the deeds of myth survive into modern times. In the absence of an effective general mythology, each of us has his private, unrecognized, rudimentary, yet secretly potent pantheon of dream.[21]

Here, in essence, is the rationale behind Campbell's metaphorical and psychological interpretation of myth. By attending to the dreams and fantasy imagery emerging within the psyche, one might access and better understand the universal archetypal determinants that shape human experience. Engaging with the archetypes can provide a source of sustaining meaning, and give to the individual life a universal significance.

There are three main components in Jung's model of the psyche: consciousness, which is that part of the psyche of which we are more or less aware; the personal unconscious, which contains complexes and the repressed contents of personal experience (memories, feelings, impulses, and so forth) that are unconsciously screened out of awareness; and the collective unconscious (or the "objective psyche," as it is also known) comprised of the archetypes—the universal organizing factors, common to all people, existing in the background of the psyche. The personal complexes in individual experience are each related to a specific archetype, such as the shadow, the anima and animus, the wise old man, the great mother, the hero, the father, the child, the trickster, the spirit, and the Self. Consciousness and the personal unconscious rest upon the collective unconscious, which is the matrix of experience.

According to Jung, one can never experience an archetype directly, but only as an archetypal image within dreams and fantasies or personified as a mythic figure. The *shadow*, for instance, might be represented by a dark figure or a wild beast that symbolizes a primitive part of one's nature that one has not been able to incorporate into one's personality and give expression to. This aspect of oneself therefore remains unconscious, appearing dark because it falls outside the "light" of consciousness. While each individual's shadow is likely to have collective elements (reflecting those values and aspects of life experience repressed and excluded by the wider culture), the shadow also functions as a personal complex, comprising one's inferior traits and a cluster of memories, emotions, and drives repressed out of consciousness.

Another common archetypal image is that of the *wise old man*—the "superior master and teacher, the archetype of the spirit, who symbolizes the pre-existent meaning hidden in the chaos of life."[22] Like all the other personified archetypes, it takes on the form of a specific character within a myth: Merlin, Gandalf, or Ben Kenobi, for example, are instances of the general archetype. Each possesses his own distinct personality, but each fulfills the universal role of wise mentor, guide, authority, and so forth, representing a ubiquitous theme and function in human experience.

The Jungian model of the archetypes and the collective unconscious provides a way of understanding the relationship between universal archetypes, themes and motifs in myth, their cultural inflections, and the complexes of individual psychology (as depicted in figure 4, below). In the Jungian view, the characters, situations, and actions in myth might all be viewed as a symbolic portrait of the archetypal patterns of the psyche. Myths arise from archetypes; they give form to the archetypal imagination. And myths symbolize the processes and dynamics of the archetypes in the psyche. Crucially,

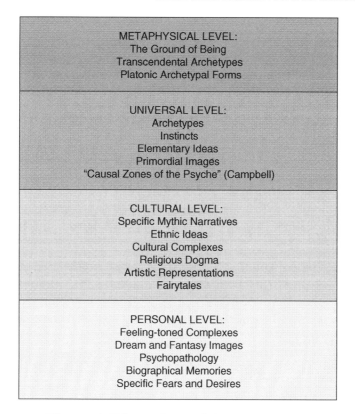

Figure 4: Dimensions of the Archetypes

myths provide clues as to how to navigate particular aspects of the individuation process.

Individuation, Archetypes, and the Persona

The individuation process, mediated by an encounter with the archetypes, effects a radical transformation of the structure of the psyche. The old form of the ego structure is destroyed, and a new more robust, more inclusive psychological structure is formed that better reflects one's psychological wholeness, the entirety of what one is—both the conscious identity and the Self, the other, unknown, greater person that stands behind the conscious personality. The Self is the center and the totality of the whole psyche, the whole human being, whereas the ego is only the center of consciousness, the part of the psyche that we are familiar with and identify with. To individuate, the ego must face that which is normally excluded from awareness. It must face the dark half of the psyche, where the Self resides. It must come face to face with the unconscious.

The individuation process can only begin in earnest when ego-consciousness has become established as an autonomous, differentiated principle. That is to say, individuation can only begin when your identity has formed, when your sense of "I" is sufficiently developed. At this point, it can happen that your own personal will has diverged significantly from the unconscious roots of your personality such that who you believe you are, and the life you are living, do not adequately reflect the totality of what you really are. During individuation, you are called by the Self, as the greater power and center in the psyche, to bring your own personal will into alignment with the Self's own intentions, which are often significantly different from your conscious plans for yourself and your life, and invariably different from what seems rational or makes sense to you.

The first archetype to emerge during the encounter with the unconscious is the shadow, the compensatory counterpart to the conscious personality. As we have seen, the shadow represents everything that is excluded from the conscious personality and everything too that our civilization excludes. It is made up of fears, taboo impulses and desires, and inferior qualities about which we feel shame or embarrassment. For this reason, it is often personified in dreams and fantasies as a foreboding, dark figure of some kind who—because we are usually unwilling to face the unconscious—typically pursues us relentlessly.

Confronting the shadow is a difficult, painful process of coming to terms with everything we would rather not face about ourselves. Yet the shadow contains many positive qualities too. Because ego-consciousness is attuned to what it takes to be the good and pleasant aspects of reality, then half of life, if not more, is excluded from conscious awareness. Accordingly, a considerable reserve of life power, passion, and vitality usually falls into the unconscious, forming the shadow. In the shadow, we might even discover our highest potentialities and our greatest possibilities, for behind the darkness lurks a plurality of other archetypes and, ultimately, the Self—the universal, archetypal human within us—the "Great Man" making itself known to the conscious ego.

If the shadow can be faced, the amorphous darkness of the unconscious can become differentiated into a multiplicity of distinct but interrelated archetypes. Of particular significance to individuation are the archetypes of the *anima* and *animus*. Indeed, these archetypes, representing one's unconscious contrasexual qualities, serve as mediators between consciousness and the unconscious. They are psychological functions by which the rational ego can attune to the living reality of the unconscious and through which one might cultivate the capacity to discern and relate to the other archetypes, such as the trickster, the hero, the child, the spirit, the wise old man, and the great mother. Ultimately, each archetype might be seen to reflect a different aspect of the teleological intentions of the Self, which, according to Jung, is both the origin and the goal of individuation.

Another important aspect of the psyche is the *persona*, which is the face we show to the world, the part of us we would like others to see, how we would like to be seen—usually our positive, happy traits. Jung describes this as a "compromise formation": it is part authentic, part pretense, showing a partial image of the true character while permitting adaptation to the requirements of the social world, providing a protective screen around the real personality.[23]

As individuation begins, the persona, the old worldly identity, dissolves or collapses—"the dissolution of the persona," as Jung called it. This occurrence can mark the beginning of a period of psychological chaos and confusion when your sense of who you are, your role in life, and your place in the world are all thrown into utter uncertainty. Often, this phase is marked by great swings of emotion, great inner struggles, high tensions, and breakthroughs. In the midst of this experience, you can feel utterly at sea, liked a ship being tossed around by the waves, as powerful emotions, desires, and drives sweep over you, pulling you violently in different directions. It is this process, this struggle, that the hero's journey symbolically refers to. It describes how we can come to terms with the deeper psyche and participate in the emergence of a new psychological center. It describes the rupturing of the shell of the ego and the reintegration of consciousness with the instinctual and emotional power of the unconscious.

Any kind of external event can trigger the undoing of the persona. It might be what Jung calls a "conflict of duties," when you have to make a major life decision between option A and option B, and you just cannot choose. The decision is irreconcilable because the same amount of drive and energy is behind both options. This produces an absolute impasse, a standstill; life is suspended and you just cannot move forward. This forces the energy inwards, downwards. You just cannot carry on with your life until the decision is resolved. And it has to be resolved at a deeper level.

The destruction of the persona could also be triggered by a traumatic experience or a deep wounding, preventing you from maintaining your assumed posture towards the world and compromising your sense of rational control; or it could occur when your former life motivation is thwarted or no longer feels meaningful. When the old persona, and the control of the ego, cannot be maintained, that is when individuation proper begins.

The journey to a condition of psychological wholeness is arduous. You must endure a death of the ego—your old identity, your former self and its will—and a resurrection into the fullness of a new life centered on the Self. When the old ego structures collapse, you must learn to withstand the onslaught of the instincts, desires, and fears that are released into consciousness. You must learn to contain these instincts, and master them emotionally, rather than repress them. You must learn to discriminate between the different drives and impulses that move you, so you can attune yourself to the promptings of the Self. In this way, the multiplicity of complexes and impulses that move you can be brought into a dynamic harmony, such that each is given proper expression in service of the Self—the principle of higher integrative unity in the psyche.[24]

Transformation and the Individual Way

The individuation process combines two key elements. On the one hand, it pertains to the challenge of becoming a unique individual, separate from the common crowd. On the other hand, it pertains to a process of deep psychospiritual transformation in which the old structure of the ego is destroyed and a new psychological structure established, centered upon the Self.

To individuate you must go your own way in life, breaking free of the social pressures and beliefs that keep you from being who you are, going off, symbolically speaking, into the dark forest or into the wilderness, finding your own unique path, thereby becoming a true individual. You must be liberated from the womb of culture and from the conditioned ego-personality and persona it supports.

The separation that takes place during individuation is from the mass, from the leveling influence of the mainstream culture. You have to break away from the collective in order to serve the will of the whole out of your own deep center, for this is a center of the cosmos too. The universe is *omnicentric*, as cosmologist Brian Swimme points out, which implies that we are each a universal center; our challenge is to realize this in the depths of our being.[25] You must break away from the limiting patterns and habits of the cultural psyche to contact what Campbell calls the "primary springs" of life—the universal archetypes. In becoming an individual, separate from the mass of humanity, you might thus simultaneously realize your universal nature.

Individuation is a uniquely individual path but it is to be realized by the encounter with the universal elements of human experience: the archetypes. Indeed, individuation is itself an instance of the rebirth archetype. It is the psychological equivalent of the death-rebirth process in nature—the same process by which the caterpillar becomes a butterfly or the fruit of the tree falls from the branch and dies, impregnating the earth with new life. The Gospel of John (12:24) expresses just this idea: "Verily, verily, I say unto you, Except a corn of wheat fall into the ground and die, it abideth alone: but if it die, it bringeth forth much fruit." During individuation, the ego finds itself in the position of the caterpillar and the corn of wheat.

One of Jung's major critiques of Nietzsche is that, in his fervor for overthrowing the religious past, he failed to recognize that he was enacting a universal archetypal pattern of rebirth that others before him had already described. Consequently, he rejected potential sources of guidance that could have helped him as he wrestled with his own transformative experiences. As a source of instruction, he could, for example, have turned to Goethe's *Faust*, exploring experiences remarkably similar to Nietzsche's own.[26] Or, as a philologist, he could have drawn on classical myths or even Christianity, which he vehemently rejected, to provide guidance. Indeed, one of Nietzsche's foremost translators, R. J. Hollingdale, has demonstrated just how closely many of the themes in *Thus Spoke Zarathustra* mirror those of the teachings of Jesus.[27] All these sources could have helped Nietzsche, Jung says, if only Nietzsche had not been so convinced he had to reject the philosophical and spiritual heritage of the culture in its entirety. For even though your experience is unique, others before you will have been through some similar experiences, which can help you make sense of your own life. But Nietzsche was too much the individualist, in a sense. He neglected to take into account the universal or archetypal nature of his experience, failing to recognize, it seems, that he was embroiled in an archetypal process of death-rebirth, the very topic symbolized and described by the Christianity he rejected and the fate of the mythic figure with which he was so closely identified: Dionysus.

As one form of expression of the rebirth archetype, individuation can be considered an inexorable natural process of unfolding, one that is occurring all the time whether or not we know it. Even if individuation is not consciously undertaken, the circumstances of our lives contrive to elicit psychological development, as surely as nature wills that a child grows into an adult or a seed unfolds into a plant. However, there is a world of difference between this natural developmental process and a conscious engagement with individuation—the later, advanced stage of psychological development, which involves a direct encounter with the unconscious psyche. Although individuation is a natural process, paradoxically it requires the overcoming of nature. It is the process by which the spirit in nature might be consciously realized. Through individuation, nature seeks to overcome and transform itself through the medium of the human psyche, which is a dangerous, unprecedented, and uncertain process. Nature brings forth the ego as the carrier of self-reflective consciousness and then, at a certain critical point in its development, the conscious ego is charged with the task of helping to liberate spirit from nature, with overcoming nature in its unregenerate form. The ego thus becomes embroiled in the continuing process of psychological evolution. The transformation is so complicated and extremely difficult to navigate because the old form of the ego must itself be overcome.

For some people, the individuation process cannot be ignored; it is intensified and brought to the foreground of experience. For others, individuation represents a potential or possibility that might or might not be acted upon. I think this difference is reflected in the Christian idea that "many are called, but few are chosen" (Matthew 22:14). In this context, to be chosen means that individuation is impressed upon you as an inescapable task; to be called means that you have the opportunity to individuate if you take it upon yourself to do so.

Individuation is also specifically related to the archetype of the hero. Indeed, according to Jung, "the archetypal forms of the hero myth can be observed in almost any individuation process," portraying both the solitary, individual nature of the journey and the death-rebirth process undergone by the ego.[28] The hero myth can thus serve as a model, a universal template, for individuation. It essentially describes the contours of a psychospiritual life journey that takes one off the beaten track, leading one to the realm of original experience of the deeper spiritual dimensions of life, beyond what one can learn from any religion, philosophy, mythology, or psychology. We can see this aspect of hero myths in the individual paths taken by the knights of Arthurian legends, in the Buddha and Jesus rejecting certain aspects of the established religious traditions into which they were born, or in Jung's quest to discover and live out his personal myth. Each person must find his or her own response to the question and challenge posed by life. In guiding one along one's own individual way, the hero myth represents the fulfillment of the Western spiritual ideal of the pursuit of one's own path through life, of trusting and valuing one's own judgment, and of becoming a unique individual *sui generis*.

As the example of Nietzsche indicates, the pursuit of an individual way through life can itself initiate psychospiritual transformation. Forsaking a life within the known horizons of the wider culture, you lose the protection and security that the collective patterns of living provide and, invariably, on your own life journey you will come face to face with the reality of the deep psyche. Consciousness, that is to say, is forced to confront the unconscious, initiating an ongoing dialectical relationship between them. Through this process, the division between consciousness and the unconscious, reason and instinct, might be healed.

Time and again, individuation will take you to your limits and beyond. But if you can see your life in terms of the hero myth this can sustain you through dark periods and crises. Periods of suffering and stress, discouragement and danger can be borne more readily because you are oriented towards the heroic struggle to bring forth the deeper Self. This has certainly been my experience. It takes an act of imagination to interpret what is happening in your life in mythic terms, in terms of the hero's journey, but if you can do this, it can provide sustaining meaning.

The "I Am" Realization

Jung saw all forms of religion as expressions of individuation symbolism. Both Christ and the Buddha are symbols of the Self—the universal human being within us, the greater personality, representing the potential for the attainment of a realized psychological wholeness. Prominent Jungian scholar Edward Edinger argues that the life of Christ might also be seen as a "paradigm of the individuating ego," symbolically describing the relationship of the human ego with the greater "spiritual" authority of the Self. "The underlying meaning of Christianity," Edinger claims, "is the quest for individuation."[29]

From a spiritual perspective, the ego serves as the vehicle for the "I Am" experience—the deep realization that one is, that one exists as a unique individual consciousness beholding the world. In *Memories, Dreams, Reflections*, Jung describes an early realization of the "I Am" when he was twelve:

> Suddenly for a single moment I had the overwhelming impression of having just emerged from a dense cloud. I knew all at once: now I am *myself*! . . . Previously I had existed too, but everything had merely happened to me. Now I happened to myself. . . . Previously I had been willed to do this and that; now *I* willed.[30]

As we saw in chapter 2, later on in his life Jung had a deeper, fuller experience of this self-awareness during his travels in Africa where he had an insight into the central role of individual human consciousness for illuminating the mystery of being.

It takes a highly developed ego to fully experience the "I Am," for it is not just a subjective individual experience, but an experience of universal, transcendental import. "Before Abraham was, I Am" (John 8:58)—Jesus's words point to a realization of an aspect of a deeper identity and consciousness that manifests within, and yet transcends, one's personal history in time. The "I Am" experience is numinous; it is close to the heart of the mystery of individual ego-consciousness and its capacity to illuminate the depths of being.

As I see it, the trajectory of the spiritual development of the West has brought forth separate ego-consciousness to support the "I Am" experience, to serve as a vehicle for this realization. The "I Am" can only be fully realized, though, at the apex of this trajectory, at the pinnacle of egoic development and separation—a point of maximum isolation at which one stands apart from all else. The "I Am" is an isolating experience because it is through this realization that one comes to know oneself and the separateness of one's consciousness from the rest of existence. The isolation accompanying ego con-sciousness can be a crushing thing to bear, as the example of Nietzsche plainly demonstrates. But the experience of the "I Am" is the foundation of a new psychological structure that supports the subsequent actualization of the Self. The teleological power of nature appears to orchestrate psychological development to bring forth the ego, and the "I Am" realization, as a prerequisite to the actualization of the Self.

With this context in mind, if we reflect again on everything we have discussed about the development of mythology, the emergence of the individual self, the alienation of the ego, the encounter with nihilism, the rejection of the established religions, and so forth, we might conclude that the entire trajectory of the Western tradition seems to be pushing us towards individuation, impelling us now to realize the deeper Self within us, to die to the old ego structure. It is almost as if at the very apex of the development of the ego, when it becomes so alienated that no further distancing can take place from the roots of the psyche, from the environment, and from nature, a "turning around" begins to take place—an *enantiodromia*. This seems to be what is happening. Ego-consciousness in some individuals is being developed to its extreme thereby necessitating a turning around to face the unconscious. The individual is thus charged with the task of bringing the power and awareness of a developed rational ego to bear on the instincts, fears, and desires in the unconscious. This is the challenge both of rediscovering and assimilating lost potentials and of coming to terms with everything that has been repressed during the emergence of the ego. It is a process by which, through deep-rooted transformation, one might realize one's wholeness.

It is to the specifics of this transformation that we will now turn our attention as we consider, in Part Two, how different phases of the hero's journey can be interpreted psychologically as a source of guidance for the individuation process.

PART II

The Journey

CHAPTER 5

The Hero's Adventure: Call and Refusal

*This path to primordial religious experience is the right one,
but how many can recognize it? It is like a still small voice,
and it sounds from afar. It is ambiguous, questionable, dark,
presaging danger and hazardous adventure; a razor-edged
path, to be trodden for God's sake only, without assurance and
without sanction.*

—C. G. Jung

The previous chapters set the stage so that we can better appreciate
the psychological significance of the hero's journey in an historical
and evolutionary context. As we have seen, without spiritual and
psychological guidance from an established collective mythology or
religion increasing numbers of individuals find themselves invited or
impelled to seek out and undertake their own unique journeys of self-
realization. Because it is a metaphorical portrayal of the archetypal
life pattern of the spiritual quest, Campbell believes that the ancient
myth of the hero's journey is especially relevant to the modern individual's life experience as a guide to spiritual transformation:

> There can be no question: the psychological dangers to which
> earlier generations were guided by the symbols and spiritual
> exercises of their religious and mythological inheritance, we
> today. . . must face alone, or, at best, with only tentative, im-
> promptu, and not very often effective guidance. This is our
> problem as modern, enlightened individuals, for whom all the
> gods and devils have been rationalized out of existence. Never-
> theless, in the multitude of myths and religions that have been

preserved to us, or collected from the ends of the earth, we might yet see delineated something of our still human course.[1]

Campbell proposes, in other words, that although we modern individuals are in some sense spiritually alone, it is possible to look at ancient myths, discern the metaphorical, psychological meaning of these myths, and thereby find guidance and instruction. This is a theme which we will consider in detail in the chapters to follow.

Beyond its import for personal experience, however, in pursuing their own spiritual journeys individuals might also contribute to the creative revitalization and enrichment of civilization. By accessing the wellsprings of spirit in the depths of the psyche, the individual might help to disseminate spiritual power to the culture at large. The hero myth has both personal and sociological relevance; indeed, one cannot properly understand the contemporary significance of mythology without taking into account the sociological context.

The Wasteland Scenario and the Renewal of Civilization

In addition to Nietzsche and Jung, a key figure in Campbell's understanding of this context was the cultural historian Oswald Spengler, famed for his magisterial *The Decline of the West*, first published in 1918, in which he heralds the coming of a phase of terminal decline and decay in Western civilization, not unlike that which befell the Roman Empire in the centuries after the death of Christ. Spengler saw this decline within a morphological model of the lifecycle of a culture, identifying a characteristic pattern within each civilization from its birth and ascendancy to its decay and death.

When a culture reaches a certain point in its development, Spengler argues that one can observe an inevitable slide into an era of "exhaustion, sterility and mechanical repetition" in which creative energy has been largely expended.[2] The once flowering *culture* becomes an increasingly complex *civilization*, centered no longer on the town and village, but on an urban metropolis. Thereafter, as is plainly evident in our own time, the logistics of life become inordinately complex and excessively bureaucratic, absorbing so much time and energy that they stifle the creative impetus of the people. Although it may endure and continue to grow for centuries, from this point the civilization enters an irreversible creative decline.

As technological functioning and practical concerns became the dominant emphases of the civilization, Spengler envisaged that the artist and creative person were to become increasingly less important than the mechanic or engineer. Indeed, in Spengler's view, an over-developed practical rationality and lack of spiritual awareness are typical of the later stage in the life of a civilization, a period when the "non-mystic"—whom Nietzsche called "Socratic Man"—flourishes. This late civilization phase is characterized by ways of living that are excessively rational and considered. It is a period in which the people live primarily from the intellect, not from natural impulses of the heart, and who therefore lack the spontaneity and playful freedom characteristic of the creative life.

From the perspective of the first decades of the twentieth century, Spengler found abundant evidence of such a decline in the modern West. He thus presents an essentially pessimistic vision of the future course of Western civilization, one that was to attain wide exposure and popularity in the decade after its publication, following the events of the First World War. Even the life-affirming Campbell confessed to be persuaded, at times, by Spengler's dispiriting vision of the future.

There is a more positive rendering of a similar cyclical organic model in the work of another cultural historian, Arnold J. Toynbee. He agreed with Spengler to a point, but suggested that when a culture starts to stagnate and go into decline, the creative individual— the culture hero—accessing the creative springs in his or her own interior depths, can renew and reinvigorate the culture, helping to give birth to a new culture from the ashes of the old. Although influenced by Spengler's prognosis, in *The Hero with a Thousand Faces* Campbell endorses Toynbee's view, on the whole, charging the hero with the task of cultural transformation as well as individual salvation, giving to the individual's journey a collective, sociocultural import. Hegel expresses a similar idea:

> The great men in history are those whose own particular aims contain the substantial will that is the will of the World Spirit. They can be called heroes, because they have drawn their aim and their vocation not merely from the calm and orderly system

that is the sanctified course of things, but rather from a source whose content is hidden and has not yet matured into present existence. This source is the inner Spirit that is as yet hidden beneath the surface; it knocks at the outer world as though that were a shell. . . . The advanced Spirit is this inner soul of all individuals; but this is an unconscious inwardness which the great men bring to consciousness.[3]

If, as Spengler believed, we are indeed in the terminal decay and subsequent death phase of modern industrial civilization, what, we might wonder, will come next? Where do we go from here? The implication of Campbell's teaching seems to be, following Toynbee, that we have entered a period of creative individualism, and it is the great calling of the heroic individual to revitalize the culture by going down into his or her own depths to recover something of value, something the culture needs to find refreshment, meaning, or a new direction. In so doing, the creative individual might effect a transition from a state of cultural stagnation and decay—a spiritual wasteland—to a state of revitalized activity.

The wasteland is an important motif in Campbell's analysis of the contemporary spiritual and mythological situation. The concept originates in the Arthurian legend of the Fisher King who is wounded in the groin by a "spear of destiny" (the so-called Dolorous Stroke), and his kingdom becomes barren—a condition symbolically suggested by the king's wound. The healing of the king and the renewal of the wasteland can only be effected by the successful fulfillment of the quest for the Holy Grail.

Inspired by the Grail legend, "The Waste Land" is the title of a poem by T. S. Eliot, published in 1922 shortly after Spengler's *The Decline of the West*. The following excerpt from a section called "What the Thunder Said" well describes a prevalent experience of modern life in a society and civilization in which there are no effective living myths:

Here is no water but only rock
Rock and no water and the sandy road
The road winding above among the mountains
Which are mountains of rock without water
If there were water we should stop and drink
Amongst the rock one cannot stop or think

Sweat is dry and feet are in the sand
If there were only water amongst the rock
Dead mountain mouth of carious teeth that cannot spit
Here one can neither stand not lie nor sit
There is not even silence in the mountains
But dry sterile thunder without rain
There is not even solitude in the mountains
But red sullen faces sneer and snarl
From doors of mudcracked houses.[4]

One has the overwhelming sense here of a kind of spiritual desert, and the barren dryness of a life without life-revivifying water. In myth and dream, water symbolizes the wellsprings of nature, the spirit within nature, and the vitality of life energy pouring forth and bringing refreshment. It is also a symbol of the unconscious and is especially related to emotions and desires. Campbell believed that the creative individual can bring a new flow of life to the wasteland of modernity, to reconnect the culture to the vital springs of life energy that reside in the unconscious. He sees this as the central sociological task of the hero. This wasteland scenario is the backdrop against which the modern individual's life journey takes place.

The Mythic Model of the Hero's Journey

Campbell refers to the mythic model of the hero's journey as the *monomyth* (a term taken from James Joyce), which is used to refer to a single mythic pattern evident within all different hero myths. He summarizes the monomyth as follows:

> The mythological hero, setting forth from his common day hut or castle, is lured, carried away, or else voluntarily proceeds, to the threshold of adventure. There he encounters a shadow presence that guards the passage. The hero may defeat or conciliate this power and go alive into the kingdom of the dark (brother-battle, dragon-battle; offering, charm), or he may be slain by the opponent and descend in death (dismemberment, crucifixion). Beyond the threshold, then, the hero journeys through a world of unfamiliar yet strangely intimate forces,

some of them which severely threaten him (tests), some of which give magical aid (helpers). When he arrives at the nadir of the mythological round, he undergoes a supreme ordeal and gains his reward. The triumph may be represented as the hero's sexual union with the goddess-mother of the world (sacred marriage), his recognition by the father-creator (father atonement), his own divinization (apotheosis), or again—if the powers have remained unfriendly to him—his theft of the boon he came to gain (bride-theft, fire-theft); intrinsically it is an expansion of consciousness and therewith of being (illumination, transfiguration, freedom). The final work is that of the return. If the powers have blessed the hero, he now sets forth under their protection (emissary); if not, he flees and is pursued (transformation flight, obstacle flight). At the return threshold the transcendental powers must remain behind; the hero reemerges from the kingdom of dread (return, resurrection). The boon that he brings restores the world (elixir).[5]

There are three main phases in this model: separation, initiation, and return or incorporation. Campbell takes these terms from Arnold van Gennep's book *The Rites of Passage* in which van Gennep argues that these stages are intrinsic to rites: an initiate is taken away from the main nexus of the tribe or society and goes through some kind of initiatory transformative experience and then returns to the social group, irrevocably changed, and fit thereafter to fulfill a designated role within that group. Toynbee, too, in his study of the role of the hero in cultural life cycles identifies a similar process of *detachment* and *transfiguration*, as he terms it. And Campbell sees this same sequence in hero stories of all mythic traditions. In the absence of rites of passage in modern society, however, these stages have now to be navigated alone.

Campbell slightly revises the meaning of some of these terms: he often refers to the separation stage as *departure*; initiation also means *transformation*; and the phase of incorporation or return is also described by Campbell as a stage of *communication*, referring to the labor of incorporating the insights and transformative experiences from the second phase back into everyday life by communicating these to others. As we saw previously, the creative artist has an experience or a vision or an insight that then has to be communicated through his or her art or craft to the wider culture. This is the essence of creative mythology, in which a new myth is shaped by the artist treating the old mythic motifs in new ways relevant to the unique demands of modern life.

A Note on Gender

Reading *The Hero with a Thousand Faces*, one cannot fail to notice that most of the heroes are male. There are some notable exceptions, such as Psyche and Inanna, but by and large the heroes are men.[6] Does this imply, therefore, that the model of the hero is inherently biased towards men, pertaining exclusively to the experiences of men? Or does the hero myth accurately reflect the experience of women too?

As I see it, to consider hero myths exclusively in terms of biological gender or socio-culturally constructed gender roles is to miss the psychospiritual import of the myth. Read symbolically, the characters in the myth, including the hero, each represent aspects of one's own psyche. In psychological terms, the hero can usually be viewed as a representation of the ego, which in its very posture is "masculine." The ego, that is to say, is always trying to *be* someone, to *do* something in the world. The ego is active and assertive; it is extraverted and intentional; it exerts its will to command and control the environment. Traditionally, these are all considered "masculine" characteristics. The nature of life in modern Western society is such that the ego is conditioned to assume a yang style "masculine" quality. Conversely, the unconscious is often depicted as "feminine," for, as we saw in Part One, in Western civilization such qualities have been repressed into the unconscious. The aim of the hero's journey is to bring together masculine and feminine—to effect a *hieros gamos*, a sacred marriage of the "masculine" conscious ego with the "feminine" unconscious. This process is also described in alchemy, as Jung has shown, as the union of *Sol* and *Luna*, Adam and Eve, king and queen. During individuation this is a challenge to be faced by men and women alike.

From a psychological perspective, then, a male hero might be seen as representing the "masculine" quality of the ego in both men and women. Jung himself appeared to entertain a similar viewpoint, observing that in the psyches of modern individuals—both men and women—the "feminine" has become increasingly consigned to the unconscious, such is the pervasive socio-cultural emphasis on "masculine" extraverted egoic individualism. The anima—the feminine principle—thus tends to remain unconscious, undeveloped, often bound up with a mother complex. Discussing the preponderance of "mother complexes" in America in the first half of the twentieth century, Jung observed: "As a result of this [socio-cultural] conditioning many American women develop their masculine side, which is then compensated in the unconscious by an exquisitely feminine instinct."[7] What was true of America then surely applies to much of the Western world now. It is worth keeping in mind, too, that many of Jung's insights into the individuation process were based, at least initially, on the analysis of the dreams and fantasies of a woman who was on the verge of a schizophrenic breakdown. This case study is the basis for his entire psychological and mythic analysis in *Symbols of Transformation*. And, of course, Jung's psychological theories were influenced and further explicated by the many brilliant women in his immediate circle, including Marie-Louise von Franz, Emma Jung, Toni Wolff, Jolande Jacobi, Liliane Frey-Rohn, and Aniele Jaffe.

Recent literature on the nature of women's individuation by Jungian authors such as Marion Woodman, Sylvia Brinton Perera, and Clarissa Pinkola Estes has focused on a woman's journey from the world of the ego, conditioned by the patriarchal values of modern industrial society, to the rediscovery of the deep feminine or the "dark goddess." For his part, Campbell believed that a woman simply has to realize that she *is* life, an insight that points to the recognition of the deeper roots of female creative power in nature. Like nature, like the Earth, woman is a vehicle for life. But what needs to be emphasized is that this realization itself involves a journey beyond entrapment within the patriarchally conditioned ego, which can leave women estranged from the deeper roots of their natural being. This journey is not merely the claiming of egoic power—emphasized so much in our own time—but a going beyond the ego to come into relationship with unconscious nature. This realization is the fruit of a journey into the depths of the psyche where one might reclaim the long-forgotten power, vitality, and wisdom of the spirit in nature and "recover the ways of the natural instinctive psyche."[8]

I do not wish to deny the important differences between the life experiences of men and women. Indeed, significant differences are apparent—in interests, temperament, developmental patterns, and more—in boys and girls from a very early age, as any parent will testify. It is hardly surprising, therefore, that certain of these differences persist, and are perhaps even exaggerated, into adulthood. However, our concerns here are the universal elements in human psychospiritual development, patterns shared by men and women alike. These might include any or all of the following:

1. bringing the ego personality (the I-principle) into a conscious relationship with the unconscious;
2. navigating a profound shift in personal identity from the ego to the Self;
3. undergoing an experience of psychospiritual death-rebirth;
4. coming into contact with the instinctual power of nature through the unconscious;
5. participating in the transformation of one's world view;
6. searching for deeper life meaning;
7. reconciling reason and feeling, spirit and instinct; good and evil;
8. encountering the numinous, spiritual dimension of experience;
9. uniting the immanent dark spirit in nature with the transcendent divine;
10. bringing the repressed feminine principle to the light of consciousness.

Clearly, none of these are unique to either gender, although one's gender might influence the way one experiences and interprets them. The mythic model of the hero's journey, I believe, is a symbolic representation of a process by which the individual—woman or man—might address each of these transformations and challenges.

The Beginning of the Journey

Campbell describes the first phase of the hero's journey as "a retreat from the desperations of the waste land to the peace of the everlasting realm that is within," although depending on the particular situation an encounter with the inner world might be anything but peaceful.[9] In every case, however, a psychological detachment from the values, expectations, and accepted patterns of life of the mainstream culture takes place.

The detachment from the ordinary world exposes one to everything that has not been confronted in one's life. The childhood psyche is rediscovered, lying unsuspected beneath the functioning world of the adult ego. In *Hero*, Campbell describes a typical dream experience accompanying or anticipating the reemergence of the childhood psyche, that of looking down into the ocean, and seeing there an assortment of childhood toys, junk, and paraphernalia lying strewn on the sea bed. Such objects from the past serve as symbols of the part of us that has remained as a child, that has not matured, and is undeveloped and forgotten at the bottom of the "ocean" of the unconscious psyche. This image describes both the lost potentiality and playful innocence of youth, often repressed amidst the harsh material pressures of life, and the residual infantile tendencies within us that must be brought to the surface, faced, and overcome. The conscious ego must descend into the depths of the unconscious (the ocean) to bring these long-forgotten elements to the surface of consciousness. The ego must establish contact with the inner child, which contains the potential for creative renewal. As Campbell puts it:

> If we could dredge up something forgotten, not only by ourselves [that is, the personal childhood contents of the individual psyche] but by our whole generation or our entire civilization, we should become indeed the boon-bringer, the culture hero of the day—a personage not only of local but world historical moment. In a word: the first work of the hero is to retreat from the world scene of secondary effects to those causal zones of the psyche where the difficulties really reside.[10]

During the phase of departure, then, there occurs a turning within to face oneself, to confront long-forgotten aspects of one's psyche. Here, in the depths of the psyche, one might encounter not just the repressed content of one's own personal past, but collective factors—the archetypes—that shape all human experience.

The individual is led through the personal and cultural to the transpersonal. Campbell believes that, by undergoing this separation from the world of the mainstream culture, the hero can forge his or her own psychological path thereby breaking through and going beyond the inherent limitations of the culture, which, let us remember, at this point has become a spiritual wasteland. In this alienated condition, economic and practical concerns dominate and stifle the spirit. There is no vitality, no living meaning, no valid myth. The culture impresses upon each of us inauthentic ways of being, life patterns that are not of our own choosing and that invariably do not serve our deeper interests, such that we become cut off from that flow of instinctual power and dynamic inspiration that is so essential to feel alive—hence the experience of dryness, which, incidentally, is not just metaphorical but actual. If you become too alienated from the life within, from who you really are and the life you want to or should be living, you can experience the dryness as a physical bodily sensation, a psychosomatic expression of what is taking place. The wasteland, in its most extreme form, is like a living death, a spiritual death. Campbell believes the hero can break through the limiting patterns of the social order to directly access the wellsprings of life, and in so doing can bring renewed vitality to a decaying culture, take the culture in new directions, bringing a new flow of life energy to the wasteland. "A vital person vitalizes," as he put it.[11] Our concern, Campbell believed, should be to make life as fulfilling, vital, full of zest, and intensity as we can. If we become truly alive, there will be an overflow that will have a reinvigorating impact on the wider culture. It is down to the individual to save society and not vice versa.

The hero's journey, Campbell notes, pertains to the process of overcoming resistances and the recovery of long lost powers from the unconscious. It is the means by which we can experience a continual birth, activating a continual flow of power from the unconscious into the daylight world of consciousness. The Jungian scholar Edward Edinger sees this exchange of energy mediated by what he calls the *ego-Self axis*—the Self, you will recall, is Jung's term for the deeper center in the unconscious that reflects our psychological wholeness, not just our consciousness. Interpreted psychologically, the journey is to do with discovering and learning to serve this deeper center within the psyche.

In chapter 2, we considered the separation that has taken place between consciousness, centered on the ego, and the unconscious, instinct, the "feminine" principle, evil, nature, and the irrational. As we saw, this separation was significantly influenced by Christianity and the entire trajectory of Western civilization: consciousness became identified with the light, the good, spirit, and reason; nature, instinct, desire, matter, the body, sexuality were seen as evil and corrupt, and were thus repressed out of awareness, cast into the unconscious, becoming dark demonic powers. Consequently, the repressed unconscious is where the source of life power now is. A spiritual wasteland in a civilization arises because the flow of life power and passion for life has been cut off and is not available to us in our conscious experience. Often, as Nietzsche stressed, life power, the potential for higher achievement, and higher spiritual values must be extricated from those aspects of our being that are deemed to be evil from the standpoint of consensus morality. "When the herd animal is irradiated by the glory of the purest virtue, the exceptional man must have been devaluated into evil."[12] It is for this reason that Nietzsche often adopts such an affirmative perspective towards evil, finding within supposedly immoral impulses an authenticity and vitality lacking in normal human experience.

Following Nietzsche, Campbell believes that the symbols, images, and teachings of Christianity are no longer vitally connected to life. The ethical duality in Christianity intensified the separation between our conscious identity, reflecting what we aspired to be, and our psychological totality, the reality of who and what we actually were and what we actually experienced. As we have seen, instinctual power and the energies of the body were denied expression because such natural impulses and desires were often seen as sinful or evil. Instinctual power was repressed into the unconscious, pushed down into the depths of the psyche. For this reason, the hero, representing the ego, has to make the decent into the depths of the underworld, into the "maternal ground of being," to reconnect to this power. Jung describes the maternal ground as seething with passions and irrational impulses, which, during the process of psychological transformation, need to be released into consciousness, controlled, and transformed.

The separation phase of the hero's adventure is essential to this transformation. If you are fully, actively involved in everyday living—working to earn money, raising a family, participating in your social life with friends, and so forth—your psychological energy is absorbed by those activities. Your worldly role and activities support your sense of identity, your sense of who you are in relation to the world. A withdrawal or separation from the world, however, frees up psychological energy and drives it inward activating the unconscious. Jung calls this process a regression of libido.[13] If you find yourself in the midst of a crisis in your life, something you just cannot cope with, when the structure of the personality in its existing form is not able to come to terms with what is happening, this can be one cause of a regression of libido. The outward expression of energy is blocked, perhaps because life feels too difficult, too painful, or the obstacles you face seem insurmountable or you are faced with an impossible decision. For whatever reason, life energy cannot flow into the world as it usually does, and is turned back into the psyche; it is driven inwards. This is why many people start to experience psychological difficulties if they lose their job, for instance. The outer world no longer absorbs their life energy and, as the unconscious is increasingly activated by the inward flow of libido, the ego and its persona start to unravel. Once activated the power of the unconscious can burst forth as a deluge or an avalanche of released fantasies, drives, passions, and fears.

The hero's journey, then, can begin at any point where one gets stuck in life or when one leaves behind or turns away from one's normal personal and worldly concerns. It may, for example, be a failure, a defeat, or a wounding that creates an opening for psychological transformation. Jung said that the first appearance of the Self is always a defeat for the ego, for it is often through a demoralizing defeat or failure that the ego is awoken to the greater reality of the psyche.[14] A new superordinate power and authority emerges in the psyche that is plainly stronger than the ego, and which dwarfs the ego. Such is Job's encounter with Yahweh in the Old Testament. Any experience that punctures the ego's confidence, that severely thwarts the will, and throws one back onto oneself can serve to initiate a hero quest. Where your life shipwrecks, that is where your treasure is, as Campbell once said.

The recovery of the treasure from the ocean-floor of the psyche takes place during the main initiation or transformation phase of the hero's adventure—the "road of trials"—as Campbell calls it. Some kind of initiatory descent into the underworld is fundamental to this phase of the adventure. The mythic underworld symbolizes the depths of the unconscious psyche, the realm of primitive instinctual drives and the archetypes. It is here, in the abysmal depths, in the pits of Hell, that the treasure resides.

Remember that Campbell always gives a psychological emphasis to the meaning of myth. From this perspective, every hero myth can be seen as relating to an inner process of psychological and spiritual transformation. These myths are not, of course, describing or advocating an actual journey over land and sea—although such a journey might trigger a psychological transformation. If there is one, the physical journey is only incidental; the essence is the inner transformation.

What Campbell describes in *The Hero with a Thousand Faces* is a quite rare experience of psychological transformation. I remember when I began studying hero myths and individuation in the work of Jung and Campbell, I was totally gripped; the ideas really captivated me. The world of myth, archetypes, and psychological transformation had a magical, almost hypnotic allure. Yet, it was only years later, in the midst of a period of prolonged psychological turbulence that I came to see directly for myself how these myths and archetypal processes were being played out through my own inner experiences. From that point, I could see that what Campbell describes in the hero's journey is directly related to what actually occurs during a period of spiritual crisis and psychological transformation. These myths, I realized, are not just fantastical ideas drawn from a magical world of ancient myth, for they describe real experiences, real processes, real inner challenges that each of us might face in our own life. They cannot be dismissed as "nothing but" metaphors. They describe a living reality, expressed through imagery and symbol, of what it is like to go on your own inner journey of transformation into the depths of the psyche. The orientation and instructive guidance these myths provide can be invaluable at such times. It is helpful, I realized, to know about these myths and models in advance, so that if you do later find yourself in a period of transformation you will be able to call them to mind.

When contemplating the relevance of this model to your own life, it is important to keep in mind that the hero's journey is not a strictly linear model. Although it obviously takes place in linear sequence through time, the nature of the journey is essentially cyclical. It is important to note, too, that the stages of the monomyth do not occur just once, but are repeated at different levels within the larger heroic adventure that is your life. You will likely experience many "calls to adventure": each time you experience a synchronicity, for instance, this amounts to some kind of call to follow a particular path. So too one must repeatedly overcome resistances to life, continually bringing forth new life energy from the unconscious, just as the labor of communicating one's truth to the world is also ongoing. There is a fluidity, then, about the major phases—separation, initiation, and return—and the subsections within these phases. Campbell articulates a formula for the model of the hero's adventure, but it is a loose one. Specific myths emphasize different sections of the journey, and different motifs just as the way of individuation exhibits significant differences for each individual.

Beginning with departure, then, let us now consider each of the subsections of the stages in detail, looking at examples from myths old and new, and from the biographies of the three figures we are most concerned with: Nietzsche, Jung, and Campbell.

The Call to Adventure

In Campbell's scheme, the first subsection of the separation or departure phase is the call to adventure. This can take several different forms. "The herald's summons," Campbell explains,

> may be to live . . . or at a later moment to die. It may sound the call of some high historical undertaking. Or it may mark the dawn of religious illumination. As apprehended by the mystic, it marks what has been termed "the awakening of the self."[15]

"But whether small or great," he continues,

> and no matter what the stage or grade of life, the call brings up the curtain, always, on a mystery of transfiguration—a rite, or moment, of spiritual passage, which, when complete, amounts to a dying and a birth. The familiar life horizon has been outgrown; the old concepts, ideals, and emotional patterns no longer fit; the time for a passing of the threshold is at hand.[16]

In fairytales, to describe to a familiar scenario, one might read of a child, playing in a forest, who accidentally drops a ball and follows it as it rolls away off the path, leading the child into a difficult situation or significant encounter. A variation on this theme is portrayed in the movie *Pan's Labyrinth* (2008). As the film opens, we witness the child hero, Ofelia, traveling with her mother to begin a new life under the tyranny of her mother's partner, the sadistic Captain Vidal, military officer in Franco's Spain in 1944. When her mother, pregnant with Vidal's child, becomes nauseous during the journey, she calls the carriage to a halt. The place of rest proves to be extremely significant, for it is here that Ofelia, wandering away from the traveling party, happens across a mysterious insect, a symbol of the archetype of the spirit that is to serve as a guide, leading Ofelia to the labyrinth where she later encounters a faun who is to reveal her true spiritual identity. The unexpected disruption of the journey at a particular place on the road and the appearance of the insect constitute Ofelia's call to adventure, which leads her into a supernatural underworld where her life destiny is to be settled.

The key motif in these kinds of examples is that through an unintentional deed or seemingly innocuous incident the hero is thrust into an adventure not consciously willed. The call to adventure is in the form of an accident, a blunder, a seemingly chance occurrence, or an error. We have all encountered synchronistic type "accidents," I am sure, where something seemingly insignificant—a chance meeting or conversation, a delay or breakdown of some sort, or reading a passage in a book—can have a profound deeper meaning and immense consequences, taking us in a different life direction. "A blunder, the merest chance," Campbell wrote in *Hero*, "may amount to the opening of a destiny."[17]

The Divine Comedy begins with a blunder of this kind. At the beginning of Dante's journey, he stumbles into a dark forest and becomes disoriented:

Half way along the road we have to go,
I found myself obscured in a great forest,
Bewildered, and I knew I had lost the way.

. . .

I cannot tell exactly how I got there,
I was so full of sleep at that point of my journey,
When, somehow, I left the proper way.[18]

The experience of losing one's way, even if it appears undesirable or traumatic, is an essential aspect of the journey of psychospiritual development, reflecting the estrangement and divergence of the conscious ego from the deeper will of the Self. The attempt to find one's way again, to get back on the "proper way," thus constitutes the ego's alignment with the larger psyche and the will of the Self.

Another form in which one's life destiny might impress itself is through an inward call, a summons to participation in the greater life of the spirit or in the unfolding drama of history. We can see this in the example of Luke Skywalker in the film *Star Wars*. As a young man, he is living on the farm with his uncle and aunt, his guardians, attending to his farm duties day by day, but he knows in the depths of his being that he has a greater destiny awaiting him; he dreams of serving the Rebel Alliance as a fighter pilot against the Empire. He just has too much psychological energy, too much life power welling up within him, to carry on in his current life situation for long. "The Force is strong in this one," his adversary Darth Vader later recognized. This inward recognition of potentiality is one aspect of the call to adventure—a realization that can come over you as a persistent restlessness, a "divine discontent," because you sense in the marrow of your bones that you were destined for something more than the standard life patterns and possibilities presented to you. When the time is right, there is sometimes a specific incident which then serves as the activating call, in which your transpersonal destiny makes itself manifest, and your ordinary personal life, as it had been, comes to an end.

Call as Spiritual Awakening

The mystical form of the call to adventure has been termed the "awakening of the self." This awakening is the revelation of a deeper spiritual identity, transcending the ego, when the dividing walls between normal waking consciousness and the divine are temporarily removed, and one attains a glimpse into the numinous. It can take the form of an enlightenment experience of the divine mystery. Obviously, such an experience can radically transform one's sense of what life is about and radically alter one's life direction.

The spiritual "awakening of the self" has been described in detail by Roberto Assagioli, the Italian pioneer of psychosynthesis and explorer of transpersonal experiences, drawing especially on the pioneering works of Richard Bucke and William James. When the soul is ready, the awakening to the divine can be triggered by a seemingly innocuous incident or thought. Typically, the awakening experience is accompanied by powerful experiences of radiant spiritual light and fire. As we read in a testimony recounted by Bucke:

> Suddenly, without the slightest warning, he found himself surrounded by a flame-coloured cloud. For a moment it seemed like a fire, an unexpected conflagration in the town, but after a moment he realized the light was inside him.[19]

Pascal's description of his own spiritual awakening could not be plainer:

> In the year of grace 1654, Monday 23rd November, St. Clement's Day . . . from ten thirty in the evening to half an hour after midnight, fire.[20]

Finally, Assagioli gives Richard Rolle's account:

> I was in such awe, indeed more than I can express, when I first felt this heat and burning in my heart, not something in the mind but a tangible fire . . . that I, in my ignorance, repeatedly put my hands to my breast to feel whether this burning had some physical cause. But when I realized that the fire was within, and had a spiritual origin, I then knew that it was a gift from my Creator.[21]

The spiritual awakening is of two basic types: it can be a sudden revelation of the reality of the immanent divine, present throughout the universe, experienced as "supreme Unity" resolving all discord; or it can be an experience of the transcendent divine, "outside" of the universe, "a real sense of the presence of . . . a great Being."[22] In both cases, the awakening, Assagioli notes, is "accompanied by a powerful indeed overwhelming flood of new feelings" and one's perception of the universe is "transfigured by the new light of spirit."[23] The experience of the mystical awakening is a radically transforming call to adventure in which one's perception and understanding of the nature of oneself and reality is utterly and irrevocably altered. Thereafter, one's life course is to be shaped by the spiritual power that has made itself known. It marks the beginning of an entirely different mode of life, even if one's outer life circumstances initially remain the same.

Further Varieties of the Call

These mystical versions of the call are the exceptions rather than the norm, of course, but they still conform to the general pattern of sudden awakening and alteration in life direction that take place during all varieties of the mythic call to adventure. In every case, the call is normally something transcendent breaking into the field of consciousness, whether a synchronicity, an accident, an inner call, or a spiritual awakening. From this moment on, one is thrown into different way of being, facing a different set of life possibilities, bringing new challenges and responsibilities.

Generally, I would say, the call to adventure is perceived as something positive, when the enthusiasm for a greater life adventure can carry one forwards across the threshold of adventure with high hopes and in high spirits, anticipating only success and positive rewards. One is lured by the unconscious to meet one's destiny.

At other times, of course, the heroic calling can seem anything but positive. It can be experienced as a titanic burden that one must assume, a cross to bear, a millstone around one's neck. It is important, then, to have certain strategies to deal with the arduous nature of the path ahead—perhaps the ability to recall a moment of spiritual uplift or a reassuring synchronicity or attuning to a vision of future fulfillment or spiritual ideal of some sort.

The call is memorably portrayed in the scene from *Star Wars* in which Luke Skywalker is suddenly, and irrevocably, cast into a new life situation, his old life having been wiped out in a stroke. After a fortuitous meeting with Ben Kenobi, the wise old man figure who rescues Luke from an attack by the sand people, Luke senses his uncle and aunt in the farm might be in danger from Imperial Stormtroopers. He rushes home to find his worst suspicions confirmed, with the building in ruins and his guardians slain. His transpersonal calling has imposed itself on him ruthlessly. For some people, it is a difficult decision to turn one's back on one's personal world and familiar life horizons. The future can seem uncertain and foreboding, as much as exciting. For Skywalker, though, there was no decision to make. To remain in his current life situation was no longer an option. In this form, then, the call announces itself as a death and sudden ending of the old life.

In *The Lord of the Rings*, to give another popular example, Frodo Baggins's call to adventure takes place when, in conversation with Gandalf, he discovers the true origin of the Ring of Power and the threat it poses to the Shire. The moment that Frodo realizes that he has to take the Ring away in order to save the Shire, represents his call to adventure—a call that had been seeded over the years by Frodo's fascination with his uncle Bilbo Baggins's tales of adventure in the wider world. What he has imagined and dreamed now becomes an all-too-real actuality, a foreboding call, when Gandalf explains to Frodo the one and only way the Ring can be destroyed:

> "There is only one way: to find the Cracks of Doom in the depths of Orodruin, the Fire-mountain, and cast the ring in there, if you really wish to destroy it, to put it beyond the grasp of the Enemy forever."

Frodo is thus called to assume a dangerous burden that he is understandably loath to accept:

> "I do really wish to destroy it!" cried Frodo. "Or, well, to have it destroyed. I am not made for perilous quests. I wish I had never seen the Ring! Why did it come to me? Why was I chosen?"

> "Such questions cannot be answered," said Gandalf . . . . "But you have been chosen, and must therefore use such strength and heart and wits as you have."[24]

Realizing there is no other possible course of action other than to guard the Ring himself and to try to destroy it by returning it to the fires of Mount Doom in Mordor, Frodo reluctantly accepts the call:

> "It seems that I am a danger, a danger to all that live near me. I cannot keep the Ring and stay here. I ought to leave Bag End, leave the Shire, leave everything and go away. . ."

> "I should like to save the Shire, if I could . . . I feel that as long as the Shire lies behind, safe and comfortable, I shall find wandering more bearable."[25]

In this situation the spiritual adventure imposes itself within an inescapable necessity; life enforces a destiny neither desired nor intended; it is thrust on the individual from without as an unavoidable task. This fate also befalls Frodo's friend, Sam, who gets embroiled in the adventure when he overhears the conversation between Frodo and Gandalf, and is discovered. Gandalf relays to Sam his punishment for listening-in on the conversation: "'I have thought of something . . . to shut your mouth and punish you properly for listening. You shall go away with Mr. Frodo!'"[26] Here again, through a chance happening, an accident, a life destiny unfolds, as Sam is unwittingly drawn into the dangerous journey ahead. This example also portrays the authoritative voice of the wise old man, Gandalf, commanding the personal ego-personality (Frodo, Sam) to assume his life task. For Frodo and Sam, the call to adventure through the encounter with Gandalf brings to an end the comfortable, sleepy, and generally uneventful life in the Shire.

In the science fiction film *The Matrix*, the call to adventure of the main character, the computer hacker Neo, takes the form of his first encounter with the sinister black-suited "Agents," and with Morpheus and Trinity, who are later to become his companions in the fight to bring down the manipulative world illusion that is the Matrix. He wakes up the following day having been through an experience that has changed him, and he feels that he cannot turn back.

In *The Wizard of Oz*, to give an example from a different genre, Dorothy's call to adventure is initiated by the tornado (the transcendental power, the power of nature), by the lost dog, Toto, preventing Dorothy from finding shelter (a variation on the lost ball motif), and then by the accident in which Dorothy is knocked unconscious, falling into a dreamlike state and triggering a stream of fantasies which comprises the rest of the film. She is thrust by a seemingly freak accident into the uncannily familiar magical land of Oz (the inner landscape of the psyche) where her adventure unfolds.

On another level, the young Prince Siddhartha, destined to become the Buddha, leaves his princely existence with its wealth and comforts, venturing out into the world where for the first time he encounters poverty, old age, sickness, suffering, and death. The future Buddha's call to adventure is in the form of an awakening to the horrors of *samsara*. He leaves behind his family and his former life, and goes off in search of enlightenment, seeking the path of liberation from suffering and the self-perpetuating cycle of death and rebirth.

In *The Odyssey*, to give one final example, this time from classical myth, Odysseus has embarked on a long sea voyage, and there has been no word of him for many years. His son, Telemachus, who has remained at home with his mother, Penelope, receives a visitation from the goddess Athena, instructing him to "seek news of your long-overdue father."[27] The call to adventure is here at the behest of a transpersonal power symbolized by the goddess. In this example, as Campbell points out, the quest for the father can be interpreted as the search for one's spiritual origin, authority, and identity—it is the quest to find where one really came from.[28]

These examples illustrate some of the variations of the call to adventure. Sometimes there is one decisive moment. Often, though, the call is ongoing; you are invited to continually respond to your own calling and remain true to your own path. This pattern is apparent when following synchronicities, those uncanny "meaningful coincidences," as Jung described them, in which the world seems to speak to you, conveying a powerful hidden meaning that can provide perspective and guidance.[29] If you are able to follow one synchronicity, another will come along in due course, and then another, and another. On each occasion you must choose if you are to follow the promptings of the spirit within the universe—a response that always requires a leap of faith, the willingness to take a step into the unknown. With each step taken, future possibilities open, drawing you further and further along your own life path. You are invited at each life juncture to put your trust in the transrational life direction suggested by the synchronicity. Goethe said that if you dare to follow your highest destiny, to attempt to do something great, the whole universe will bend to your aid. But to do this requires placing your trust in life, and accepting and embracing your own life journey with all the challenges and suffering it entails. It will ask of you everything you have got. It will take you past all of your existing limits. It will force you to face everything in your psyche, good and bad, for on the path of spiritual transformation, as we read in the words of Jesus (Matthew 10:26), "there is nothing concealed that will not be revealed, or hidden that will not be known."

Real-life biographies provide further examples of the call. Jung's call to adventure, certainly in terms of his outer professional life, was the intuition of his future vocation when he was a medical student in Zurich, affirmed by his decision to pursue psychiatric studies, much to the consternation and puzzlement of his advisers and peers who could not understand his attraction to what was then such an obscure, fringe subject that promised little in the way of future career advancement.[30] The choice was precipitated by the reading of a preface to a psychiatry textbook—the specific triggering event that, seen in retrospect, was the culmination of many preparatory life experiences from earlier in Jung's life, and the catalyst for his future life's work. Upon reading the opening lines of the preface, Jung describes the sheer exhilaration as his life destiny opened up to him—an experience familiar to all those who choose to follow their own deep interest:

> My heart suddenly began to pound. I had to stand up and draw a deep breath. My excitement was intense, for it had become clear to me, in a flash of illumination, that for me the only possible goal was psychiatry. Here alone the two currents of my interest could flow together and in a united stream dig their own bed. Here was the empirical field common to biological and spiritual facts, which I had everywhere sought and nowhere found. Here at last was the place where the collision of nature and spirit became a reality.[31]

A significant point of departure in Friedrich Nietzsche's life was the decision, forced upon him by his worsening physical and psychological condition, to abandon his scholarly career as a classical philologist at the University of Basel. Nietzsche's own nature demanded of him an altogether different type of life, one in which he would be able to detach himself from the culture, breathe the rarefied mountain air of the Alps rather than suffocate in the stuffy halls of academia. Only in isolation—in his life of wandering through the Swiss mountains, Italy, and the Côte D'Azur on the Mediterranean—would he be able to look upon Western culture, religion, and philosophy as if from the outside, and to find, in his own psychological depths, the redeeming vision of the *Übermensch*.

In Joseph Campbell's case, his call to adventure seems to have been significantly influenced by his experiences in Munich and Paris as a student during the 1920s. During his sojourn in Munich, Campbell quickly learned the language, enabling him to read Freud and Jung in their native German. Although Campbell had encountered Freud previously, it was at this time he truly immersed himself in the writings of these depth psychologists. He was also profoundly influenced by Schopenhauer and Nietzsche, in many respects the philosophical forefathers of the psychology of the unconscious.

Campbell's mind was ignited by the new ideas he encountered in Europe. Upon his return to New York, he found he could not settle back into his Ph.D. program with its specialized focus on Medieval literature, so he dropped out. It was 1929, the beginning of the Great Depression. With little of hope of finding employment, Campbell spent the next five years in the wilderness—literally. Four of those years were spent living in the woods near Woodstock on the East coast of America, during which time Campbell embarked on a disciplined, self-imposed program of reading and writing. It was a period of hermetic pedagogy, to use a term Campbell would later employ to describe a withdrawal from the demands of the external world when one can discover oneself and follow one's own line of interest. It was a creative incubation period in Campbell's life. He threw off the demands of the external world, with its pressures to find a job, get married, buy a house, raise a family, and so forth, placing his trust in his own experience, with its unknown, unfolding direction. He allowed the life within him to shape his experience, and to guide his reading and reflections. He opened himself to the unconscious, one might say. In mythic terms, Campbell entered the dark forest, trying to find his own way, pursuing those ideas that really excited him.

The other year in this five-year period was spent in California, living with a group of writers and scholars that included novelist John Steinbeck and Ed Rickets, the marine biologist. The events of this period were famously captured in Steinbeck's novel *Cannery Row*. As in Paris, during this period Campbell was living among artists, bohemians, and other creative people who, by stepping outside of the pressures of modern life, were able to tap into the wellsprings of creative energy that such periods of withdrawal can activate.[32]

Thereafter, Campbell's own heroic journey seems to have been played out through, and mediated by, his writing and scholarship: Writing *Hero* seems to have constituted a vicarious descent into the underworld and transformative journey, taking place within the relatively safe confines of the intellect and imagination rather than as a direct personal experience.[33] As we have seen, the creative process is closely connected to individuation. The imagination can serve as a vehicle for psychospiritual transformation and provide a way of accessing and processing energies and emotions from the depths of the psyche.

The Actualization of Destiny

For some people, it is often the case that the pattern and the future course of life are prefigured and anticipated by particular early experiences or the circumstances of the childhood years, as if our future destiny were already shaping us from birth, if not before. James Hillman calls this the "acorn theory": the kernel of what we are, and what we have the potential to become, is there from the start, just as the pattern of the oak tree is present from the first within the acorn.[34] In some sense we are drawn forth to meet our already determined life path and calling—a perspective that contradicts the usual way of thinking of life as being shaped by causal factors or circumstances in the past or by our own acts of will.

In an essay entitled "On an Apparent Intention in the Fate of the Individual," Arthur Schopenhauer argues that if we look back on our life, especially from the perspective of old age, it can seem as if the events and experiences have been crafted and written by an unseen author—that there is a power behind the scenes determining our life course. In retrospect, it seems that everything fits into a pattern, and that we have been unwittingly pulled along a particular path.

Jung came to a similar conclusion: "What happens to a person is characteristic of him. He represents a pattern and all the pieces fit. One by one, as his life proceeds, they fall into place according to some pre-destined design."[35] From this perspective, the individual is not the self-willing creator of his or her life destiny; rather, ego-consciousness, responding to the call of the deeper being, brings into actualization an already ascribed life path or destiny.

Schopenhauer proposed that human nature is comprised of an *intelligible character*, which is the person we are in potential, and an *empirical character*, which is the ego, the person we are becoming, realizing in the acts of life. The intelligible character (which roughly equates to Jung's concept of the Self) is the orchestrator of our experiences. To see the workings and the "intentions" of this orchestrating principle in moments of illumination, it can seem like there is a transcendent fatality at work in life, arranging our experiences and our life circumstances, even expressing itself through what we consider to be our own acts of free will. Jung made a similar point: "The Self . . . is an a priori existent out of which the ego evolves. It is, so to speak, an unconscious prefiguration of the ego. It is not I who create myself, rather I happen to myself."[36] In a similar vein, Friedrich Nietzsche suggests it is possible to arrive at a condition of "joyful and trusting fatalism" that rests on realization of the inextricable connection between one's own life and the whole—the totality of all that has been and will be.[37] Paradoxically (to the rational mind, at least), although one affirms a fatalism in life, one is also actively involved in bringing into existence a self and a world that are present in the beginning as mere potentiality. In the final analysis, fate and free will might be perceived as opposite sides of the same coin.

The Refusal of the Call

The negative counterpart to the call to adventure is the refusal of the call—the "dull case of the call unanswered," as Campbell describes it.[38] It is dull in terms of its impact on the individual's future life experience, but as a phenomenon I find the refusal of the call extremely interesting. Why would someone not want to follow the call of life? Why would someone refuse to follow the path of his or her own transpersonal destiny with all the rich life meaning and adventure this promises? In refusing one's life adventure, what happens next? This is a fascinating situation. Here first is Campbell's description:

> Often in actual life, and not infrequently in myths and popular tales, we encounter the dull case of the call unanswered. For it is always possible to turn the ear to other interests. Refusal of the summons converts the adventure into its negative. Walled in boredom, hard work, or culture, the subject loses the power of significant affirmative action and becomes a victim to be saved.[39]

Campbell gives the example of King Midas who builds a vast empire, accumulates immense wealth, but as this is outside of his true life purpose it thus proves wholly unsatisfying, a snare and an entrapment rather than a fulfillment. In *The Way of Myth*, Campbell talks about the realization that one has "climbed the ladder against the wrong wall," a realization, typically occurring later in life, that you have given your life energy and attention to something that did not reflect your real vocation.[40] The climb might well have been successful, but was that particular ascent what you originally intended? Was it what life intended for you?

There are several reasons someone might refuse the call to adventure. The first is *rationalization*, which means dismissing the call as unworkable, irrational, impractical. Following the call to adventure can often seem crazy from the standpoint of common sense, or economic sense. Committing to your life adventure will inevitably cause a lot of disruption in your life. The world is built on seemingly rational, pragmatic concerns, often in the service of an underlying motivation to avoid pain and suffering, and to make life as pleasant and as comfortable as can be, which, in practical terms, usually translates into making as much money as possible. If this is your life aim, you will not be able to follow your call to adventure, which invariably entails giving up all that is secure and comfortable, going against common sense, contravening even the pleasure principle and the self-protective impulse to avoid pain. Common sense is largely dictated by the norms and expectations of the culture; it often reflects what everybody wants you to do to keep the world orderly, or it reflects what everybody else does. Since the majority of people do not choose to follow their spiritual calling (or that calling has not yet made itself known to them with sufficient force), the accepted collective life patterns must inevitably impress upon us inauthentic, limiting ways of being. To live authentically, we often have to leave behind the reasonable, sensible option, and learn to live with the pervasive uncertainty and, sometimes, the seeming madness of the unique path and calling presented to us. This is not an easy task, and in my experience this factor prevents many people from accepting and following their own call to adventure.

The second, closely related, reason is emotional sensitivity, and not wanting to upset people. This concern is exacerbated by the often deeply ingrained Christian moral emphasis on the consideration of others—the love of one's neighbor—which can easily become a hindrance, preventing you from pursuing what it is you must do in life. Faced with this concern, it might be helpful to reflect on the discrepancy between the espoused Christian morality and the actual deeds and words of Jesus. For contrary to the popular image of the Son of God as an all-loving pacifist, the words of Jesus emphasize the necessity of strife, conflict, and division if one is following the way of the spirit: "Perhaps men think that I have come to cast peace upon the world, and they do not realize that I have come to cast divisions upon the earth: fire, sword, strife."[41] Divisions within the family as much as on the cultural level, are seemingly inevitable: "For there will be five in a house, three will be against two, and two against three, the father against the son, and the son against the father."[42] In order to realize the Christ within, which in Jungian terms means becoming a unique manifestation of the universal Self in your particular culture at a particular time of history, you will inevitably, unavoidably, upset people. If your life aim is always to be thought well of and never to cause conflict, you cannot become who you are and fulfill your potential. No one has yet lived a life without conflict, much less a deeply meaningful life infused with spiritual purpose. This is part of the test of the hero. You have to be able to live with your own uncomfortable feelings if your words and actions cause offense and go against the grain of conventional morality. As we saw earlier, if positive values have fallen into the darkness, and have become what is considered taboo or even evil, then to access these values often requires contravening the collective morality, going against what is generally deemed good or acceptable. This is not easy, especially as many people who are trying to follow a spiritual calling of some kind are often sensitive, caring, thoughtful people who do not by temperament like to cause upset. Nietzsche is very good at helping with this problem. He is so extreme. He denigrates the mass, the common crowd, and consensus morality, pointing out that much of what masquerades as morality, charity, and altruism actually conceals an unconscious power drive—it is self-interest in disguise. "Your love of your neighbor is your bad love of yourselves," he said with his eye for unmasking deception.[43] You need some of what is ordinarily considered selfish energy if you are to become who you are—a healthy selfishness, one might say. But it is a selfishness based on a transcendental authority beyond your personal will, sanctioned by a power beyond your own choosing. It is not mere egotism.

The third reason for the refusal is fear of the unknown. In ordinary life, perhaps with a job and family and a stable place to live, you generally believe you know who you are; you know to a large extent what is coming; things seem fairly well under your control (although this is often more apparent than real, of course). However, as soon as you go off the well-trodden path, you can find yourself in the dark forest, in a frightening place in your life, where you just do not know what is going to happen, where there seems to be nothing certain to hold on to. This pervasive uncertainty is often tied in with fear of dying, the fear of going insane, the fear of ridicule, or the fear of solitude and destitution. Such fears can keep you imprisoned in a life situation that is far beneath your potential. Fear can serve as the guardian of the threshold making it difficult for you to overcome psychological and environmental obstacles and to continue your authentic life adventure. If you are not able or willing to face your fears, you cannot meet the archetypal challenge of the hero, and you might well spend your life avoiding your deeper wishes and ignoring your highest possibilities as a result. You have to believe in yourself and in the deeper spiritual power that sustains you and your life. The passion that inspires your journey can help to carry you along; it can help to consume the fear that you will feel at various stages of your life adventure. Hard material necessity, too, can be a great help, forcing you to do and to face that which you might otherwise avoid.

A fourth reason for an inability to act on a call to adventure is a "conflict of duties"—a theme we touched on earlier. If, for example, the young Buddha's care and concern for his family, his wish to stay with them in his princely existence, were of absolutely equal intensity to his desire to seek enlightenment and eliminate the roots of suffering, he would have found himself at a total standstill, a total impasse, not being able to decide between the one course of action and the other. This would have meant he was unable to accept his call to adventure, at least until the matter could have been resolved on a higher level. Such conflicts, as Jung realized, often prevent the extraverted expression of life energy. The condition of total impasse drives energy inwards stimulating deep psychological transformation.

A fifth reason, and the final one we will consider here, is an unwillingness to deal with the burden of responsibility and the disturbance that the acceptance of the call entails. The call to adventure itself is often exciting, inspiring, carrying you along on a wave of energy. However, to act on the call, you will invariably have to attend to many things in your life and be willing to make radical changes. You have to be master of yourself, to a certain extent, so you can direct your energies where they need to go to accomplish the tasks before you. Acceptance of the call can be delayed by a lack of psychological and emotional readiness for the journey ahead. You need to be able to retain a firm sense of psychological control as the journey involves facing powerful energies, passions, and fears that can easily overtake you, and, if unchecked, lead you to wrack and ruin.

I am intrigued by the phenomenon of refusal because I think many of us encounter this in one form or another. It is rooted in the defenses of the ego, which might need to be systematically deconstructed before the life adventure can proceed. Mishaps and misfortune, illness and sustained psychological tension, jolting shocks or close brushes with death can all serve to deliver hammer blows to the resistances of the ego and to galvanize the will to affirmative action.

Campbell also points out, however, that the refusal itself can be heroic. He gives the example of what he calls "willed introversion," which occurs when a spiritually aspiring person becomes utterly disinterested in the life possibilities presented to him or her, and thus rejects everything—effectively roaring "no" to life like Nietzsche's lion.[44] There is just no life path, option, or goal that appeals sufficiently to mobilize such a person's energies. Campbell describes this condition as "a deliberate, terrific refusal to respond to anything but the deepest, highest, richest answer to the as yet unknown demand of some waiting void within: a kind of total strike, or rejection of the offered terms of life."[45] If you are destined to do something that is not in your current sphere of awareness or interest, you are obviously not going to be satisfied by other, lesser alternatives offered to you. It might happen, however, that people who find themselves called to a greater destiny try to avoid the truth of their situation, desperately seeking alternatives or palliatives, only to find themselves relentlessly pursued by the one thing, the true calling, that could provide the only authentic and satisfying resolution. For some people, to respond to the call is a matter of choice. For others, running from the call of destiny is ultimately futile. Life has placed on them an inescapable task to be fulfilled. The only alternative to doing this is not to live at all. "Many are called, but few are chosen." As we have seen, to be "chosen" in this sense means that your life is not your own, but must be given up to the service of a higher destiny.

Another mythic rendering of the positive, heroic version of the refusal of the call is portrayed in what Campbell calls the "refusal of suitors," exemplified, he suggests, by the romantic adventure of Prince Kamar al-Zaman and Princess Budur from the *Arabian Nights*. Al-Zaman, the Prince of Persia, continually declines his father's wishes that he should take a wife, defiantly declaring that he would rather die than marry a person not of his own choosing. Humiliated by his son's actions, the king has the young man imprisoned in a dark tower.

Meanwhile, in another kingdom far away in China, a beautiful princess follows a similar course of action, declining all proposals of marriage by the suitors presented to her, much to the consternation of her own father. Refusing one potential proposal after another, preferring even to take her own life rather than wed, the king's patience with his daughter eventually runs out, and, in fear that she might come to harm, he holds her captive within her palace chamber. The situation seems impossible to resolve. Behind the scenes, however, unsuspected powers are at work, which are ultimately to bring the realization of the royal couple's romantic destiny.

By remaining true to their sense of what is right for them, in spite of the pressure of circumstance, the powers shaping the destinies of the prince and princess see to it that circumstances bring them together, albeit through the greatest trials and adventures. "For when a heart insists on its destiny," Campbell notes,

> resisting the general blandishment, then the agony is great; so too the danger. Forces, however, will have been set in motion beyond the reckoning of the senses. Sequences of events from the corners of the world will draw gradually together, and the miracles of coincidence bring the inevitable to pass.[46]

This example applies not just to romantic affairs, of course, but to any aspect of life: the search for the right vocation, the right place to live, the right program of study perhaps. It takes a lot of courage and faith to continually hold fast to a course of action that reflects your own sense of truth and your highest potential, and thus to turn down lesser, more readily available substitutes. To do this, you have to be willing to live with uncertainty, and to face the risk that things might not work out. You have to be able to handle the negative emotions that arise during those periods when your life energy has no immediate means of satisfactory expression. Your will and inner calling are pitted against circumstance. By turning down one life possibility after another, energy builds within you, and this provokes a response on the part of nature, and the unconscious.

In ordinary life, it is often the case that our circumstances have to become very uncomfortable and oppressive before we can find sufficient motivation to make the difficult changes required to restructure our lives around our deeper interests and passions. Indeed, this is one of the reasons why "it is easier for a camel to pass through the eye of a needle than it is for a rich man to enter the Kingdom of God" (Matthew 19:24). With money at your disposal, you can easily absorb yourself in all manner of distractions and diversions thereby avoiding the risk, self-discipline, and exacting demands for self-consciousness that inevitably come with individuation (the wealthy Jung seems to have been a rare exception to this rule.) The rich person is able to use wealth to buy any number of easier, more attractive life possibilities rather than face the arduous demands of individuation. Wealth can thus be a barrier to spiritual realization. It can enable you to satisfy your desires in the world, but in so doing you might also be possessed by these desires to the detriment of your conscious self-awareness and spiritual direction. "Truly, he who possesses little is so much the less possessed," as Nietzsche said, giving a positive spin to relative poverty.[47] Those people without a surplus of money are forced to commit themselves to a path and stay on it. They do not have the luxury of being able to buy alternatives. This singular commitment is often necessary to bring forth something of worth. If you have money in abundance, it is easy to act on desires and thus be "possessed" by them.

The psychology of the refusal of the call is bound up with the ego. The ego is built upon the self-preservation instinct; it is a psychological expression of this instinct. The system of ego defenses belongs to the part of us that is concerned with preserving our well-being, and with ensuring we always have reassuring answers to questions such as "will I be alright in a year's time?" and "will I be alright in a week's time?" The boundaries of the ego are built by fear. As soon as you jeopardize your place in the world and your personal and economic security, the ego becomes agitated, anxious, fearful, and more rigid. In *The Gospel of Thomas*, this aspect of the ego is portrayed as the "strong man" seeking to remain in control, protecting, forcing, retaining a tight grip on your personality and life circumstances to ensure your well-being. In so doing, the soul and the child within you are kept imprisoned by the "strong man." To liberate the soul, the "strong man" within you has to be recognized and kept in check or "bound."[48]

Living according to the dictates of a controlling ego can only occur at the expense of an authentic existence, an insight encapsulated in Jesus's teaching (Luke 17:33) that "whosoever shall seek to save his life shall lose it." If your life motivation is built around a fearful self-preservation (trying to save your life), which prevents you from living authentically with freedom and trust, out of the passion and spontaneity of your deeper being, you will attract into your life circumstances and events that undermine and destroy the life structure that you have built. Life intends that you be who you are and that you do not remain in an inappropriate limiting situation out of fear of what might go wrong if you dare to take a chance on your life adventure. You will lose your life, your authentic life, if you try to cling on to what you have, barricading yourself behind material trappings or some safe worldly identity and life structure. You will have already forsaken your real life and, moreover, you will attract circumstances and events that seek to "liberate" you from this situation, by destroying your existing life structure, or perhaps even making you sick, destroying the part of you that resists life. "Even what little he has will be taken away," Jesus further cautions (Matthew 13:12). Often, in this situation, it can seem like one is the unfortunate victim of a capricious fate, or that one has been singled out by the wrath of God from some unpardonable sin. Yet it is, in truth, the lawful consequence of not living in accordance with the imperatives and dictates of one's deeper nature. If a lion tries to live the life of a lamb, the lion's nature will be crippled, ultimately to its own demise.

You must dare to commit to your life adventure and accept the uncertainty, fear, and challenging emotions that arise as a result. There are no guarantees of success, of course; there is no insurance olicy or safety net to fall back on. But not to dare to be who you are is to have lost before you have begun.

During individuation, there has to be a transition from an attitude of self-will and a wary, protective self-interest—the belief that you always have to be in control of your life, making absolutely certain you will be alright—to an attitude of trust in a higher authority: the Self, in Jungian terms. You have to overcome the little person within who is trying to manipulate and control everything; in spite of any fear you might feel, you have to let go of your rigid control, and move forward in life one step at a time, placing your trust in what is going to happen. Campbell noted that if you do not have your own life adventure, in time cynicism and bitterness can set in, and you might then become one of "the world's policemen," the enforcer of laws and consensus value judgments, patrolling your little world like a Freudian censor to ensure everyone and everything stays in place.[49] If you are not experiencing your life adventure, you might well find yourself compelled to make sure that no one else does either. One can see this phenomenon wherever one looks in life; it is so common. It is important, then, to have your life adventure while you still can, to discharge your life energy in the direction it is intended to go so the energy is not locked up inside you. The essence of this theme is again captured in _The Gospel of Thomas_: "if you bring forth what is within you, what is within you will save you; if you do not bring forth what is within you, what you do not bring forth will destroy you."[50]

If you are not able to accept the call to adventure, for whatever reason, energy starts to build. The energy that you should be expressing in following your call is damned up, and from the resulting accumulation of energy there arises a corresponding increase in psychological pressure and tension in the body, more stress, more anxiety. The energy from your unactualized life destiny becomes a negative or destructive force, and there is no way to discharge it through other activities; nothing feels satisfying, nothing feels right.

This situation is at the core of the existential crisis, with its characteristic experience of angst or dread. When the rational ego is persistently opposed to the spontaneity of the instincts, consciousness becomes cut off from the larger psyche and the person might then be subject to a crippling state of anxiety. This condition often afflicts intellectual types in which there has been an overdevelopment of rationality such that intellectual development has become out of balance with the needs of the larger psyche. One feels, in this condition, that one must conquer everything by thinking, reading, learning, analyzing. For the intellect in service of the ego, life becomes a problem to be solved, a riddle to be figured out. Of course, there is no formula or recipe for living that will ensure success, prosperity, and happiness. Life does not require a solution. It just is. Life cannot be accommodated within a rational program or spiritual path or religious practice or any philosophical system, however grand or integral. The call to adventure leads the individuating person beyond the ivory tower of the intellect into the more intense, extreme, ambiguous reality of the larger psyche.

Existentialism, Sin, and the Dark Side

The entrapment within the rational ego in this particular phase of psychospiritual development is explored in the work of existentialist philosophers such as Søren Kierkegaard, Jean-Paul Sartre, and Albert Camus (although existentialists generally do not see it as a stage of development but as a reflection of the unalterable facts of human existence). Existentialism explores the condition in which the individual has become utterly disillusioned with conventional life, feels tragically alienated from the world, and often can do no more than endure existence under protest or in distress and resignation. Life is experienced as agonizingly meaningless, absurd, crushingly banal, causing the emotions of ennui (existential boredom), angst, and nausea (a pervasive non-specific anxiety and state of apprehension)—a condition famously portrayed in Edvard Munch's painting, *The Scream* (1893). These are authentic responses of an ego alienated from the instinctual dynamism of the larger psyche. To reject them, and take refuge behind some social role, is to live, as Sartre observed, in a condition of bad faith. Such reactions only become genuinely pathological if they are avoided, denied, or uncritically accepted as reflecting the nature of reality itself.

Fyodor Dostoevsky's *Notes from Underground* does much to illuminate the state of alienation that characterizes the existentialist condition. With penetrating insight, it takes the reader into the heart of the existential predicament as it explores the individual's experience of a heightened self-consciousness that is pathologically distant from an instinctive, natural way of living. This type of ego-consciousness does not trust instinct. It questions everything, analyzes, seeks ever more fundamental causes and reasons, forms endless associations between ideas—in short consciousness becomes stuck in thinking, set against the dynamism of instinct. One becomes divided against oneself. In such a condition, one can feel just like the pitiful office worker and anonymous narrator of Dostoevsky's novel. The unnamed civil servant describes the twisted torment of a life under the tyranny of reason, experiencing the negative consequences of drives and impulses that cannot be expressed, leading into the absurdity of self-deception, loathing, and resentment. All conviction is lost, all is uncertain. "The direct, lawful, immediate fruit of consciousness," Dostoevsky observes, "is inertia"—the inability to act.[51] Divorced from instinct, one's conscious capacity for affirmative action is lost. At the collective level, this condition gives rise to the wasteland scenario characterized by a painful disjuncture between how one behaves and how one actually feels.

The individual in the midst of these psychological states often has an acute sense of the inescapable burden of freedom of choice that self-consciousness entails, the agonizing freedom of existing as a self-aware being within the vastness and apparent purposeless indifference of the universe. This can be a crushing experience to bear. Having not yet found a source of greater meaning and life direction, and having not been able to connect to a flow of life-renewing power from the unconscious, at this stage one can feel oneself to be utterly alone in the universe, existing without meaning, without support from a spiritual principle or a greater power beyond that of one's personal will. Existential crises of this type often tend to arise, I would say, when the individual is approaching the endpoint of ego development, possessing a highly developed intellect often coupled with a sensitive temperament, but with no apparent way out of the prison of the ego personality. The psychological reality of this situation is invariably projected onto or disclosed within the world itself, which can feel oppressive, claustrophobic, and banal to the point of absurdity—a situation that Jean-Paul Sartre famously described as one of "no exit." In this existential prison, the individual can get utterly caught up in his or her own reflective awareness, rational analysis, and thought processes, tied up in knots, unable to see any way out of the current psychological and existential predicament. The result can be an acute neurosis—a state of painful inner division when consciousness becomes split off from the larger reality of the psyche, exacerbating the person's sense of alienation. Properly understood, however, this situation is not intrinsically pathological but a symptom of a stage of psychospiritual transformation that might be passed through en route to a fuller, more deeply meaningful life in service of the Self. As Jung pointed out, neuroses only occur in people of a "higher type," with a far greater potentiality than the average person.[52]

From a Christian perspective, it is illuminating to think about the origins of the existential crisis in terms of good and evil, and sin and temptation. Sin is related to ego-consciousness, with its own personal will that deviates from the Will of God. Every act that is not in accord with God's Will is, strictly speaking, a sin. To develop ego-consciousness, as we must, is to develop one's own capacity for freedom of will and thus to fall inevitably into sin.

We also often think of sin and evil as being closely related or even as synonymous. In the popular understanding, sins are acts that contravene the ethical standard of what is good, and therefore seem to be evil acts. Aldous Huxley, analyzing the meaning of the Lord's Prayer, throws an interesting light on this topic. He considers the two lines "And lead us not into temptation, but deliver us from evil." On reading these words, one automatically assumes that temptation (leading to sin) and evil are closely related, perhaps even the same thing. However, Huxley draws attention to the connecting word *but*, which implies that temptation and evil are in some sense opposed. The implication is that by avoiding temptation we are more susceptible to fall into evil, and thus in need of deliverance from evil. The meaning would be wholly different if it were "lead us not into temptation, *and* deliver us from evil."

In depth psychological terms, in the prayer we are asking first not to be possessed by the flow of desire and instinct from the unconscious ("lead us not into temptation"); and, second, we are asking not to become closed off to the flow of desire and instinct and thus fall into the evil of personal will and ego-consciousness ("but deliver us from evil"). Temptation might be construed as consenting to desire or being unconsciously possessed by it; evil might be construed as alienation from desire, from instinct, in which, because of this alienation, we are subject to the tyranny of personal will and rationality (the existentialist condition) such that our desires and life energy turns negative. These lines in the Lord's Prayer point to a middle way, courtesy of God's grace, between possession by desire and the repression of desire.

Campbell suggests that the "dark side," as portrayed in *Star Wars,* refers to a state of being in which you have strayed too far over to the consciously intentional side of life, when you are living exclusively according to your rational ego, and not from the spontaneity of your heart—which is exactly what often occurs before the onset of the existential condition described above. Living this way, natural desires and impulses are repressed and can proceed to dominate you unconsciously. The "dark side" thus refers to the over-controlling intentional ego that is possessed by the unconscious drives it has not permitted to be expressed and which have therefore become negative forces in the psyche. This condition is obviously vividly conveyed in the character Darth Vader—a controlling, power-driven figure who is out of touch with his own humanity. Darth Vader, Campbell suggests, is an arch personification of mechanical man, the machine man, suggesting an extreme of conscious rationality, out of touch with the naturalness of the body—indeed, he cannot even breathe without the assistance of his mask.

State Power, the Herd, and Mechanical Man

Campbell also sees Vader as a personification of state man, fulfilling an empire position. He has forsaken his natural authentic being and even his humanity in favor of a state power role—a theme, Campbell believed, that is especially relevant to our time. The new forces of mechanization and computerized technology, on the one hand, and the political-economic power of global corporations, on the other, pose a grave threat to the integrity and freedom of the individual, as many commentators have stressed.

The Grapes of Wrath by John Steinbeck contains a striking description of this motif of the mechanical man. The passage in question poignantly describes the fate of families of Oklahoma farmers who are being displaced from their land by "the Bank." The farmers, who have owned and worked the land for generations, are facing the loss of their livelihood and their way of life. "The Bank" now owns the land, which has become barren due to drought, and has sent in the tractors to plough up the earth and evict the farmers from the property. When the tractors roll in, the farmers confront the tractor drivers, pleading with them not to proceed, appealing to their better nature. In the following exchange, we read the tractor drivers' response and explanation:

> "We're sorry, it's not us. It's the monster. The bank isn't like a man."

> "Yes [the farmers reply], but the bank's only made of men."

> "No, you're wrong there—quite wrong there. The bank is something else than men. It happens that every man in a bank hates what the bank does, and yet the bank does it. The bank is something more then men, I tell you. It's the monster. Men made it, but they can't control it."[53]

Steinbeck then gives a description of the Darth Vader figure at the helm of the tractor:

> The man sitting in the tractor did not look like a man: gloved, goggled, rubber dust mask over nose and mouth, he was part of the monster, a robot in the seat. The thunder of the cylinders sounded through the country, became one with the air and the earth, so that air and earth muttered in sympathetic vibration. The driver could not control it—straight across country it went, cutting through a dozen farms and then straight back. A twitch at the controls could swerve the cat', but the driver's hands could not twitch because the monster that built the tractor, the monster that sent the tractor out, had somehow got into the driver's hands, into his brain and muscle, had goggled him and muzzled him—goggled his mind, muzzled his speech, goggled his perception, muzzled his protest.[54]

> The driver sat in his iron seat and he was proud of the straight lines he did not will, proud of the tractor he did not own or love, proud of the power he could not control.[55]

In this alarming passage, we are presented with a description of someone who has given his volition, his power to live his life as he chooses, over to "the Bank," for money, for security, for a place in the world, for the material trappings and comforts of life, perhaps for the "good" of his children. Steinbeck's tractor drivers and Darth Vader are representations of the tendency and potential within each of us to give our freedom, individuality, and integrity away in the fulfillment of a worldly position for any number of seemingly well-intentioned reasons. Yet in choosing this life path, one risks losing one's identity in the herd, effectively becoming a meaningless statistical unit, a cog in an impersonal power-driven machine, and impervious to the plight of the soul. This is the potential fate of "mass man."

Campbell derives some of his analysis of the dehumanizing dangers of state power from Nietzsche (and also, no doubt, from his one-time friend Steinbeck). Nietzsche was fervently anti state:

> The state is the coldest of all cold monsters. Coldly it lies, too; and this lie creeps from its mouth "I, the state, am the people."[56]

> I call it the state where everyone . . . loses himself: the state where universal slow suicide is called—life.[57]

The state, having become invested with immense power, is able to cater for virtually all the basic needs of the population—for material goods, food, clothing, housing, forms of entertainment, and so forth. Imperceptibly, however, this arrangement can give rise to a condition of childlike dependency on the "nanny state" and blind subservience to the system in which people relinquish their moral autonomy and individual responsibility for their own lives. Like a child, one can look to the state to provide for all one's needs and blame the state when things go wrong. As Nietzsche says, "It will give you everything if you worship it, this new idol."[58] Of course, the price one pays for this generosity might well be the sacrifice of one's individuality, autonomy, and creative freedom. Even one's humanity, ultimately, might be lost, as in the Darth Vader example. As Campbell points out, at the end of *The Return of the Jedi*, when Vader is unmasked by his son, Luke, he appears wormlike, an undeveloped human being who had been hiding behind his mask, power, and authority. The human part of him has atrophied.

The sacrifice of spiritual and moral integrity for the order, security, and known horizons of some well-defined role within the established order of a life managed by the state—and this could be any number of roles within society that are not necessarily related to government or municipal activities—is but one way in which genuine individuality can become lost in the collective. For there can be no true individuality while the individual remains within the confines of the "herd," while his or her sense of identity comes not from within but from participation in the collective world of the anonymous "they," to use an expression from Heidegger. The power of the state remains indifferent to the claims of the human spirit.

It is important to keep in mind when you are reading myths, or watching movies with mythic themes, that to interpret the myth psychologically you need to see the myth or the entire film, including all the cast of characters and everything that happens, as expressions of your psyche. We are all potentially Darth Vaders just as we are all Luke Skywalkers or Princess Leias. This approach is the standard practice for interpreting dreams in which all dream characters are viewed as aspects of one's own being. The natural tendency, of course, is to put yourself on the side of good—to identify with the good characters—against what is deemed evil, rather than trying to appreciate both those elements within you. Beyond any affinity with good against evil, however, we each are potentially the Vader character, in that we each have to face up to the part of us that would willingly, for money or security or power, turn away from our deeper calling. The pressures to conform to society are great, the roads to loss of soul and loss of meaning are many. As we read in Matthew 7:13, "For wide is the gate and broad is the road that leads to destruction, and many enter through it. But small is the gate and narrow the road that leads to life, and only a few find it." You should also keep in mind as you watch films such as *Star Wars* and *The Lord of the Rings* that these challenges and themes can manifest at any stage. You are probably not going to resolve the Darth Vader issue once and for all at the beginning of your own journey. Similarly, the pressure to turn away from the incessant struggle of your life journey and to resign yourself to an easier life within the bounds of tradition is present all the time.

The spiritual challenge today calls for people who, steadfastly faithful to their own deeper calling, can stand alone—not in isolation from the wider world, of course, but as true individuals who can resist the overwhelming pressure to conform to mass-mindedness, state power, and cultural conditioning.[59] "Blessed are the solitary [or "those who stand alone"] and the elect," we read in *The Gospel of Thomas*, "for you shall find the Kingdom."[60] The individual can realize the Kingdom of Heaven only by eschewing social and cultural patterns in favor of living his or her own life. This is an immense challenge, but it is that is supported and assisted by the spiritual powers within nature.

CHAPTER 6

Beyond the Threshold and Through the Opposites

The descent into the depths always seems to precede the ascent.

The shadow is a tight passage, a narrow door, whose painful constriction no one is spared who goes down into the deep well.

—C. G. Jung

Responding in one way or another to the call, the hero is drawn forth to the threshold of adventure by transcendental powers lying beyond his or her personal will. The call is from the Self to the ego; it is a call from the depths of being. Even if the hero does not really understand what is taking place, the departure phase reflects the workings of this greater power, often experienced as the inescapable force of destiny. This greater power makes itself known through the experience of supernatural aid.

Supernatural Aid

On the spiritual journey, if you attempt to find and follow your own life path, powers that you did not know existed will come to your aid. Even though you are indeed on your own, the powers of the unconscious symbolized by gods and goddesses, amulets and weapons, helpers and guides—will be there for you. To the individual open to such assistance, supernatural aid comes as grace; to the individual excessively attached to exclusively personal aims, however, supernatural aid might be unrecognized, overlooked entirely, or mis-interpreted as an unwelcome intrusion, impeding his or her chosen aims and intentions. As Jung pointed out, like a mirror the unconscious reflects back the attitude one takes towards it.

An influx of grace can be triggered at the point of exhaustion of the individual will. If you find yourself in a desperate situation, for instance, when you feel you have reached the absolute limit of your capacity to cope, making a genuine heartfelt appeal can result in a helpful rush of emotional-spiritual power, a confirming conviction that all will be well. Or aid might come in the form of a reassuring voice within, or a synchronicity perhaps, in which the outer world communicates something of importance to you about your situation. Obviously, the appeal for aid is not something that can be intentionally willed. It comes over you spontaneously when, and only when, you are at the point of surrender. There is something inherent in the act of surrender that takes place at such times that empties your being of personal will permitting an influx of a transpersonal power. When the ego has no resources left at its disposal and surrenders, transcendent aid appears bringing salvation.

Another version of supernatural aid manifests through the figure of the wise old man such as Ben Kenobi and Yoda in *Star Wars*, or Virgil in Dante's *Divine Comedy* who personifies the principle of spiritual reason that guides Dante on his journey through Hell and Purgatory. The wise old man (or its female equivalent, the fairy godmother or helpful crone) provides guidance and instruction when it is needed. "The old man knows what roads lead to the goal and points them out to the hero."[1] He is a guide, that is, to individuation, representing the principle of established wisdom, the superior knowledge of the total personality, that can guide the individual ego (hero) on the way of individuation. As Jung has shown, in dreams the appearance of this archetype is often accompanied by a "voice" speaking with absolute spiritual authority, which announces what is to be done and what is to come to pass.

In *Star Wars,* we might think, for example, of Ben Kenobi, having died in combat with Darth Vader, reaching out as a spirit guide to Luke Skywalker at the memorable climax of the film, beseeching the young Jedi to "trust the Force" as he makes his approach to the Death Star. Or we might call to mind the pearls of wisdom coming from Master Yoda when he is instructing Skywalker in the ways of the

Jedi, teaching him to go beyond his personal will and effort to place his absolute trust in the Force. The wise old man represents the principle of spiritual wisdom that can guide the inexperienced ego on its transformative journey.

Sometimes the guide takes on the form of a spiritual guru who has the aspiring yogi or apprentice perform seemingly ridiculous, pointless tasks. This is often rather amusingly conveyed in martial arts films. In *The Karate Kid*, for example, Mr. Miyagi has Daniel Larusso, his adopted student, spend endless hours washing cars, painting fences, and waxing floors, much to the teenager's frustration, since he did not realize that these repetitive activities were conditioning precisely the moves he needed for karate combat. I remember as a teenager watching the old Jackie Chan films in the 1980s, which feature a similar old Chinese master-guru, assigning his young disciple excruciating exercises that seem to serve no ultimate purpose. Characters of this type suggest the capacity of the wisdom of the deeper psyche to give to the often foolhardy and reckless ego, fueled by youthful enthusiasm, just the instruction it needs to develop the necessary virtues and powers of self-discipline for the life journey ahead.

The guru can also be an imaginal or disincarnate figure, as in Jung's spirit guide, Philemon, who led Jung through his confrontation with the unconscious. And even if there is no figure, real or otherwise, to fulfill this role, the guide can be life itself, educating and instructing, testing one's patience, faith, and steadfastness through circumstance.

In myth, transcendent or supernatural aid can also be mediated by an amulet or charm or magical weapon of some kind given to the hero to aid his or her journey. On the quest for the Golden Fleece, as portrayed in the film *Jason and the Argonauts*, Jason is given a necklace by Phineas with a carved likeness of the goddess Hera, which later comes to his aid. As a gift from the gods, another Greek hero, Perseus, receives a helmet that makes him invisible and a reflective shield, which he uses in the slaying of Medusa. Odysseus is given a magical herb by Hermes to protect him from Circe's deadly spell. In *The Lord of the Rings*, Frodo is given a protective vest by Bilbo that ultimately saves his life in the Mines of Moria, and he is able to draw at crucial moments on the power of the Ring to become invisible or to gain extrasensory abilities. In *Star Wars*, Luke Skywalker receives his light saber, a symbol of the power of psychospiritual discernment, by which he is able to do combat with the forces of darkness (unconscious complexes and resistances, the tyrannical ego and superego). Again, these scenes and images, however removed they might appear from the actual deeds of ordinary human life, symbolize real experiences that you can have when you are in contact with the depths of the psyche.

When you have embarked on your adventure, leaving behind the old certainties and securities of the everyday world, you are exposed to all manner of unsuspected dangers and challenges. Following the way of your desire, your bliss path, as Campbell would say, with a heightened instinctual charge coming from the unconscious, the ego is no longer in its position of strength. This is a dangerous period for all of us until we become accustomed to handling the powers of the unconscious. Amidst the danger, however, you can often have the sense that you have transcendent protection and guidance. If you align yourself with the intentions of the Self, if you sincerely follow your life calling without holding anything back, you can get the sense of divine benediction, almost to the point of feeling bullet-proof. Buoyed by a flow of power from the unconscious, you can feel yourself to be virtually indestructible. Skillfully handled, this flow of power nerves one to accomplish great deeds that would be impossible by willpower alone. The sense of invulnerability comes from the conscious self's empowerment by the unconscious; it is almost as if you were riding the back of a wave. Accessing the power of the unconscious puts you in great danger, but it also activates forces that can support you, empower you, carry you along, and protect you. Nature unconsciously strives for your individuation and supports you on your task, even as it simultaneously resists. This is the paradox.

For Nietzsche, the intercession of a greater power, imposing upon him the intense suffering of psychospiritual transformation and sporadically leading him beyond this to joyful self-overcoming, came in the form of his own will:

> Truly, I have gone my way through a hundred souls and through a hundred cradles and birth-pangs. I have taken many departures, I know the heartbreaking last hours.

> But my creative will, my destiny, wants it so. Or, to speak more honestly, my will wants precisely such a destiny.

All feeling suffers in me and is in prison: but my willing always comes to me as my liberator and bringer of joy.[2]

The will is imagined here as a power beyond Nietzsche's conscious control—something that comes over him with an intent and purpose of its own.

For Jung, supernatural aid came in the form of powerful dreams, visions, and synchronicities, or was mediated through his spirit guide, Philemon. Campbell speaks of "invisible hands" coming to your aid when you are following your bliss, powers working behind the scenes to assist you on your adventure.[3] For it happens, sometimes with unerring regularity, that the events of life conspire to shape your life direction providing guidance just when you need it: the right book falls into your hands at the very moment you are ready to read it; a chance conversation directs your thoughts just where they next need to go; a synchronicity or moment of spiritual opening renews your faith in times of discouragement; or circumstances thwart a misguided attempt to move in the wrong direction. In hundreds of small but significant ways your hand and eye can be guided by unseen forces.

As these examples make clear, the mythic motif of supernatural aid is not just a metaphor for an entirely inner experience; rather, it describes a principle of higher assistance that influences one's whole life, having a direct impact on the outer world too. The unconscious is connected to the whole of reality; it is not just an encapsulated region in the mind. Supernatural aid—both within and without—is activated if you take the first step, courageously moving forward into your adventure. Apart from in exceptional circumstances—births, deaths, marriages, and the like—it does not tend to make itself known to those who choose to stay within the bounds of conventional life patterns.

The Guardian of the Threshold

At the beginning of the spiritual adventure, buoyed by the exciting rush of newly found spiritual energies, it is tempting to imagine that one's life will readily move towards states of increasing enlightenment, ascending towards higher levels of spiritual realization.

Caught up in the enthusiasm of first discovering spiritual teachings or myths or philosophies that convey profound truths, we often do not anticipate the struggle that inevitably comes later on the spiritual journey. But a struggle it invariably is.

Sooner or later, one will hit the limits of one's own ego, and find oneself facing an obstacle that one is not able to overcome. After the initial joy of spiritual awakening, the emergence of such obstacles might take one by surprise, and be experienced as a sobering defeat that is difficult to understand. Perhaps for the first time, one becomes aware of an authority in the psyche greater than that of the conscious will. The first experience of the Self, as we have seen, brings "a defeat for the ego." The ego might be left weakened and wounded by this encounter, unable to perform its daily business as it once did, as the Self imposes a labor of transformation that absorbs all one's time and energy. In mythic terms, this first deflating or prohibitive experience of the Self is suggested by the motif of the "guardian of the threshold."

After following the call to adventure, then, the first challenge of the hero's journey, according to Campbell, takes the form of an encounter with a threshold guardian—perhaps represented by an insurmountable obstacle, such as a mountain or rock face that is too steep to climb, or perhaps suggested by dreams of being driven back from one's chosen path by adverse conditions. The threshold guardian might also be symbolized by an indestructible beast—such as a lion, snake, leopard, or wild dog that cannot be overcome—forcing one back on another route. Here the beast symbolizes the instinctual power of the unconscious that the conscious will cannot as yet master. At this stage, the appearance of such motifs in dreams and fantasies suggests that desires or fears are too strong to be bypassed or overcome, even by the most strenuous of efforts; the threshold guardian cannot be conquered by an act of will. In order to overcome the beast that bars the way or the insurmountable obstacle, psychological transformation is required. You have to learn to tame the beast within you, as it were, humanize it, and incorporate it into the emerging wholeness of your psyche. The wild animal, then, or perhaps a dragon or monster of some kind or a shadow figure, represents the instinctual power of the unconscious, which is experienced through your desires, passions, and appetites for the good things of life—for food and drink, pleasure, sex, prestige, success, riches, excitement, and so on. Mastering your passions, taming the beast within, is a fundamental challenge of the hero's journey.

In *The Divine Comedy*, Dante aspires to make the ascent to Heaven, but, as he begins his journey, he is confronted in turn by a leopard, a lion, and a she-wolf, which each drive him back. The animals cannot be killed, and cannot be passed. They block the way, and prevent him following his chosen path:

And, almost at the point when the slope began,
I saw a leopard, extremely light and active,
The skin of which was mottled

And somehow it managed to stay in front of me
In such a manner that it blocked my way so much
That I was often forced to turn back the road I had come

. . . a lion appeared before me, as it did.

When he came, he made his way towards me
With head high, and seemed ravenously hungry,
So that the air itself was frightened of him;

And a she-wolf, who seemed, in her thinness,
To have nothing but excessive appetites,
And she has already made many miserable.

She weighed down so heavily upon me
With that fear, which issued from her image
That I lost hope of reaching the top of the hill . . .

So I was transformed by that restless animal
Who came against me, and gradually drove me down
Back to the region where the sun is silent.[4]

Dante is forced to undertake a descent into Hell and an arduous voyage up the Mount of Purgatory, symbolizing the long and painful process of psychospiritual purification that one is subject to on the path of mystical realization and individuation. The descent describes the ego's journey through the realm of the unconscious, where one encounters all the desires and fears not yet addressed and mastered, all the complexes and resistances that need to be worked through. The initial spiritual awakening and elevation is followed by an arduous process of transformation—a veritable Herculean labor, as Jung put it.

Assagioli describes this process as a journey through the "lower unconscious" after the initial euphoria of the spiritual awakening caused by an influx of the "superconscious"—the spiritual dimension of the psyche. When the initial joy of spiritual awakening (the mystical call to adventure) subsides, he explains,

> the lower urges are reawakened with renewed energy; all the sharp rocks, the rubble and the waste that had been covered over by the high tide now reappear. . . . On occasions certain lower tendencies and impulses, which had laid dormant in the unconscious, are reawakened and aroused into violent opposition against the new lofty spiritual aspirations, thus constituting a challenge and a threat.[5]

In *The Lord of the Rings*, to give another example of this aspect of the journey, Frodo and his companions, attempting a high, treacherous mountain pass (ascent), are forced back by violent blizzards summoned by the evil Saruman. The harsh weather conditions and the wild power of nature here point to the violent emotions and desires that must be brought under conscious control before any spiritual progress can be made. These conditions also suggest the difficult psychological circumstances in which the ego finds itself. In this scene we witness the party being driven back from the threshold of the mountain track, having no option but to make the pass underneath the mountain instead, through the Mines of Moria. They are forced, that is, to make a descent into the underworld, there to wrestle with the powers of the unconscious psyche. The guardian of the threshold bars the way for aspiring spiritual heroes, forcing upon them the labor of psychospritual transformation and an underworld descent. A threshold is indeed crossed, but it does not lead to where one thought it would.

The Point of No Return

The fourth part of the departure or separation phase Campbell calls the crossing of the first threshold. This theme is memorably conveyed in the science fiction film *The Matrix* when Neo is presented with a choice between two pills, one blue and one red. Choosing the first (blue) would enable Neo, who is reluctant to accept the new reality he has been exposed to, to forget everything he has experienced and to return to his former life and his former identity; the second pill (red) would reveal the truth, from which there could be no turning back. Swallowing the red pill, he passes through a kind of perinatal death-rebirth process, and we witness Neo crossing over a threshold that takes him from the illusory comforts of the world he knows into an unsuspected dark reality beneath the computer-generated façade in which he had been living. As he passes through a slimy, sticky substance, everything is stripped away from him, and he emerges in a grim underground civilization, which again reflects the fact that the direction of the hero's spiritual journey leads down into the depths before any ascent can take place. The spiritual seeker finds himself or herself on a descent that was not anticipated. Though it promises much, the adventure typically takes the hero into a more difficult situation, a harsher reality, in which the full horrors of *samsara* are revealed. Ostensibly, it is the same world, but all appears strange, uncanny, different. In myth and in dream, the first approach into the realm of the unconscious is often symbolically suggested by the hero or dreamer entering an alien land—perhaps a desert or a forest or a jungle—and there encountering strange powers and arduous trials. The hero has to adjust and adapt to the new environment, to become familiar with the landscape of the unconscious.

The threshold crossing marks a point of no turning back. Often the crossing can be a struggle, involving a painful loss of a more innocent life. I call to mind here the lyrics of Jimi Hendrix's "Are You Experienced?": "I know you'll probably scream and cry / that your little world won't let you go."[6] It is a painful transition from the ordinary personal world of the ego to the transpersonal dimension of life and an encounter with the ominous powers of the unconscious. In this new world, you have to deal with potent energies, archetypal images, and powerful instincts that need to be recognized and controlled. You are up against the tyranny of your own ego. You find yourself in a difficult psychological landscape where you must pass through all kinds of trials and hazards. There is little wonder, then, that part of us would like to avoid all of this and remain in the sleepy comfortable world of childhood with its known horizons, familiar patterns, and securities. The ordinary, personal part of us does not want the extra level of suffering and intensity—this is the personal "little world" not letting you go to begin your transpersonal adventure. In the New Testament (Luke 13:28), Jesus declares that at the end of the world there will be much "weeping and gnashing of teeth," which conveys the same idea. Jung puts it in no uncertain terms:

> When a summit of life is reached, when the bud unfolds and from the lesser the greater emerges, then, as Nietzsche says, "One becomes Two," and the greater figure, which one always was but which remained invisible, appears to the lesser personality with the force of a revelation. He who is truly and hopelessly little will always drag the revelation of the greater down to the level of his littleness, and will never understand that the day of judgment for his littleness has dawned. But the man who is inwardly great will know that the long expected friend of his soul, the immortal one, has now really come . . . a moment of deadliest peril![7]

The idea conveyed here, to put it simply, is that you have to let go of the lesser to receive the greater. You have to relinquish the little world of the ego in which you were master and ruler in order to enter the larger world of the greater psyche in which you are a rank novice, knowing nothing, stumbling from one misfortune to another, one difficult psychological state to another. This is a humbling experience. "Many who are first shall be last" (Matthew 19:30), to put this reversal in the familiar words of the Bible.

The transformation from personal control to transpersonal adventure amounts to dying to the life you think you should be living, to the old ideas and fixed images of what you thought your life should be about, and opening yourself to what the Self—the divine within you—has in store for you. It is no small matter to do this for we are conditioned from the very first to take control of our lives, to go after what we want, to earn money to buy ourselves opportunities, to make something of ourselves through our own efforts. It comes as a painful shock to entertain and learn to adapt oneself to a new way of being in which the ego does not determine the life direction, but has to serve.

Since none of us, I imagine, would claim to be directly privy to the biddings of the divine, we must constantly apply spiritual discrimination to determine what the next step should be. One must consistently and repeatedly overcome the pull of the past, which takes one back to a simpler, more natural, but less conscious way of living.

In *The Lord of the Rings*, amidst the ceaseless turmoil and exhausting dangers they face, Frodo and his hobbit companions often yearn to go back to the Shire, where life was simpler, easier than it is on this very demanding adventure. It is a curious fact that before we embark on the adventure the inner being craves it, craves the intensity of experience, the fullness and the excitement that the adventure promises to bring. But when one is on the adventure and things become difficult, one comes up against one's resistances, and nostalgia for the simple, peaceful life sets in. Each experience draws forth its opposite.

Campbell suggests that the controlling part of the ego is symbolized by a tyrant ogre, the antithesis of the hero. "The hero of yesterday," he warns, "becomes the tyrant of tomorrow unless he crucifies himself today."[8] Life is always in a process of being broken down; as soon as the form of something crystallizes it becomes anti-life. The hero therefore has to undergo a continual death and rebirth. A figure like Palpatine in *Star Wars* is a symbol of the tyrannical ego within each of us—desperately clinging to power, manipulating, attempting to control all it surveys. The extent to which we are unconsciously dominated by this aspect of the ego only becomes apparent during the process of psychospiritual transformation we are considering here. Ordinarily we cannot notice this part of the ego at work; we remain unconsciously identified with it. During individuation, however, all the complexes in the psyche become amplified and intensified, such that they cannot be ignored. At the same time, some kind of psychological separation occurs that allows consciousness to see the controlling dimensions of the ego as a subject to an object. The tyrannical part of the ego becomes a separate split-off complex that, with psychological vigilance and resolute determination, can be seen more objectively, and thus confronted and overcome.

A further feature of crossing the threshold, which Campbell discusses in *Hero*, is symbolized by the god Pan, who, as the name suggests, is related to the experience of panic. In the early stages of the individuation process, after the collapse of the persona, consciousness "falls" into the unconscious and finds itself in a strange world, where everything is charged with intense emotion, a world in which the ego barely has any control over the fantasies and impulses that threaten to take over the personality. Realizing that it is impossible to control what is happening, one might become panic stricken, or even enter a state of relentless trauma such that even the slightest sound or movement can be jolting and jarring. Just the snapping of a twig, Campbell notes, or the rustling of the wind in the trees, could be enough to cause panic. Dreams of alarm bells often convey a similar idea in modern form. The god Pan is thus the personification of the threatening power of nature, pressing in on the all-too-human ego-personality unaccustomed to such fateful intrusions.

In the moment of "grave peril" when the "One becomes Two," the original unity of the psyche is torn asunder such that the ego becomes radically detached from the rest of the psyche, cast adrift in the unconscious, and you can find yourself in a potentially terrifying existential crisis and a dangerous psychological condition. This amounts to a threshold crossing from the natural state of human existence to a condition of profound alienation when the old psychological structure collapses and disintegrates, as a prelude, ideally, to the formation of a new, higher unity during the work of individuation. Needless to say, we are concerned here with a psychological and spiritual transformation that very few people directly experience and even fewer successfully navigate.

The primary emotion accompanying the onset of this experience is that of dread, which is explored in the work of Kierkegaard. Dread can perhaps best be described as a fear that has no particular object; in its most extreme form it manifests as a panic fear that extends into eternity. Dread is the emotion that arises as a result of the ego's alienation from the original unity of the psyche. As we have seen, when this takes place the person feels, perhaps for the first time, that he or she is utterly alone in the universe, staring into an abyss of nothingness. Dread can be characterized by an intense combination of claustrophobia and agoraphobia. It is an experience of utter isolation with no apparent metaphysical or psychological support, with nowhere to turn for relief. Nothing in life can prepare us for this. Dread is a numinous religious experience, but it is also dark, powerful, and extremely disturbing. As we have seen, in spiritual terms, the realization of being an independent point of self-consciousness, standing utterly alone in the world, is related to the profound experience of the "I Am." This experience is in some sense a culmination of the trajectory of the Western path of spiritual development, a supreme realization of individual selfhood and at the heart of the teachings of Jesus in the New Testament gospels. It is the conscious realization of the immensity of a spiritual selfhood that transcends space and time: hence Jesus's enigmatic statement that "before Abraham was, I Am." It is the enormity and isolation of the experience of this conscious-ness that is, initially, difficult to bear.

As you proceed to face the psyche during individuation, the emo-tion of dread gradually subsides. What was the overwhelming dark-ness of the unconscious as shadow is transformed; more of the shadow is brought into awareness and the darkness loses its terrify-ing, abyss-like quality. Dread seems inescapable at first, but if you can face it a little at a time, you can overcome it. The experience of dread cannot be reversed, however. It is not something you can opt out of. You can numb the experience with medication, perhaps, but this will not solve the problem. It might even put you into a state of more or less permanently arrested development. The only construc-tive way out of the dread or nausea felt by the alienated conscious-ness is for the old ego to be destroyed as a prelude to a rebirth into a deeper identity. This process is exactly what seemed to be taking place in Nietzsche who passed from existential alienation through nihilism to the promise of spiritual renewal with the realization of the coming *Übermensch*. That Nietzsche's own life ended so tragi-cally perhaps testifies to the great dangers involved in this process.

In Greek mythology, the theme of dread is well conveyed by the figure of the gorgon Medusa, who symbolizes the dark (because repressed) instinctual power of nature, here personified in female form. To those who look directly into Medusa's eyes, the sight is so fearsome that they are instantly turned into stone. Staring into the darkness of the unconscious, that is to say, one can become paralyzed by fear. It is an utterly terrifying experience when you first have to turn to confront the darkness within you. Remember, the shadow has been created by centuries, even millennia, of psychological evolu-tion. Consciousness and civilization are relatively new phenomena that merely mask all that remains primitive, brutal, evil, chaotic, and terrifying in the human psyche. Consequently, you have to overcome great fear and resistance to look into the darkness of your own depths. The darkness can easily overtake you. As Nietzsche observed, "He who fights with monsters should be careful lest he become a monster; if you stare into the abyss for too long, the abyss stares back at you."[9]

Nietzsche's existence was, in a sense, one of continual threshold-crossing, forged by experiences in which he was driven beyond his psychological limits into and through the pain of self-overcoming. One particularly significant transition in his intellectual life, however, was his separation from the ideas and life philosophy of Schopenhauer. Another was his break from his one-time friend Richard Wagner. Both separations had the decisive affect of pushing Nietzsche ever deeper into his own emerging individual truth, compounding his spiritual and intellectual isolation.

For Jung, the point of no return was his decisive break from his mentor Sigmund Freud occurring in late 1912 and early 1913 following the publication of the original version of Jung's *Wandlungen und Symbole der Libido* in which he set out his own mythological interpretation of incest theory—a bold deviation from the established Freudian position. Prior to this Jung had been a follower and supporter of Freud, and had assumed the role of the first president of the International Psychoanalytic Association. Contravening the patriarchal authority of Freud, however, Jung chose to remain true to his own insights and experiences, and this meant professional and, to a certain extent, psychological isolation: "When I parted from Freud, I knew that I was plunging into the unknown. Beyond Freud . . . I knew nothing; but I had taken a step into darkness."[10] Indeed, it was this threshold crossing that led directly to Jung's "confrontation with the unconscious"—an underworld descent we will consider later.

The Belly of the Whale

Sometimes, if the hero cannot proceed voluntarily across the threshold of adventure, the unconscious will assume control, and the hero will be taken, against his or her conscious choosing, into an experience of the depths. The belly-of-the-whale motif pertains to this experience of being engulfed by the unconscious, of being suddenly swallowed and pulled underwater into an inescapable dark place, where the light of consciousness is all but extinguished. There are several well-known illustrative examples of this type of experience in the Bible: most obviously Jonah being swallowed by a whale, but also Joseph been forced into a well, Daniel in the lion's den, and Jesus's three-day entombment in a cave after his crucifixion—the cave symbolizing the bowels or the belly of the Earth, as it were. This motif was also incorporated into the Disney version of Carlo Collodi's tale of Pinocchio in which the young puppet, on his own journey of transformation (to become a "real boy"), is swallowed by a whale. The belly serves as an incubating vessel of transformation, initiating the individual into a deeper reality.

As water represents the unconscious, the whale, periodically surfacing from the depths into the daylight world above, is a symbol of the animal part of us, the instinctual power lying within the unconscious emerging into conscious awareness. The hero, representing the conscious ego, is engulfed by the whale, swallowed alive, and taken to the depths. This means that consciousness, which is normally attuned to the daylight world of everyday concerns, is pulled down into the unconscious. The entire focus from this point is inward, on what is occurring in the psyche. The hero has effectively disappeared from the outer world, which implies that one's will is no longer active and effective in the world, as it used to be, for it has been overpowered by unconscious desires and fears. To prevail in this situation, you have to control and overcome the instincts and thus free yourself from the inside of the whale.

A similar meaning is implied in the motif of being devoured by a wild animal, which suggests that your consciousness has been possessed by an unconscious complex, taken over by a powerful stream of desires. The complex effectively devours you, consumes you like a fire, until you are able to muster the psychological strength and sufficient self-awareness to tame the beast.

Again, the experience of being swallowed, pulled underwater, or consumed is what it actually feels like when you encounter the power of unconscious. When you are going through this process of transformation, the ordinary world appears very different. It is the same world, of course, but everything seems to have inexplicably changed. The environment is at once familiar and yet now alien, uncannily different. You can feel like a stranger in your own land, even in your own home, around friends and family. Because the unconscious has been activated, it changes the ego's perception of the world; the ego falls or is taken down into the unconscious, and from this psychological vantage point you see the world filtered by the distorting lens of unconscious complexes. Not unlike the experience of being underwater, you feel yourself to be submerged such that you cannot see things in the clear light of day. Your conscious will and capacity to clearly discern what is happening are severely compromised. You feel yourself to be held captive in the dark depths, unable to free yourself. This experience can last for a considerable length of time—months, or even years. It requires a gargantuan effort over a prolonged period to overcome the unconscious, to free yourself of its power.

The well-known trash-compactor scene in *Star Wars* is one modern rendering of the belly-of-the-whale motif. As they flee the Stormtroopers, Skywalker, Leia, Solo, and Chewbacca inadvertently find themselves in the trash compactor of the imperial spacecraft. Wading knee-deep in murky waters of sewerage and trash, Skywalker is suddenly pulled underwater by a monster from the depths and appears to have met his end, only to miraculously emerge unscathed. As soon as has he passed through that ordeal, however, the walls of the trash compactor start to close in, threatening to crush them, one and all, until a last-second intervention by Skywalker's robot R2-D2.

In psychological terms, there are several different motifs suggested in this scene. First, the underwater creature pulling Skywalker down into the sewerage represents the animal-instinctual power of the unconscious, pulling the hero (ego-consciousness) into the dark water (the unconscious)—a variation on the whale motif. Second, the trash and sewerage represent the rejected aspects of the psyche, everything that has been excluded from consciousness, which, as Jung has shown, must be brought to consciousness, accepted, and purified during individuation, a task well symbolized in Greek myth by the fifth labor of Hercules, that of cleaning the Augean stables.

Passing Through the Opposites

The third motif in the trash-compactor scene is that of being crushed between the opposites. The crossing of the threshold is a passage from the old mode of being within the confines of the ego to a new reality centered on the Self. This passage leads one between pairs of opposites: good and evil, light and dark, consciousness and the unconscious, male and female, reason and instinct. The compactor scene conveys in psychological terms what it is actually like when the ego is confronted by the unconscious and is subject to a titanic crushing pressure. The instincts, long submerged in the unconscious, enter into an intense struggle with the repressive control of the ego. Repression is intensified as instinct gains in power and the ego fears it is losing control; the more instinct is repressed, the stronger it gets. Amidst this standoff, the sense of psychological and even physical pressure can reach extreme levels. You can get a sense of this extremity reading Nietzsche and Jung. You will recall that the entire religious and metaphysical history of the Western world converged on Nietzsche, who attempted to reject it, cast it off. His was a life of alienation, however. Nietzsche had become acutely alienated from the unconscious, from the world, from people. In this condition, he experienced crushing pressures, intense and prolonged headaches, near blindness at times, and found himself embroiled in a ceaseless and painful tussle between his will and his emotions and instincts. This intense crushing pressure is characteristic of the process of deep psychological transformation. If you have undertaken any breathwork or rebirthing sessions, such as the method of holotropic breathwork pioneered by Stanislav Grof, or if you have found yourself in a psychospiritual crisis, you might have a sense of what this psychological pressure is like. The old structure of the ego is effectively destroyed by the extremity of pressure exerted on it from the repressed instincts. The *Star Wars* compactor scene is a powerful metaphor for this experience.

The motif of the jaws of the whale is another symbol of the opposites—a modern variation of this image might be elevator doors opening and closing, or the clamp of a vice. During a death-rebirth experience, you have to pass through the opposites in the psyche. The inner being, emerging as a new focal point of consciousness, has to pass through the "doorway" of the old ego structure, which is being forced open and progressively destroyed as the inner self moves into a fuller existence, into a larger world of experience. During deep psychospiritual transformation, this passage happens again and again.

Such a passage is suggested in the 1960's film *Jason and the Argonauts*, which provides a fine illustration of mythic themes relevant to the individuation process. Jason embarks on a voyage to the other side of the world on a quest for the Golden Fleece, the magical animal-skin that has the healing power to cure all ills and bring prosperity to the land. During his adventure, he has to lead his ship, the Argo, along a narrow stretch of water that passes between clashing rocks (the Symplegades) on either side. As the Argo makes its approach, the crew witnesses another ship being utterly destroyed by falling rocks and boulders. To follow the same course seems certain to invite disaster. Placing his trust in the gods, however, Jason gives the order to proceed, only for the mighty rocks to rumble and shift, and once more begin to collapse into the sea. It appears Jason and his crew are doomed. In desperation, as the rocks continue to fall and the crashing waves violently toss the ship around, Jason makes a desperate appeal to the gods for help and throws the amulet, given to him by Phineas, into the water, more in anger than expectation. Lo and behold, however, at the behest of Hera the great sea god Triton, son of Poseidon, surfaces from the depths of the ocean, holding the collapsing rocks in place, protecting the Argo, and allowing its safe passage to the other side.

Breaking down the psychology of this scene: the boat represents the vehicle of life and of consciousness, Jason is the hero representing ego-consciousness (or the heroic part of the ego), and the crew members represent other parts of the psyche that Jason is trying to control and direct. The narrow passage leads between the opposites, the rocks represent the crumbling old psychological structures that crash into the water (representing the unconscious). At the same time, the collapsing rocks cause the water to whip up, lashing the Argo, tossing it from side to side, suggesting the turbulence of the desire nature and instincts when the old psychological structure starts to collapse and long-repressed drives, fears, and passions are violently released into consciousness. Throwing the amulet into the water and the desperate appeal to the gods is a call for supernatural aid. Again, it often happens that at the very moment all seems lost, and you curse the gods in an act of despondency or surrender, some kind of aid or help or revelation comes to your rescue when you did not expect it. In this scene, Triton represents the supernatural aid, the intercession of a transcendent power into the normal sphere of human experience—perhaps the guidance or intervention of the Self, in psychological terms. Triton here effectively midwifes the individual's birth passage through the opposites—an experience that can actually take place in deep psychological transformation. One can have the sense that something like a cosmic midwife is pulling one's inner being with a giant hand through the closing walls of the old ego structure into a fuller reality. Amidst the intense psychological and physical pressures and agonies of rebirth, one is eased through the opposites, as the inner being moves into the foreground of conscious experience.

The psychological validity of such an experience has been confirmed by recent research in transpersonal psychology by Stanislav Grof. His work demonstrates that, in non-ordinary states of consciousness, the experience of being pushed or pulled through the opposites is mediated by the reliving of the biological birth experience. The individual experiences the intense pressure of contractions in the womb, a life-and-death struggle in the journey through the birth canal, and the annihilating then ecstatic emergence through the vaginal opening—a veritable passage through the opposites leading to a bright new world beyond. The successful resolution of this experience, over many rebirthing sessions, can bring about a profound psychospiritual transformation. Such experiences, Grof has found, are typically accompanied by archetypally resonant images drawn both from the storehouse of world mythology and actual events in our individual past and collective history.[11]

What we are doing here, to reiterate, is trying to discern within an extraverted heroic adventure the inner significance of what is taking place. By interpreting myths in this way, we are looking for the psychospiritual implications of the physical acts of heroism, in trials and battles, and in episodes of high adventure and danger portrayed in myth. This is not an easy thing to do of course. Centuries ago, it seems unlikely that many people would have seen myths in these terms. However, because myths are expressions of the imagination, shaped by the archetypal dynamics of the psyche, myths, like archetypes, apply to many different levels of human experience such that physical adventures have their inner, psychological correlates.

The passage through the opposites marks the end of the departure phase, as Campbell defines it, but it should be kept in mind that this experience continues to occur all the way through the hero's adventure; indeed, it is intrinsic to the transformation occurring during the individuation process. The old psychological structure is broken apart, instincts and drives are activated and released into conscious-ness, needing to be controlled, and then, in order to assimilate the released energy, one must pass through the opposite walls of the old ego structure into a new brighter world, and a fuller and deeper way of being. Through this process, the "existential gap" between ego consciousness and the larger psyche is progressively closed and the ego is able to gradually yield to the Self.

In the modern West, experiences of deep psychological transfor-mation of the kind we are exploring here are generally seen as patho-logical, requiring medication to control and subdue. In this respect, individuals in the modern era are much more on their own than in the past, when cultures supported these kinds of transformative spiritual experiences. The isolation, the harsh judgment of one's peers, and the diagnosis or misdiagnosis of those in the medical profession cre-ate an added burden, a greater challenge. Usually, when a person experiences deep psychological transformation of the kind described by Jung or Stanislav Grof or John Weir Perry, he or she just simply does not know what is happening, and there is nothing in the imme-diate environment that will help. Perhaps this isolation is itself part of the evolutionary strengthening that has to take place. On the heroic journey, you must be able to handle the incredulity and judgment of people close at hand who have no understanding of what is happen-ing or what you are experiencing. You must learn to control your emotions and instincts yourself, develop confidence in your own judgment, trust your deeper sense of what is happening. Ultimately, even if you benefit from a supportive environment, no one can do it for you.

The hero's journey, as a symbolic portrayal of individuation, can be seen as the expression of the same dynamic power that drives the entire process of cosmological evolution. Human psychological transformation is the very tip of the evolutionary process, which is perhaps why it involves such a prolonged struggle and is so difficult to navigate. Individuation entails the overcoming of centuries and even millennia of conditioning—the archetypal habits of nature and of culture that compel us to behave in certain ways. Through the human being, nature, or the spirit in nature, is striving to overcome itself, to transform itself. The individual human being is a protago-nist in this epic cosmic drama. There is much more at stake, I believe, than only one's own psychological transformation. For what happens to each and every one of us can have a decisive effect on the evolutionary transformation of the whole. If we can overcome our own unconscious habitual tendencies, which pull the human spirit back, we can add consciousness and freedom to the world. A single individual might thus be the one, or one of many, that is the catalyst for a revitalization, renewal, and transformation of the wider culture, perhaps even the entire civilization.

CHAPTER 7

Dual Threats: The Empire of the Ego and the Beast Within

It is possible for a person to attain totality, to become whole, only with the co-operation of the spirit of darkness, indeed . . . the latter is actually a causa instrumentalis *of individuation and redemption.*

—C. G. Jung

Between two modes of being, one centered around the ego and the conscious will, the other around the Self and a deeper transpersonal will, there lies the dangerous journey of individuation, a "night-sea journey" down into the depths of the psyche for renewal and rebirth. The decay and death of what Jung called the "conscious dominant," the old principle of ego control and will, brings with it the temporary collapse of the mechanism of repression by which the autonomy and control of the ego is maintained.[1] This collapse unleashes into consciousness the long-repressed power of the instinctual unconscious, which can be experienced both as a tremendous creative daemon and a terrifying, destructive force. During individuation—on the way of psychospiritual transformation—one faces two main challenges, which occur simultaneously: first, overcoming the old dominant, ruling principle in the psyche; and, second, controlling and taming the Dionysian power of the instinctual unconscious. In this chapter, we will consider these challenges in more detail.

tiation and Transformation: Overcoming the Ego

During the second phase of the hero's adventure, that of initiation and transformation, one has to overcome the dominance and control of the old ego. The ego is that psychological function, related to the principle of personal will, which enables us to manipulate the environment, to change things to our liking, protecting us from undesirable experiences and emotions. The ego is created by a conditioned "no" response, which separates us from the flow of life, and from aspects of the psyche and reality that we do not like, do not wish to experience, and do not identify with. To individuate, to move towards wholeness, we must also experience the negative side of life, the shadow side of the psyche. We cannot remain in the pleasant and the good, living out some ideal image of ourselves and our life. The psychological equivalent of the "no" response is resistance and repression. This resistance must be undone; the negativity, fear, and pain behind the repression must be experienced and subsumed within the newly emerging psychological totality. This is a process that occurs again and again.

To overcome the ego, then, is to overcome resistance to the experience of life as it is. In our culture, there is typically a controlling, fortified quality to the ego, which makes the struggle to overcome it that much more intense, and more prolonged. I think we are at a moment in our evolution, collectively, where the ego has reached or is nearing an endpoint in its development. The ego is the vehicle for self-reflective consciousness, but it is also in some sense an accidental by-product of the emergence of this consciousness. It has become an alienated ego that needs to learn to serve the greater being from which it emerged. The ego is not an end in itself but a function of the deeper psyche.

As we have seen, in myth the old ruling principle of the ego might be portrayed as a tyrannical empire or emperor, as in *Star Wars* with Palpatine and Darth Vader in command of the Stormtroopers; or in *The Lord of the Rings* with the dark controlling power of Sauron and Saruman and the ferocious armies at their disposal. In female form, one might think of the Queen in the fairytale *Snow White*, desperate to cling to her powers and to retain the position as "fairest of them all." Emperor Ming in the science fiction comic strip (and later television series and film) *Flash Gordon* is another fine example of the tyrannical ruler. Or the terrifying force of the old ego might be suggested by the figure of the ogre or giant that must be slain, as in David felling Goliath or Odysseus blinding and outwitting the Cyclops.[2] As suggested by these figures, the defensive controlling element of the ego—the "no" response to life—can assume gargantuan proportions. During deep psychological transformation, the unconscious defenses and operations behind the ego are magnified and intensified such that they cannot be ignored. The hero aspect of the personality—the intentional consciousness, with its intelligence, self-awareness, and power to choose—has to slay the giant or the ogre, or destroy the ruling empire.

One example of the destruction of the empire of the ego is a scene from *Star Wars* in which Luke Skywalker, leading a fleet of Rebel Alliance fighter jets, is being pursued by Imperial fighters, one of them manned by his adversary, Darth Vader. Skywalker has one shot at destroying the Death Star and saving his home planet from destruction. As Skywalker prepares to lock into his target using a computer tracking device, he hears the voice of his deceased mentor, Ben Kenobi, the wise old man, instructing him to "trust the Force." Going against his rational judgment, and following what seems like a reckless course of action, Skywalker turns off his computer guidance system, and uses his feeling or intuition to guide his hand and eye as he delivers the missile with pinpoint accuracy.

The idea conveyed in this scene is that, on the spiritual journey, or during the course of individuation, you must let go of rational control and tune into a transrational source of guidance; you must put yourself in harmony with the greater wisdom of the Tao, the Logos, the Will of God, "the Force." Your own personal will based on rational analysis, subjective considerations, and cultural conditioning has to be made subservient to the transrational authority of the Self, which, we noted, sometimes discloses itself through the authoritative "voice" in dreams or fantasies. During individuation, then, there is a gradual thwarting of, overcoming of, and letting go of egoic will. Rational self-determination is transcended. The course you are called to follow often seems to be irrational, going against common sense. In truth, however, as often becomes apparent in retrospect, this seemingly irrational path actually reflects a higher ordering that is initially beyond our ken.

Jason and the Argonauts provides another example of the battle with the old ego, portrayed in the scene in which members of the crew of the Argo awaken the bronze giant Talos. The party, having arrived at the Isle of Bronze, is instructed by the goddess Hera not to take anything apart from essential provisions of food and drink—a variation on the "one forbidden thing" motif. Immediately, of course, two members of Jason's crew happen across a hidden cave full of treasures. Enticed to enter, and against the express instructions of the goddess, they remove a golden javelin. The theft brings to life the guardian of the treasure, Talos, the giant man of bronze, in vengeful pursuit of the thieves. Symbolically, the treasure represents both the distraction of life pleasures that can pull consciousness along a path to ruin, and, at another level, it represents the "jewels" to be found in the psyche, the spiritual riches that are to be attained with the promise of a new life centered on the Self, the lost potentials that are to be recovered from the unconscious. It is a form of "boon theft" that provokes a destructive vengeful reaction on the part of the rigid old ego (symbolized by Talos), which wants to keep things as they are.

The giant or tyrant is an especially apt symbol of the challenge to be faced. The old ego personality is based on a false personal will that has been developed primarily to help the individual adapt to living in the world. It is supported by the old persona. Attuned to social expectations, the ego's persona enables the individual to behave in certain socially conditioned ways and in so doing to fulfill its desires in the world. An inner censor monitors the individual's inner responses and presents to the world a mask and a socially acceptable set of responses that are perhaps even the opposite of what was actually experienced within. In this way, the persona serves as protective screen over the true personality, enabling the ego to function by keeping threatening and unacceptable feelings out of consciousness, and out of public view.

Fundamentally, the human ego structure, which has evolved century by century, is based on the self-preservation instinct: it responds fearfully to perceived threats in the environment; in its more exaggerated form of expression it controls the emotions with an iron grip, pushing the inner self around. The tyrannical ego is itself empowered by the instincts, enabling it to assume a formidable character, such that it can seem impossible to liberate yourself from the oppression of the ego's rule. When you see the workings of the ego during individuation, it does indeed feel like you are confronting a monstrous giant.

Another way this challenge is portrayed in Greek myth is in the figure of the many-headed Hydra, the terrifying beast confronted by Hercules on his second labor. According to the myth, each time one of the Hydra's heads is cut off, another two grow back, which is a fair approximation to how it feels when consciousness is struggling to overcome the ego and the instincts. The more control you seek to exert, the more forcefully you try to overcome yourself, the stronger the ego gets, the stronger instinct gets. Using your personal will to destroy the ego and forcibly deny the expression of the instincts cannot work. Strength of will is insufficient and actually works against your intentions; it tends to promote repression, which merely increases the psychological tension you are likely to be experiencing. In practice, however, such a course of action is unavoidable. To overcome repression, one must first endure the experience of repression being driven to an extreme. To overcome the instincts, one must first grapple with them and contain them, even if this entails considerable psychological tension and torment.

At first, in the struggle with the unconscious, the controlling part of the ego becomes ever more powerful. The moralizing superego or "strong man" or "topdog," to use a term from Gestalt psychology, bullies the personality, fiercely controlling, forcing it to meet certain standards, and judging every thought or feeling that arises. This is an absolute tyranny of the ego suggested by the rule of the tyrant emperor, the Herod figure, desperate to remain in control, to hang on to power, crushing all possible threats to his position. Herod, let us recall, tries desperately to prevent the coming Christ—the Self, in psychological terms—by issuing the decree that all newborn boys in Bethlehem be killed.

During this phase, when you first become aware of the workings of the ego and are trying to become free of it, it can feel like you have to be constantly on guard, catching every thought, every feeling, before it takes over consciousness. The superego as censor serves a positive function in that it can prevent us being possessed by a desire or feeling. Taken to an extreme, however, this censorship becomes a huge problem itself, crippling the personality, tying the psyche up in knots of fearful repression. Again, the way out of this condition is through it, moving deeper into it. Knots tighten to unbearable proportions, but then they dissolve; censorship and self-judgment feel remorseless and relentless, but they are progressively burnt out.

Self-acceptance and the existential freedom this brings can only come when the psyche in its entirety consents to life as it is. While certain parts of the psyche judge and repress, control and censor, trying to keep the ego in control, or trying to attain pleasure and avoid pain, one is not truly whole. As Jung noted, human beings prefer to follow their own desires rather than discover God's intention for us, which is tantamount, in Jungian terms, to discovering the will of the Self.

The Double Bind of Consciousness

Exploring the question of how the ego can liberate itself and come to an unconditional affirmation of life and the realization of freedom, Alan Watts suggests that ego-consciousness finds itself in a "double bind" situation.[3] Spiritual realization requires an unconditional acceptance of life as it is, but this acceptance cannot be willed or engineered. The ego in its very nature is the antithesis of this state of acceptance. Even spiritual practice can reflect a subtle ego-centered response to life, for everything the ego does, Watts observes, every attempt to liberate itself, to find enlightenment, inevitably creates more ego; it strengthens the ego by reinforcing the idea that there is a separate person in need of liberation. One feels that life needs to be altered in some way, or that one's personality needs to be altered, that one must become more spiritual. Attempts to find enlightenment or to alter oneself are a subtle form of the ego's impulse to control life, rather than accepting life as it is. The practices of meditation and prayer, for instance, however well intentioned, can often come out of an egoic, self-oriented motivation.

This subtle form of ego defense is what Alan Watts meant by the double bind of consciousness. It is at the heart of the Zen koan through which the inherent contradiction of the ego trying to free itself but in so doing creating more ego is worked out. All spiritual paths lead to this paradox. Indeed, one way spiritual transformation can be effected is to drive the contraction of the ego to an extreme, until the raveled, ever-tightening knot of self-conscious effort associated with the ego spontaneously uncoils and relaxes into an acceptance of life.

Meditation, contemplation, prayer, and any spiritual discipline are, of course, all quite the opposite of the childlike playful spirit and unconditional affirmation of life that is the desired goal. Can you imagine a child, utterly lost in the play of life, feeling the need to meditate or to pray? As we read in *The Gospel of Thomas*, Jesus is quizzed by his disciples: "Do you wish that we should fast? And in which way should we pray? Should we give alms?"[4] Jesus warns that to give alms or to pray would be to commit a sin. His only instruction is: do not do that which you dislike (or hate). This cuts through all the supposed rules as to how one should live spiritually.

One way to bypass this double bind is to follow your passion— "follow your bliss," to use Campbell's expression.[5] If you follow your passion, by aligning yourself with the flow of life power coming through you, the transformation of the ego-structure can occur obliquely. Living this way, you will have no time or cause to think about your spiritual development, whether you are becoming enlightened or individuated, and so on; you will be totally caught up in the life force that is coming through you, totally absorbed in what you are doing. If you remain consciously aware, intentionally allowing yourself to ride on the back of your passion, as it were, it is something quite other than blind extraverted activity; it is an intentional, but oblique, self-transcendence in the joy and zest of life. By focusing on your passion, doing what you love, you can divert your attention away from the incessant struggle and periodic suffering of psychological transformation and self-overcoming. If you are pursuing what you love in the world, the allure of your passion draws you forward, activating an inexhaustible flow of vitality and life energy that can carry you past psychological sticking points and give you the motivation to continue to strive, to keep on going.

As you follow your passion in the world, you might well activate deep reservoirs of psychological energy previously dormant in the unconscious. The released energy becomes the agent of psychological transformation. The two elements go hand in hand: the inner journey of transformation and the outer vocation or life calling. This approach balances an introverted focus on the workings of the psyche with an extraverted calling in the world. You can easily get so hung up on your own transformation and spiritual growth that inner concerns become obsessive and all-consuming such that you are always thinking about yourself and your individuation—a form of spiritual narcissism. But if you have a purpose in the world, something to absorb all your energy and attention, this can be your central life focus, and your psychospiritual transformation is then just part of your overall life, rather than the be all and end all.

In *The Gospel of Thomas*, we find a parable that relates directly to this life strategy:

> The Kingdom of the Father is like a woman
> who was carrying a jar full of flour
> while walking on a long road;
> the handle of the jar broke
> the flour streamed out behind her on the road.
> As she did not know it
> she could not be troubled by it.
> When she had reached her house
> she put the jar on the ground;
> she found it empty.[6]

The implication here is that the jar of flour represents the burden of the ego, which is gradually and imperceptibly discharged on the journey through life. The focus is on the life task (carrying the jar) and the destination (going to the house). No thought is given to transformation, which occurs obliquely.

When the spiritual call comes later in life, as it does for many people, often the demands of the ego have already been partly overcome. In the innumerable daily acts of personal, family, and professional life, when one has to put aside one's own needs, delay gratification, work without reward for others or for some greater cause or enterprise, the ego is eroded and the instincts subdued, little by little. Then, when the spiritual journey begins in earnest, the path can proceed more smoothly than it would otherwise. On the other hand, however, with increasing age, the shell of the old ego personality can harden; one can become closed off to new possibilities. Secure in one's kingdom, it is more difficult for the energies of the unconscious to initiate positive psychospiritual change.

In those cases when the old ego is particularly dominant, you might have to confront the fearful control of the ego more directly— to slay the giant, to overcome the strong man. Myth gives a clue as to how this can be done through the motif of the Achilles's heel. The Achilles's heel or chink in the armor (a variant on the same idea) refers to the area of life where the ego's control is at its weakest, the point of inferiority, the aspect of experience that one has feared or disliked the most and has therefore consciously or unconsciously avoided. Typically, this is the area of life where fear, guilt, shame, and pain are experienced most acutely. These experiences provide the way to the ego's undoing because it is here that the controlling part of the personality can exert the least amount of influence. The way to transformation, as the old alchemists realized, is through the despised and rejected aspects of ourselves symbolized by discarded waste products, feces, trash.

In Jungian terms, the way out of the tyranny of the ego is through the shadow. The exit route is through those areas in which the ego does not exert total control. In Frank Darabont's film *The Shawshank Redemption*, the portrayal of Andy Dufresne's escape from many years of wrongful imprisonment by crawling through a sewerage pipe illustrates this point. The old ego-structure is the prison. The journey to freedom is through our psychological sewerage, as it were. The crack in the structure of the ego is an opening that leads down to our psychological depths and on to freedom in the larger reality and transformed psyche on the other side. As the ego structure is prized open, or begins to collapse, one can then make the descent into the underworld. The immense resistance everyone feels to making this descent reflects both the acute pain of having to face one's shadow weakness and the daunting prospect of having to stare into the dark power of nature.

The Relationship Between the Ego and the Unconscious

Before we continue with our analysis of the journey and look specifically at the descent into the underworld, it might be helpful to reflect in a little more detail on how this descent may be described in terms of the Jungian understanding of the individuation process.

You will recall the Jungian model of the psyche from chapter 4. For Jung, the psyche is divided into consciousness centered on the ego, which is the "I" principle, relating to personal identity; and the unconscious, with personal and collective dimensions (see figure 5, below). Normally, the ego is supported by a flow of energy from the unconscious in the form of drives and desires. Ordinarily, the ego's identity is not jeopardized by the unconscious, but exists in a kind of dynamic harmony with it, as shown in the first diagram. Thus, if you experience a desire, for example, you can decide either, yes, I will act on the desire or, no, I will not. In other words, you have, or you appear to have, quite a large degree of control of your desires and psychological states. At this stage, the unconscious mechanism of repression or censorship screens most of the unwanted or unacceptable desires, drives, and fears out of consciousness, which enables you to function without having to be concerned with the larger reality of the psyche. You do not at this stage really have to face the challenge of directly wrestling with your desires, other than meeting the ordinary demands for self-control required to live in society. Indeed, at this stage, people generally have little knowledge of the psyche, except for the surface personality.

In the second diagram (stage b in figure 5), the ego has become alienated and closed off from its desires, too narrow and one-sided in its focus, such that the unconscious gains in power. Energy that might ordinarily be discharged in the acts of life, if you are giving expression to your desires, here becomes dammed up; a reservoir of energy accumulates in the unconscious. This might happen, and indeed it often does, if you are living in a way that is at odds with your true feelings and impulses, or you are living too rationally, or doing what you think you should do rather than what you really want to. We all make this compromise to a certain extent, but if it becomes too extreme, as sometimes happens, you can easily find yourself in a condition of psychological alienation.

The circles in the diagram represent complexes, clusters of emotional energy—feelings, desires, impulses, thoughts, and memories—each organized around a specific archetype. In Jung's model, the archetypes are the collective aspect, manifest in all people, and the complexes are the personal aspect, unique to each of us. The more alienated the ego becomes, the greater the power in the unconscious complexes. Little by little the tension between consciousness and the unconscious increases, in some cases reaching a climax when the ego can no longer retain control, and the division from the unconscious that had enabled consciousness to function autonomously collapses (see diagram c in figure 5). The mechanism of repression fails, and the separation of the ego from the unconscious dissolves. As we have seen, Jung calls this the "dissolution of the persona" or the "collapse of the conscious attitude." When this takes

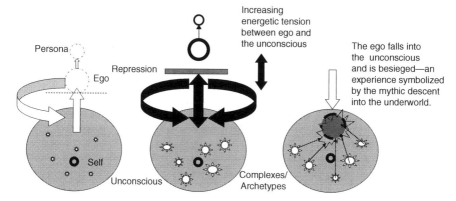

Increasing energetic tension between ego and the unconscious

The ego falls into the unconscious and is besieged—an experience symbolized by the mythic descent into the underworld.

A. Normal functioning ego. There is a continual flow of energy from unconscious to the ego in the form of desires, instincts, impulses. The ego's boundaries are relatively permeable. The individual is not aware of the Self and archetypes.

B. Alienated ego. The flow of energy from the unconscious is blocked; repression intensifies; energy accumulates in the unconscious. This is the apex of the "no" response to life. The ego's clings to its increasingly narrow persona identity.

C. Dissolution of the persona. The repression that sustains the ego's separation from the unconscious collapses; the persona is dissolved; the ego "falls" into the unconscious and is besieged by the instincts and complexes connected with the archetypes.

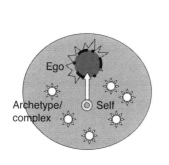

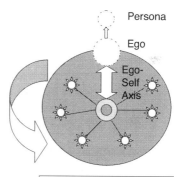

D. The emergence of the Self. Amidst the turmoil of a confrontation with the unconscious, ego consciousness becomes aware of the archetypes and the new center in the psyche: the Self.

E. Self realized as new center and totality of the psyche. The ego re-emerges from the underworld encounter, re-establishes a persona. But the ego is now in relationship with the Self. The ego and the archetypes circle around the Self.

Figure 5: The Ego's Relationship to the Unconscious

place, ego-consciousness no longer retains the position of control it once had; it "falls" into the unconscious where it discovers, to its great distress, that it is just one complex among many. What this means for personal experience is that whereas you could formerly maintain a degree of rational control of your personality, now you feel yourself to be violently pushed around by different desires and impulses, as first one desire and then another overwhelms you. It is extremely hard, if not impossible, to maintain a rational distance from your desires in this condition because they "possess" your consciousness. The conscious personality is like a small vessel tossed around by the crashing waves of the sea.

When the old structure of the personality collapses and the persona dissolves, and consciousness falls into the unconscious, a number of different responses are possible, some of which are explored by Jung in *Two Essays on Analytical Psychology*. The possibilities discussed are not mutually exclusive; indeed, during the reorientation of the psyche, one can expect to move between each type of response until one begins to recognize and understand the dynamics of the process.

The first response is evident in those tragic cases of the schizophrenic dissolution of the personality. The individual, subject to the sudden influx of desires and fears from the unconscious, is utterly terrorized by them, becoming panic stricken and losing all control. In this desperate condition—truly a state of hell—the individual personality is effectively drowned in the turbulent waters of the unconscious. While this condition need not inevitably lead to medical intervention, unless one can retain some degree of conscious control and gain some understanding of what is happening, it often does. As Stanislav Grof and John Weir Perry have pointed out, in an ideal situation these kind of transformative experiences, which are not unlike a shamanic illness, would be supported by a community specifically set up to help individuals move through the process. Alas, at present such communities are extremely rare if not non-existent.

A second dangerous possibility is that, in a dissociated condition, the individual becomes possessed by the power of the instincts and archetypes, unconsciously inflated by the energies surging out of the depths of the psyche, and the insights and feeling of empowerment these energies bring. Jung uses the term *mana personality* to describe the condition in which the conscious personality is empowered by the deeper forces of nature, infused with life energy, or *mana*. The onset of individuation activates and releases tremendous powers which, if they can be mastered, give the ego a sense of titanic uplift and power. The ego has unwittingly accessed energies lying unsuspected in the depths of nature, and has thus become a being of superior power and insight. This attainment inevitably carries the grave dangers of psychological inflation. Swelled by the numinous power of the unconscious, without critical discernment one can easily become a puffed up, inflated superman, claiming the new powers as one's own. We see examples of something like this phenomenon in popular culture in the plight of many young pop stars, actors, and sports stars instantly propelled to celebrity status, yet ill-prepared psychologically to cope with all the spurious power, wealth, and adulation this brings.

If one loses one's sense of balance and critical discernment when dealing with the collective unconscious, identifying with the new, intoxicating energies and experiences, this jeopardizes the integrity of the individual self. When archetypal imagery and instinctual drives flood into consciousness, bringing insights and tremendous energetic empowerment, without the necessary critical discernment it is easy for the individual to believe that he or she is a special being with access to great truths and a powerful message of world historic significance. In these circumstances, under the influence of the activated unconscious a person might even become an estranged prophet, a crazed visionary, serving as a mere mouthpiece of the unconscious, or perhaps, in extreme form, a psychotically inflated madman, like Hitler.

The condition of unconscious possession, when one is literally engulfed by intoxicating life power from the unconscious, contrasts markedly with the state of existential alienation, when everything is experienced as barren, dry, and lifeless. During the crisis preceding individuation, one can move between these two extremes. Indeed, the two states might be recognized as different aspects of the same psychological condition in which consciousness in an alternating pattern is alienated from and then possessed by the unconscious. The sojourns in one state or the other vary in length; one can, for instance, go for long periods feeling utterly disconnected from one's life energy, utterly alienated from oneself.

The possession state is characterized by episodes of high, perhaps excessive, emotional arousal and the intoxication of desire. The drought experienced during an existential crisis is ended by the flood, as it were. It is important to retain the integrity of your conscious self at this time. The "flood" might be welcomed with open arms, but if consciousness is lost the flood of instinct can begin to strike you as empty and meaningless, leaving you feeling burnt out, scorched, and hollow.

In an alienated condition, the possibility of recapturing the vitality and zest of the old life by looking back to what you once had, or even to the enchantment and glories of earlier times of human history, can be appealing indeed. You might reason that you have gone badly astray, made some terrible error, and you just need to get back to how things used to be, to how you once lived. The drives and desires you used to feel, perhaps now no more than memories, seem to contain all the intoxicating passions and pulsating life energies you are so tragically lacking. If you could reconnect with and give free reign to the passions and desires, the reasoning goes, you would feel again the sought-after invigorating rush of life energy. At this most critical phase of psychological development, the temptation to return to nature or to look back to a simpler life, a life more in harmony with the instincts, more in tune with your feelings, is extremely powerful. The danger here, however, is succumbing to a mere reversion to the natural, instinctive mode of life that has been outgrown with the development of rational ego-consciousness. The temptation to give yourself away to your old desires invariably comes at the expense of your individuality, your self, and your consciousness, and is therefore to be resisted.

During the onset of psychospiritual transformation, there is a danger, too, of succumbing to nostalgia for a romanticized past: whether the heroic glories of ancient Greece, the majesty of Rome, the magic and enchantment of a misty Celtic Britain, a primal existence in the bosom of nature, or simply the "good old days"—all of which are very much alive within us. These longings express the constructive impulse to reconnect to the lost potentials of the past, but also the regressive tendency to turn away from the unique challenge and potentials of your own life here and now. Individuation requires moving forward into your own future, not reverting to past achievements and ways of life. Through individuation you are bringing forth something new and unique. Your life leads into uncharted territory, even as it unfolds according to universal archetypal patterns.

DUAL THREATS: THE EMPIRE OF THE EGO AND THE BEAST WITHIN   171

A third possibility, after the psychological collapse that precedes and instigates individuation, is what Jung calls the "regressive restoration of the persona," which basically means reverting to an earlier stage of your personality. The onset of psychospiritual transformation can manifest as a jolting shock, leaving the personality shorn of psychological resources to cope with the ensuing crisis. You can feel wounded, incapacitated, and perhaps defeated. In this scenario, you might well be inclined to think you have made some grave error in how you have been living, perhaps by attempting too much, aiming too high. The natural tendency therefore is to pull in the reins, to cut back your activities and aspirations, and so to adopt altogether narrower life horizons, more modest aims. This strategy, though understandable, is ultimately to the belittlement of the personality, severely impairing psychological development, and generally arises from an incorrect assessment of what has happened.

During the onset of the death-rebirth experience that accompanies individuation, all well-meaning advice to take it easy, rest, and so on is usually quite the opposite of what is required. This crisis marks the transition to a higher, more demanding mode of existence; it is not a signal to turn back and reverse what is taking place. Because this process is so difficult to bear, and brings with it many deeply disturbing experiences, it is tempting to think of your emotions as inherently wrong, pathological, and thus needing to be prevented, corrected, or reversed. It is imperative at this stage, however, to affirm what is happening as being absolutely valid and ultimately constructive. You must affirm the alienation, challenging psychological states, and the intense struggle accompanying this stage of individuation as positive challenges that are essential parts of your psychospiritual development.

The optimum path, therefore—the fourth type of response—is a critical engagement with the unconscious such that consciousness maintains its integrity and its position even against the onslaught of desires and fears from the unconscious. The power of the unconscious, symbolized by the monster or dragon, must be controlled. As Jung explains:

> It is precisely the strongest and best among men, the heroes, who give way to their regressive longing and purposely expose themselves to the danger of being devoured by the monster of

the maternal abyss. But if a man is a hero, he is a hero because, in the final reckoning, he did not let the monster devour him, but subdued it, not once but many times. Victory over the collective psyche alone yields the true value—the capture of the hoard, the invincible weapon, the magic talisman, or whatever it may be that myth deems most desirable. Anyone who identifies with the collective psyche—or, in mythological terms, lets himself be devoured by the monster—and vanishes in it, attains the treasure that the dragon guards, but he does so in spite of himself and to his own greatest harm.[7]

This passage, for all its gendered heroic language, identifies the key challenge to be faced: namely, that of slaying the monster, overcoming the beast within. The same surge of instinctual power that initially spurs one to high ambitions and supports the quest to throw off the demands of society in the pursuit of one's deepest passions has later to be controlled. To refer again to Nietzsche's parable of three metamorphoses of the spirit, one could say that the lion has to become immensely powerful to emancipate the individual from the false authority of inherited values and dogma. It is the power of the lion (the ego supported by the instinctual unconscious) that propels the individual self to victory over the dragon "Thou Shalt." But, having won through to freedom, how then is the lion itself to be tamed? Unrestrained by the containing structures of society or of any philosophical system or any religious dogma, or indeed of any supporting mythological context, the lion becomes a monster, a law unto itself. Set free of all restriction, the lion devours the personal human being, and roars at everything and everyone.[8] It has won freedom for itself from subservience to false values but, untamed, it prevents any kind of relationship to the social group, to humanity, or to a higher spiritual authority. It is the principle of individualism *par excellence*.

In Nietzsche's third metamorphosis (from the lion to the child), he describes this transformation as if it were inevitable, or straightforward, when it is, perhaps, the most perilous and demanding transition of all. The heroic will that can liberate the individual from consensus morality and collective values is unable, through force of will alone, to deal with the primitive drives of the unconscious. The inner beast cannot be tamed by the repressive control of a heroic ego. As we will see, it is only through the cultivation of the feminine principle that one can gain mastery over the emotional power of the instinctual realm.

Romanticism and the East

There is an important distinction to be made here as to how one chooses to respond to the existential crisis that can accompany the onset of individuation. It is often imagined that all spiritual paths ultimately lead to the same goal or serve the same purpose. I do not believe this is the case. Among many different spiritual paths, at least two markedly different overall approaches may be identified: the first, which we have focused on here, might be loosely characterized as Romantic, affirming the Will, the instincts, and the passions, while seeking to transform them; the second approach draws on Eastern perspectives, especially Buddhism, and emphasizes the development of a meditative consciousness that stands outside of the passions.

Confronted with the deep anguish of an existential crisis, you can either affirm the suffering as a necessary phase of your life experience or you can seek to detach yourself from it by stepping outside the activity of the Will. One response to the pain of the alienated ego, is to turn to the East, as it were, adopting a life philosophy of self and world abnegation, obliterating individual selfhood through the realization of *nirvana*, extinguishing all the desires and fears associated with being a separate distinct human being. One can derive considerable benefit from Eastern meditative practices, designed to effect spiritual liberation, but these can also be dangerous and inappropriate if used incorrectly. As we have seen, one must be careful that a spiritual path is not part of the ego's controlling program for life, a means of escape from life. What appears to be spiritual transcendence might be a subtle form of ego defense and repression.[9] Liberation from life and from the world is not the goal of individuation.

From the Romantic and Jungian perspective, you are to engage with your deepest urges and drives, to follow your passion, committing yourself wholeheartedly to the world. Spiritual life, as Campbell said, is the "bouquet of nature."[10] Spirit comes out of natural life; it is not a substitute for it. The aim of the Romantic approach to life affirms the passions and desires; it does not seek to extinguish them. The goal of life (to paraphrase Campbell) is to learn to ride the back of the Dionysian leopard without getting torn to pieces.[11]

Dionysus, as we have seen, is the god of impassioned intoxication or frenzy, symbolizing the annihilating and blissful quality of the full experience of the power of your own desire nature. Campbell thus advocates an approach to life in which you follow what it is you really want to do—your deepest desire (which is in some sense akin to your highest potential)—and you follow it wholeheartedly, with conviction, to the end. You keep your mind in control, as far as possible, so that you can prevent yourself getting scorched, destroyed, and dismembered by the force of your passion. The passion is all-consuming, but you have to learn to ride it, which is an art that can only be mastered through experience. It cannot be taught.

The aim of psychospiritual transformation, in the Romantic view, is to forge a consciousness that can handle the full power of the unconscious, the full power of the gods, as it were. Desires are to be affirmed, participated with, engaged with. The Buddhist perspective, favored by a number of prominent transpersonal theorists, promotes a disengagement with desires in favor of the development of consciousness in the direction of spiritual enlightenment. The focus, one might say, tends to be on the ascent of consciousness rather than descent into the underworld of the unconscious. Without the descent, however, whatever states of enlightenment might be attained, the passions will remain untransformed and wholeness out of reach. "A man who has not passed through the inferno of his passions," Jung notes, "has never overcome them."[12]

The Descent into the Underworld

In mythic terms, the irruption of the unconscious into conscious awareness is suggested by the motif of the "descent into the underworld." The underworld signifies the "inferno of the passions" lurking beneath the ordinary threshold of consciousness. The descent portrays the ego's encounter with the shadow dimension of experience. The division between the light of consciousness and the shadow is itself a manifestation of the split between the opposites of light and dark, good and evil, spirit and nature, consciousness and the unconscious, which need to be reconciled and resolved. This reconciliation is to take place during the process of individuation

In terms of personal experience, the descent into the underworld takes you to a dark place psychologically; your life energy and consciousness are dragged down into the depths; you are pulled away from the daylight world as your energy and attention are forced inwards. The descent into the underworld, passing through Hell, going on a night-sea journey to the bottom of the ocean, crossing the river Styx—these motifs are all symbols of this process. On the journey through the Mines of Moria in *The Lord of the Rings*, Frodo, Gandalf, Aragorn/Strider, and the party, traveling in almost total darkness, are besieged by one challenge and attack after another. This episode powerfully conveys the experience in which the light of consciousness—often symbolized by a flickering torch—has gone down into the dark depths of the unconscious. Everything here is oppressive, tense, dangerous. The fragile light of consciousness, kindled in the darkness of being, must be guarded at all costs. Facing an assault from the unconscious, which threatens to utterly smother your individuality and extinguish the spark of consciousness, and amidst the suffocating pressures of the external world and mass culture, you have to defend with all your might the precious light of conscious selfhood. During the descent, everything is amplified: desires, resistances, and fears assume gargantuan proportions. The stability and integrity of the sense of the "I" is severely challenged. *The Lord of the Rings* well conveys the incessant quality of a confrontation with the unconscious—a confrontation portrayed in the form of an attack by wild beasts, hostile enemies, and huge monsters surfacing from the depths (such as the fearsome Balrog in the Mines of Moria), which each have to be confronted. Such episodes are a symbolic, mythic representation of the struggle to control and transform the instincts.

When the ego falls into the unconscious, you can find oneself in a situation not unlike the Sorcerer's Apprentice in *Fantasia*, desperately trying to keep a lid on everything that is boiling up inside you, struggling to control the different impulses as they rise up. Different desires erupt in turn pulling you in one direction and then another. As soon as you have managed to control one part of yourself, another begins to boil up and overflow. As we have seen, parts of your psyche that were previously dormant become powerfully charged, magnified, and thus begin to flood into consciousness. If, for example, you had been harboring a desire to break free from your current situation and throw off everything, this urge can totally take over you for periods of time, such that your power of rational determination and your good judgment are temporarily lost. Or if you have been craving power or experiencing the desperate need to exert influence in the world and to achieve fame, these urges, too, can become overwhelmingly powerful, utterly captivating your consciousness. This experience, in which consciousness is uncontrollably gripped first by one desire and then another, borders on that of schizophrenia or psychosis. It marks a dangerous time. The major difference from these pathological conditions is that the hero, representing the ego, usually makes the descent with at least a modicum of conscious awareness of what is happening, or subsequently realizes what is happening and exerts some degree of conscious control, whereas in a schizophrenic break consciousness is utterly dominated and engulfed, and a panic fear from loss of control can take over.

This is one reason why Jung advocates undertaking the descent into the underworld of the psyche intentionally, to prevent blindly stumbling headfirst into a dark pit.[13] It was Jung's strategy to encourage individuals, for whom this path was probably unavoidable, to consciously take on their own individuation in order to mitigate the chaotic and dangerous experience of having psychological transformation unexpectedly thrust upon them. It is better, Jung believed, to give conscious attention to your own individuation process while you are able to remain in relative control.

Jung's own description of his "confrontation with the unconscious" is a striking example of an underworld encounter. Consider this following passage, relating to an experience in 1913:

> An incessant stream of fantasies had been released, and I did my best not to lose my head but to find some way to understand these strange things . . . . I was living in a constant state of tension; often I felt as if gigantic blocks of stone were tumbling down upon me. One thunderstorm followed another. My enduring these storms was a question of brute strength. Others have been shattered by them—Nietzsche, and Hölderlin, and many others. But there was a demonic strength in me, and from the beginning there was no doubt in my mind that I must find the

meaning of what I was experiencing in these fantasies. When I
endured these assaults of the unconscious I had an unswerving
conviction that I was obeying a higher will, and that feeling
continued to uphold me until I had mastered the task.[14]

As we have seen, the "incessant stream of fantasies," desires,
impulses, and so forth is often represented in dreams as water—an
"avenging deluge," as Jung described the experience of consciousness being swept along by the stream of libido flowing out of the
unconscious. Jung continues: "I stood helpless before an alien world;
everything in it seemed difficult and incomprehensible."[15] This captures the experience of the conscious ego when it first falls into the
unconscious. One is living in the same world, of course, but one is
now directly confronted with the inner reality of the psyche, about
which, in modern times, we know virtually nothing; we have no edu-
cation to prepare us for this experience.

The "constant state of tension" in which he "felt as if gigantic
blocks of stone were tumbling down" is another example of the
crashing rocks motif, describing the experience of the old structure
of the ego crumbling under the immense pressure exerted upon it by
the long-repressed instinctual power of the unconscious. We can also
see in the above passage a number of other themes we have touched
upon: the transcendent supernatural aid and support (obeying a
higher will, being upheld by this), the calling ("there was no doubt in
my mind that I must find the meaning of what I was experiencing"),
and the instinctual empowerment giving Jung the demonic strength
to see the experience though to its resolution.

These kinds of experiences—dramatic, intense, dangerous, numinous, and relentless—are well personified by hero myths. During deep
psychological transformation, it actually feels like you are the mythic
hero struggling against overwhelming forces; and indeed you are, it is
just that the action takes place in the psyche not on the battleground.

The year 1913 also brought a decisive breakthrough for Jung:

I was sitting at my desk once more, thinking over my fears.
Then I let myself drop. Suddenly it was as though the ground
literally gave way beneath my feet, and I plunged down into the
dark depths. I could not fend off a feeling of panic. . . . Before
me was the entrance to a dark cave, in which stood a dwarf with

a leathery skin, as if he were mummified. I squeezed past him through the narrow entrance and waded knee deep through icy water to the other end of the cave where . . . I saw a glowing red crystal. I grasped the stone, lifted it, and discovered a hollow underneath. At first I could make out nothing, but then I saw that there was running water. In it a corpse floated by, a youth with blond hair and a wound in the head. He was followed by a gigantic black scarab and then by a red, newborn sun, rising up out of the depths of the water.[16]

Jung's recollection of letting himself drop, of falling into his own psychological depths, is a vivid example in personal experience of the descent into the underworld. In this vision, following the sudden descent, Jung makes his way past a guardian of the threshold (the dwarf) through a narrow passage (passing through the opposites, crossing the threshold) to discover, concealed beneath the rock, the springs of running water, symbolizing the spiritual wellsprings of life. The dwarf often represents the little person in us, the smallness of the ego, yet it can also symbolize a part of us that has atrophied or failed to develop and remained locked away deep in the unconscious, remaining primitive. The wise old man, Jung points out, can also appear as a dwarf (think of Yoda, for instance), and in Hindu mythology the dwarf is a symbol of spiritual ignorance, crushed under Shiva's foot.

Of the other motifs in this passage, the scarab is an Egyptian rebirth symbol, and the red color of the crystal and the sun suggest the blood that animates life in the body. Jung alludes to the relevance of this vision for what was to happen on a collective level during the First World War—relating the wounded blond youth to the German hero Siegfried and the bloody fate that was to befall Europe in the years to follow. This vision pertains both to the collective situation and to Jung's personal experience of rebirth, which were inextricably entwined.

At the collective level, the Western ego now appears to be faced with the prospect of some kind of initiatory descent as the prelude to its transformation. The herald is sounded by Nietzsche's visionary prophet, Zarathustra, in his address to the Sun, the "Great Star," that descends each day into the dark ocean:

I must descend into the depths: as you do at evening, when you go behind the sea and bring light to the underworld, too, superabundant star!

Like you, I must go down—as men, to whom I want to descend,
call it.[17]

The Sun, a symbol of the light of consciousness awareness, whose
ascent to the noontime position in the sky symbolizes the voyage
of the Western ego to its pinnacle, is now faced with an imminent
descent into the unconscious depths for transformation and renewal.
Just as surely as night follows day, the rise of the light of reason and
consciousness, as the dominant principles and powers of Western
civilization, must turn to face the instinctual unconscious, the maternal ground, the origin from which they emerged. Indeed, Goethe
called the underworld of the unconscious the "realm of the Mothers,"
the place to which Faust descends during his own transformative
adventure.[18] The transcendent, rational, spiritual principle—God the
Father, of Christianity—is to be brought into relationship with what
Jung called the "maternal abyss" and the dark spirit in nature.[19]

Alchemy and the *Nigredo*

One symbolic system that explores the processes of psychospiritual transformation in extraordinary detail is alchemy. For the last
three decades of his life, Jung devoted considerable time and energy
to interpreting the psychological significance of numerous arcane
alchemical texts, finding in the obscure writings of the alchemists
descriptions in another language of the individuation process.
Although ostensibly describing attempts to transform base metal
into gold, the alchemical texts, Jung demonstrated, symbolically
describe psychospiritual processes. The alchemist, arduously seeking to effect the transformation of the metal through various chemi-
cal procedures, unconsciously experienced an inner, psychospiritual
transformation that was symbolically mirrored in the alchemical
work. The choice of alchemical operations, that is, seems to have
unconsciously reflected the psychological process the alchemist was
going through at the time. Thus, when the alchemist decided to apply
heat to the metal, for instance, this seems to have reflected what was
happening in his psyche—suggesting, perhaps, that the base material of his natural personality was being transformed by the fire of
instinct and desire. What was happening psychologically was projected onto the matter in the alchemical vessel.

A number of the alchemical texts describe the death and resurrection of the king or *Sol* (the Sun), which, like the hero, represents the ego and the light of consciousness. The descent into the underworld in myth coincides with what is known as the *nigredo* in alchemy, a phase within the transformation process that leads to the *mortificatio* (death) of the king. The *nigredo* is a period of darkness, of a "black blacker than black," during which the king undergoes immense suffering, dismemberment, and a mystic death or crucifixion comparable to what St. John of the Cross described as the "dark night of the soul."[20] The *nigredo*, according to Jung, is instigated by the "boundless concupiscence and egotism" of the king who, in an alienated state, is "thirsty" for life-renewing contact with the unconscious, symbolized by water.[21] The ego, that is, having become alienated from the instincts, is unconsciously possessed by desire. This desire originates in the king's unconscious shadow side—his undifferentiated, primitive feeling nature. By drinking, and therefore indulging his desire, the king is overwhelmed as unconscious contents flood into consciousness, a process metaphorically portrayed, Jung explains, as the king drowning or being swallowed by a sea monster—the vehicle of his renewal.[22]

The renewal is necessary because the daylight world of consciousness inhabited by the king, without a life-giving connection to the unconscious world of feeling, has become a wasteland. The ego's existence has become arid, barren, inauthentic, and lifeless. The king's submersion and drowning in the waters of the unconscious symbolize a return of the conscious ego to the oceanic state of undifferentiated unity.

In alchemy, dissolution in water enables the discovery of, or return to, the *prima materia* from which the alchemical gold may be produced.[23] The return to the *prima materia* symbolizes a state of psychological fragmentation and dissolution, which is described by the alchemists as the king's return to the "dark initial state" of the "chaos," a condition in which, Jung explains, "all connections are dissolved."[24] In order to be transformed, the old conscious identity has to be sacrificed and must return to the source from whence it came: "Dissolution," Jung notes, "is the pre-requisite for redemption."[25]

In psychological terms, this chaotic state arises when the old sense of order based on the dominant rule of the old ego is destroyed.

In alchemical lore, what is initially solid matter has to be transformed into a fluid, undifferentiated liquid by the process of *solutio*. This is a metaphor for the dissolution of the crystallized form of the ego-structure that, over time, has become insulated and detached from the flow of life energy emerging from the unconscious.

As we have seen, during the onset of the dissolution of the persona and the collapse of the structure of ego consciousness different parts of the psyche are broken apart and function autonomously, with no coherent relationship to the other parts. It is a dissociated state in which everything feels chaotic, like a raging battle is taking place between the different parts of the psyche. It is the work of individuation to bring the antagonistic parts into a dynamic harmony, to bring about a new wholeness. In the teachings of Jesus, this dissociated, fragmented condition is suggested by the idea of a "kingdom divided against itself" that "cannot stand" (Mark 3:24). This inner division might also be suggested in modern dream imagery by a world war, for example, with different countries and regions (representing parts of the psyche) in tumultuous conflict.

The dissolving waters that perform the *solutio* and also perform a symbolic baptism of the king are known as the *aqua permanens*, the "wonderful waters of transformation," which are described as the liquid form of the philosopher's stone itself—the end product of the alchemical opus.[26] Water in alchemy is both the agent of transformation by *solutio* and, at the same time, the precious liquid to be extracted from matter. The king's submersion in water is a version of the mythological night-sea journey; it is a descent into the darkness of the waters in order to find the "treasure hard to attain" and thus to be regenerated.[27] The treasure is the symbolic equivalent of the alchemical gold, which was the "physical goal of alchemy," representing, Jung reports, "the panacea, the elixir of life."[28]

When one first experiences the *nigredo*, the instinctual power of the unconscious is primitive, dark, uncivilized. According to Jung, the imagination first conceives of this instinctual power as a cold-blooded reptile or dragon. During the course of individuation, there follows a progressive evolution in this animal imagery, from reptiles to birds and then to warm-blooded mammals. As the instinctual power of the unconscious emerges into consciousness, and is controlled and transformed, it becomes ever more civilized, tamed, moving nearer to the human state. In *The Lord of the Rings*, to give one example of this theriomorphic symbolism in film, Gandalf's encounter with the Balrog in the Mines of Moria features the most primitive, dark, powerful creature one could imagine and it thus symbolizes an early form of manifestation of the unconscious as it confronts the conscious ego.

Transformation and Purification in Alchemy

The alchemists draw interchangeably on imagery of water and fire to represent the destructive, purifying, and transformative action of the unconscious on the conscious ego. The psychological death (*mortificatio*) and subsequent rebirth can be described by the metaphors of drowning in a watery grave, baptism, and a second birth out of the waters; but they can also be described as the consumption and purification in the flames of an underground hell. Fire is associated with the alchemical process of *calcinatio*, which leads in time to a psychological death experience and then to a phoenix-like resurrection out of the ashes in a spiritual ascent (*sublimatio*). The heating of the *prima materia* in the alchemical vessel burns out impurities and releases the "spirit" trapped in the containing structure of the matter.

In psychological terms, according to Jung, the process of *calcinatio* symbolizes an "inflammation by desire," the torturing flames of the frustrated and repressed instincts and desires in which the ego is consumed.[29] The heat of desire, when contained, is turned back onto the self and becomes the agent of transformation. After the collapse of the old ego structure and with it the sense of personal control of the psyche, the flow of desires and drives cannot be halted, as before. This situation might be compared to a gas leak that cannot be turned off or an electric current that cannot be broken or a flow of water that cannot be stopped. This new reality feels relentless and exhausting. One has to come to terms with a psychological wholeness that includes the full power of the unconscious. When one is adapting to this condition, it can really feel like one is subject to the torturing flames of Hell. Naturally, this experience brings with it the grave possibility of being permanently scorched and scarred, which we see in the fate of Anakin Skywalker in *Star Wars*: He is scorched and mutilated by force of his own vengeful feelings and desires, experiences suggested by the scenes of conflagration and destruction in his duel with Ben Kenobi in *Revenge of the Sith*. Unable to master his own nature, he tragically succumbs to his own negative emotions and the dark force of his desire for power. Ultimately, the humanity is all but crushed out of him when he takes on the character of Darth Vader.

Ideally, confronting deep-rooted desires and fears is a process that can both purify one's motivations and effect a transformation in the psychological structure of one's being. The element of purification is especially emphasized in the mystic form of the hero's journey. After the initial spiritual awakening (the call to adventure), the second phase of the mystic hero's journey—initiation or transformation—amounts to the mystic's purification of the self. In Christian imagery, the process of purification is depicted as a descent into Hell and a passage through Purgatory, a journey which receives its finest literary articulation in Dante's *Divine Comedy*. In the state of purgatory, the drives, desires, and instincts that were formerly submerged, hidden from consciousness, are made conscious and purified. In modern dream imagery, the need for purification might be suggested by scenes of filth and grime that need to be cleaned, not unlike the stable-cleaning task facing Hercules.

The Test of Power

The hero's journey constitutes a "road of trials," rightly described as a "razor-edged path"—it is dangerous and uncertain, ever poised on the brink, always hanging precariously in the balance. In *The Lord of the Rings*, as the party crosses the bridge over the abyss-like depths below in the Mines of Moria, the bridge collapses behind them, and they survive by a hair's breadth. This episode is a fair reflection of what it feels like on the journey of individuation: the past falls away behind you; there can be no looking back.

One of the main challenges to be overcome is the test of power. The ego is subject to the lure of power, but must not succumb to it. Nietzsche, as we have seen, identified with Dionysus, the god of impassioned frenzy, representing the onrush of the instinctual power of the unconscious. The Dionysian energy seems to have taken possession of him, inspiring his euphoric vision of the *Übermensch* (which suggests a condition of overflowing godlike power) but inflating his own sense of egoic individualism and, by the time he wrote

Ecce Homo, ultimately consuming his individual personality. "Dionysus," as Jung notes, "is the abyss of impassioned dissolution, where all human distinctions are merged in the animal divinity of the primordial psyche—a blissful and terrible experience."[30] The Dionysian experience is blissful because the person is temporarily released from the pressures of conscious selfhood, losing themselves in ecstatic release in the annihilating onrush of the power of nature; it is terrible because the spark of ego-consciousness is lost by the total abandonment to the intoxication of desire. You can get a sense for what this experience is like when you listen to stirring music and are swept along by it, when your deepest emotions are activated and you are liberated from your ordinary state of being for a short time. But the experience of dissolution and euphoric abandonment is not the aim of the hero's journey and individuation. The aim, rather, is to pre-serve the precious spark of conscious selfhood, while activating and transforming the Dionysian power locked away in the unconscious.

The instinctual possession state is superbly conveyed in *The Lord of the Rings* by the power of the Ring to control and corrupt even the noblest characters when they come into close contact with it. As soon as anyone puts on the Ring, or comes within its sphere of influ-ence, he or she is subject to a titanic flow of power that can take over the personality—a veritable possession in which the individual's power of self-control and awareness is severely compromised. Succumbing to the its influence, the carrier of the Ring invariably betrays his or her higher ideals and falls prey to its intoxicating power. No one is immune. Even the otherwise honorable and virtu-ous Boromir becomes susceptible to its power. As we read in *The Fellowship of the Ring*, Boromir, finding himself alone with Frodo, employs all manner of arguments, plans, and protestations to con-vince his hobbit companion to relinquish the Ring:

> "I need your Ring: that you know now; but I give you my word that I do not desire to keep it. Will you not at least let me make trial of my plan? Lend me the Ring!"[31]

Frodo is acutely aware, however, that all is not right, and that Boromir is not himself, for he appears somehow changed, his "eyes lighting" with a "strange gleam" and his hand "trembling with suppressed excitement."[32] As Frodo stands firm, Boromir becomes more force-ful and insistent:

"It is not yours save by unhappy chance. It might have been mine. It should be mine. Give it to me!"[33]

Desperately lunging at Frodo, Boromir displays the hallmarks of possession: "His fair and pleasant face was hideously changed; a raging fire was in his eyes."[34] Characteristically, as soon as the episode of possession has passed and his normal consciousness restored, Boromir is filled with remorse:

> "What have I said?" He cried. "What have I done? Frodo, Frodo!" he called. "Come back! A madness took me, but it has passed. Come back!"[35]

Madness indeed, for only the childlike Frodo can carry the Ring without being utterly overcome, although even he is adversely affected by it. The Ring of Power represents the rush of desire, the possessive quality of the instinctual power of the unconscious that time and again irrupts into consciousness during individuation.

Jung likens this encounter with the unconscious to touching a high-voltage cable: the personality becomes dangerously "charged" with energy. When dealing with the unconscious, therefore, it is imperative, first, to maintain critical self-awareness such that you realize what is taking place and thus avoid becoming unconsciously possessed; and, second, to maintain an ethical stance and a commitment to your personal relationships. The world of human concerns—with its many duties, relationships, established moral standards, laws and norms, cultural learning, religious wisdom, and so forth—must be brought to bear on the uncivilized nature of the unconscious, which can initially manifest as feverish desire or panic fear or as violent swings of mood or as irrational impulses and convictions.

The innocent, childlike part of us, represented by Frodo, is the part that is incorruptible by power. The child suggests the "still, small voice" within that remains constant and steady even amidst the earthquake, wind, and storm of the powerful emotions released from the unconscious. The character of Gollum, by contrast, represents the condition of being utterly possessed by the power, to the point of being tortured by it, consumed by it. We must reckon with and integrate the power of the instincts lest they possess us. As we read in *The Gospel of Thomas*:

> Happy is the lion which the man will eat, and the lion will be-
> come man. Abominated is the man whom the lion will eat, and
> the lion will become man.[36]

The power, that is to say, will emerge through us in one way or
another (the lion will become man), so we must come to terms with
it and express it as consciously as we can (eat the lion). If we do not
give expression to the creative power within us, it will possess us in
negative form as instinct (eaten by the lion). Where instinct reigns
morality is lost, conscious discrimination is lost. Desires and passions gain the upper hand. But if instinct can be contained, it can be
transformed into spirit. The power of nature might then be directed
to elevated cultural and spiritual aims to the betterment both of the
individual and society.

A similar theme to that suggested by the character Gollum is portrayed in a scene from *Jason and the Argonauts* in which the blind
seer, Phineas, is tormented daily by the Harpies, giant bat-like crea-
tures who descend from the sky to steal the blind man's food and
spoil his banquet, leaving him to feed off scraps. In psychological
terms, this torment well reflects a condition in which split-off psychological energies ruin every attempt to find pleasure and enjoy-
ment in life. Until the split-off energies have been brought back into
relationship with consciousness, controlled, and overcome, nothing
works out as you would want. You can feel yourself to be tormented,
sabotaged; dominated by these energies, you will be driven to grasp
after what you desire and thus spoil the pleasure you are seeking. In
this condition, you can feel driven to distraction.

Before you can continue with your life, therefore, you have to deal
with these split-off psychological energies. This is a painful and
painstaking task, requiring constant vigilance of changes in consciousness and a disciplined resistance to the pull of desire. Because
a kingdom divided against itself will not stand, you must first make
yourself whole—"seek ye first the Kingdom of God," (Matthew
6:33) "make thine eye . . . single" (Matthew 6:22)—for then, and
only then, will "all these things be added unto you"(Matthew 6:33).
This is not an arbitrary divine decree, but the lawful consequence of
the state of one's psyche. It is a psychological insight.

In the New Testament, in response to the Devil's temptations, three
times Jesus gives the retort "It is written," followed by reference to

specific aspects of the scriptures, such as "Do not put the Lord your God to the test" (Matthew 4). Such a response relates to the archetypal function in the psyche symbolized by the wise old man, who has assimilated the spiritual wisdom of his tradition, and is thus able to use the moral authority of that wisdom ("it is written") against the dark power of the unconscious (the Devil). The whole trajectory of Western religious history has differentiated good from evil such that now, when we modern individuals are confronted by the uncivilized energies of the unconscious, we can draw on our knowledge of good and evil, thus making us less susceptible to fall prey to desires or power drives.

Jung makes a similar point in *Mysterium Coniunctionis*, his last major work, in which he explores the psychological significance of alchemy and its relationship to Christianity. As we have seen, the unconscious is fundamentally amoral so it requires a differentiated consciousness attuned to standards of right and wrong, good and evil, to give constructive expression to the unconscious. Consciousness, with its capacity for moral discernment, is required to transform the expression of the Self from an archaic, undifferentiated wholeness to a consciously realized, higher wholeness.

The encounter with the nature-power of the unconscious can also have positive effects, providing not only a sense of empowerment for a difficult life path or the resources to fulfill some momentous life destiny, but also furnishing the individual with psychic abilities, foreknowledge, and the sense of being able to influence reality from a deeper psychological level. The mind-control powers of the Jedi in *Star Wars* or the magical powers of Gandalf in *The Lord of the Rings* or the wisdom of the goddess Hera in *Jason and the Argonauts* are representative examples of this phenomenon. In each case, the encounter with the unconscious gives access to the submerged powers of nature, which raise the individual above the normal level of abilities and knowledge. You might think here of the popular superhero figures, such as the Hulk, Spiderman, and Batman, in which the ordinary human being is imbued with the magnified power of the animal or natural world, the source of the superhuman abilities.

Rather than fall victim to the demonic power from the unconscious, if you can assimilate it consciously, master it psychologically, the more power you can consciously wield in the world. By bringing the power of your desires under your control, rather than being dominated by them, you are able to win ever more freedom from the instincts. This enables you to serve your highest calling rather than be bound by the lower drives within you. "The demon that you can swallow gives you its power," as Campbell put it.[37]

A conquest of this kind is suggested by the Greek hero Perseus's encounter with the gorgon, Medusa, depicted in the film *Clash of the Titans*, in which Perseus, using his shield to reflect Medusa's image, manages to behead her without gazing directly upon her face. In this well-known episode, we can recognize some now familiar themes: the magical shield represents supernatural or transcendent aid; Medusa represents the dark feminine principle and she thus embodies many of those elements that were repressed by patriarchal Western culture: her serpent hair connects her to the uroboros and the natural, instinctual life of the unconscious, as well as to the serpent of Eden; and the look that turns to stone, as noted, relates to the paralyzing effect of staring into the demonic power of the unconscious. In its reflective capacity, the shield symbolically suggests the role of human self-reflective consciousness, making known the dark power of the unconscious, reflecting it in the light of conscious self-awareness.[38]

With Medusa's power under his control, the hero carries away the gorgon's head and uses it against an even mightier foe: the monstrous Kraken, released from the dark ocean depths by the gods. Holding the severed head aloft, the gorgon's paralyzing stare turns the Kraken to stone, and Perseus is able to liberate the princess Andromeda, who had been chained to the rocks as a sacrifice. From a psychological perspective, this rescue symbolically suggests the liberation of the soul (or anima, in Jungian terms) from the desirousness of the animal passions and the tyrannical rule of the ego (motifs suggested by the Kraken). During individuation, as desires, fears, and powerful emotions are subdued, you can then access your true feeling nature and attune to the innocent child part within you, discerning the voice of your soul, which can serve to guide you further along your own spiritual path. To know the soul, the deepest inmost experience of self, is to have everything; without it, every success and pleasure in life, every achievement, amounts to little. "He who understands the all, but lacking himself, lacks everything," in the words of Jesus.[39] Or again, "what shall it profit a man, if he shall gain the whole world but lose his own soul?" (Mark 8:36).

In Greek myth, the winged horse Pegasus, born from the blood of Medusa's decapitated head, represents the power of nature in its positive aspect. It represents nature and instinct supporting consciousness. Thus, in Pegasus, the animal world is no longer portrayed as dark and threatening, but as white and helpful. Wild horses, on the other hand, suggest instincts and drives that need to be consciously controlled. Horses, of course, have been used more than any other animal to serve human ends. As they can be "broken in" and tamed, in dreams horses often represent instincts that can be mastered and harnessed to serve higher spiritual ends. Every victory over the instincts brings a sense of a sense of triumphant mastery, an experience well suggested by soaring flight and uplift of the majestic Pegasus.

The Inner Child

For the person in the midst of a death-rebirth struggle, the conflict between the displaced ego, desperate to reestablish its control, and the instinctual power of the unconscious is the cause of great suffering. The inner self is kept prisoner within the claustrophobic confines of the ego, and suffers as it is gradually released by the action of the Will, the "liberator and bringer of joy," as Nietzsche described it.[40] For Nietzsche, as we have seen, this struggle is rendered meaningful and bearable by his sense of the impending emergence of the *Übermensch*. He recognized something new was taking shape and being born within him and through him, and he thus aptly chose to describe his experience using perinatal metaphor:[41]

> For the creator himself to be the child new-born he must also be willing to be the mother and endure the mother's pain. Truly I have gone my way through a hundred souls and a hundred cradles and birth-pangs.[42]

Simultaneously, as the old outer shell of the personality is broken open, the inner child emerges, coming to the forefront of consciousness. The child has been protected by the ego during the course of development, but, with psychological resources directed primarily to the ego, has therefore remained undeveloped, lying dormant in the depths of the unconscious. During individuation, the child is brought back into relationship with the conscious ego to assume a place at the center of the new personality.

The first appearance of the child can be challenging. It is quite a shock, to say the least, having reached adulthood, forged a place in the world, formed relationships, established a career, and so forth, to then discover that on some level you are still a child, helpless and exposed, lacking a strong directed will, the power of self-determination, and worldly awareness. The emergence of the child thus brings with it certain dangers. Unless one remains vigilant, under the influence of the child archetype one's consciousness can be unwittingly pulled into a childlike world of undifferentiated consciousness, devoid of responsibility. Decisions made and actions taken in this state of mind will obviously not reflect your best interests or highest potentialities.

During individuation, the child is becoming established as a new differentiated function within the psyche, and it is the ego's job, initially, to protect the child at all costs—to protect it from outside pressures, other people's opinions, and the overpowering force of desires and fears arising inside you. The hero must protect the child until it becomes acclimatized to the often crude, insensitive nature of the external world, with its crashing noises and its ceaseless whir of activity. Yet, paradoxically, the archetypal child itself, as Jung stresses, is graced with power and strength that belies its innocent character and small size. In dreams, for example, one might witness the child overpowering a wild beast, such is the high value the psyche places on preserving its offspring.

In its positive aspect, the child suggests continual creativity, spiritual freedom, and playfulness, as in the final metamorphosis of Nietzsche's parable in which the child represents "innocence and a new beginning," and "a wheel moving out of its own center." Indeed, as individuation proceeds, interspersed with periods of struggle and suffering your life experience can recover the unique, fresh quality of childhood. This transformation represents the fulfillment of Jesus's teaching to become again as little children. It marks the discovery, in conscious awareness, of a higher state of spiritually transformed naturalness. The ultimate prize of the hero's journey in psychospiritual terms is the Self and the full realization of your unique individuality in the world. By individuating, you become a type unto yourself. The unique potentiality of the child is realized in the empirical personality.

Individuation requires the sacrifice of the natural instinctual state of being, the death of our animal nature, the sacrifice even of our ordinary humanness that we might realize a state of higher-than-human godlikeness, and realize our inherent divinity. For this to take place consciousness has to become detached both from the instincts and from the old structure of the personality. When this detachment happens, you are able to relate to your instincts as an object, outside of yourself, rather than unconsciously identifying with them, as before. No longer will you experience a desire and automatically identity with it ("I want to do this or that"), but you experience the desire as something other, something outside of your conscious will that you that must be engaged with and related to in a critical dialogue. So too consciousness becomes separate from the old structure of the ego and the old dominant principle of egoic willpower, which are progressively destroyed. In Christian terms, the old Adam dies that the coming Christ might be realized. This amounts to a profound psychospiritual death and rebirth, vividly conveyed in the epic adventures of the hero. The human being is realizing a greater identity, becoming something other, evolving, transforming. Hero myths can serve as your guide through this process. The scenes depicted and recounted in myths are real experiences that you can have during individuation. If you think of your experience in terms of these myths, you can get a better sense of what is happening to you. The imagination can become your guide even when rational understanding fails you.

CHAPTER 8

The Encounter with the Goddess
and the Sacred Marriage

*Once the masculine consciousness has attained its height, it
comes face to face with its feminine counterpart, the anima.*
—C. G. Jung

The first appearance of the unconscious is in shadow form, which
is why everything appears dark, difficult, threatening, and uncertain. But eventually a light is kindled in the darkness, and out of the
shadow other archetypes emerge: the anima and animus, the mana
personality, the wise old man, the trickster, the great mother, the
child, and the Self.

The transition from the shadow to the Self, in Jungian terms, takes
place through the anima and animus. In myth, the anima is often
symbolized by the goddess. Although the goddess is obviously
female, and although in Jung's view the anima relates to the inner
feminine principle of the male psyche, this archetype is relevant to
us all. I noted earlier that while myths reflect the inherent gender
biases of the culture from which they originated, it is a mistake,
I believe, to think of myths exclusively in terms of biological gender.
The ego, in its posture of extraverted self-assertion, is "masculine"
in quality, so the encounter with the archetypal feminine in myth is
to do with the need for each of us, irrespective of our gender, to get
in touch with the feminine principle within and thus to come into a
more conscious relationship with the deeper powers of the psyche.

It is also the case that the archetype of the animus, the inner masculine principle, is within us all. According to Jung, when the

animus remains unconscious, it is initially the source of irrational opinions carrying tremendous conviction, which we must learn to detach from and then subject to rational scrutiny. The susceptibility to irrational opinions of this kind applies to both men and women, of course, just as both men and women are subject to the irrational moods associated with the anima.

Before it is engaged with during individuation, an unconsciously functioning animus can often manifest as a lack of critical discernment and the tendency to accept and espouse all manner of unedifying preconceived opinions and assertions that have not been subjected to critical reflection, but that nevertheless masquerade as wisdom. In this condition, a person may serve as a mouthpiece for the prevailing attitudes of the day, which, reflecting the beliefs of the common crowd, are invariably opposed to the way of individuation. Such ideas form something like an unreflective folk psychology, unconsciously passed on from person to person, generation to generation.

Equally prevalent is the tendency to find oneself dominated and possessed by the animus. In this case, one is subject to a deeply ingrained habitual tendency to make and accept damning judgments about oneself and the world, such that one is crippled by remorseless doubts, lacerating self-criticism, and a morass of confusing and contradictory ideas. In women's dreams, especially, such critical voices and dominant opinions are often symbolically portrayed as men, perhaps crowding around the dreamer or relentlessly pursuing her.[1] By uncritically accepting these voices as valid, and identifying with them as one's own thoughts, one becomes the victim of an unintegrated and unconscious animus. Both these tendencies—lack of critical discernment and excessive self-criticism—might be simultaneously present.

The development of the animus also entails the cultivation of the capacity for self-assertion and creative independence. In cases of an underdeveloped animus function, there is a tendency to project power and control in one's life onto outside figures, often serving as a substitute for the father. We might think here of the person longing to be swept up and rescued by some all-powerful hero figure, traditionally conceived as a damsel in distress waiting for her knight in shining armor. Or we might think of the collective faith in Jesus as the spiritual savior for whom the believer waits in hope and expectation of salvation. Prior to its development during individuation, then, the animus function relates to the tendency, in each of us, to project our own capacity for self-assertion, individual authority, independence of thought, and decisive action onto powerful external figures who embody those qualities one might recognize and cultivate in oneself.

Individuation requires the development of both anima and animus. Indeed, in Jung's model of the psyche there are four psychological types or functions: sensation (relating to the given facts of your life circumstance), thinking (relating to rational analysis and reasoning), feeling (an emotional evaluation of how you feel about something), and intuition (apprehending the hidden significance and unfolding possibilities or meaning of experience). The ego tends to utilize two of the functions in its approach to life, a dominant function and an auxiliary one. As the ego develops its dominant psychological functions, the inferior functions remain in the shadow, primitive and undeveloped. During the descent into the underworld of the unconscious, if you are to prevail, you have to face up to your weaker side. Indeed, cultivating these inferior functions is imperative for overcoming the tyrannical element of the controlling ego. These undeveloped functions lie outside the old ego's sphere of dominance and thus provide ways to break out of its control.

To move towards greater psychological wholeness, then, you are obliged to cultivate your weaker or inferior functions. One might think here of the intellectual who has a deficiency in feeling, or of the idealistic intuitive dreamer, the *puer aeternus* or *puella aeterna* character, unable to face the practical facts of his or her life situation, ever escaping into a fantasy world of unactualized possibility. Or again, one might envisage the hard-nosed materialist, with a dominant sensation function, accepting as real only that which can be seen and touched—a trait that characterizes the understanding of the nature of reality prevailing in the modern West. To become less one-sided, each character needs to cultivate its complementary opposite.

Regarding the thinking function, on the spiritual path it is essential that you scrutinize the ideas and assumptions shaping your approach to life. You must subject the stream of unreflective "wisdom" or critical judgments flowing from the animus, which are invariably based on false ideas about reality, to careful critical evaluation. You have to formulate your own world view based on your own experience and knowledge, in so doing challenging those inherited or irrational beliefs that inform your emotional patterns and ways of being in the world.

In itself, however, a transformation of one's world view is not enough; it is merely a prelude to the incomparably more demanding challenge of psychospiritual transformation. Consciousness has to come to terms with the inner world of the desires and feelings, and with the archetypes and instincts. It is here that the anima takes center-stage. The anima is the source of emotional wisdom and intuitive guidance that must be coupled with the faculty of rational-critical evaluation to guide the hero on his or her journey through the unconscious. Thus, in *The Divine Comedy* Dante has to rely on both the male guide Virgil, the personification of rational-spiritual wisdom, and Beatrice, who personifies spiritual guidance derived from intuition and feeling.

Jung portrays the encounter with the shadow as the "apprentice-piece" of individuation and the encounter with the anima as the "masterpiece."[2] At the more advanced anima stage, the moral challenge of facing one's point of weakness and the titanic struggle with the dark forces of the unconscious subside, to an extent, and are accompanied by a new challenge—the meeting with the goddess—which is the next manifestation of the problem of opposites, now personified as male and female, in addition to light and dark, and good and evil.

The Goddess as the Great Mother

The Great Mother goddess simultaneously nurtures and destroys, nourishes and annihilates. Individual ego-consciousness is born from the Great Mother's womb and sustained by her, but her negative aspect is that of the dark goddess, the Terrible Mother, who threatens the integrity of the conscious personality and the independence and ongoing development of the ego. Both these aspects are well represented by the Hindu goddess Kali. In mythic terms, the lure of the Great Mother represents the peril of a return to the oblivion of primitive unconsciousness, the grave danger that ego-consciousness will undergo a dissolution, merging back into the faceless impersonal anonymity of the unconscious processes of nature. The ego must therefore struggle against the power of the Great Mother if it is to maintain its independent existence and autonomy.

The dynamics at work here were especially evident in the early phases of the collective development of the ego, when, millennia ago, human consciousness was first struggling to stand apart from nature. At this early point in development, human consciousness needed reinforcing against the pull back to nature. In the West, we noted, the separation of consciousness from nature was effected and fortified by the patriarchal Yahweh's Ten Commandments and harsh punishments for transgression of his will. Yahweh's stringent moral authority and commands meant that the Jewish people were to follow a set of imperatives imposed from without rather than live naturally. Obedience to these laws meant going against natural instincts thereby reinforcing the autonomy of ego-consciousness, further separating it from the state of unconscious natural wholeness.

With the spread of Christianity, the same struggle was to be played out within the psyche of each individual, having to curb natural instincts and desires and to exercise self-awareness and self-control in order to meet the requirements of a social, religious, and moral code. As we saw in Part One, the Christian morality impels people to become more aware of the impulses arising within them, purely to avoid falling into sin, or to recognize sin that they might become absolved of it during confession. When the old ego structure starts to fall apart during onset of individuation, the individual must confront a similar challenge but at a deeper level. Now, the instincts, desires, and fears cannot be held in check and repressed in favor of a commitment to a moral code, as they were before; these drives and impulses have to be fully experienced, contained, and transformed.

As we have seen, on the journey to psychological wholeness there is a period of dangerous transition when one's old personal willpower is rendered impotent and the structure of the ego collapses. With the shell of the ego broken, consciousness is once again exposed to the maternal abyss. At this stage of psychological transformation, when the old way of being has fallen irrevocably away and the old self seems to be dying, life can feel extraordinarily difficult and overwhelming. The unrelenting pressure of being an individual, with separate ego-consciousness, can feel too great, and the temptation to return to the blissful condition of pre-consciousness can be powerful indeed. There is a temptation to just give in, surrender, and let go of the burden of individual existence. Returning in surrender to the Mother, the struggle associated with ego-consciousness is brought to an end but this comes at the highest price: the tragic loss of one's individuality. During individuation, the hero has to come back into contact with the Great Mother as source, but one must not lose one's self in the process.

Transpersonal theorists make a helpful distinction between what is *pre-personal* (the state prior to the development of a separate ego) and *transpersonal* (a higher spiritual realization beyond the ego). These states can easily be confused. For genuine transpersonal development to occur, one needs to maintain the integrity of individual consciousness, and not allow it dissolve back into a prepersonal unity, devoid of all self awareness. Although individuation involves a death of the old ego structure, a new ego is forged, a new more fortified personality structure, and with it a more powerful will. Individuation does not lead to the absolute dissolution of the ego, but its transformation. This transformation leads to a higher, incomparably more demanding way of being than normal life; it does not consist in a letting go or relinquishing of the pressures of individual selfhood but brings a tremendous increase in the pressure and responsibility of conscious self-awareness.

The lure to return to the arms of the Great Mother goddess at this stage, then, is to be resisted and overcome. The hero must fight against the tremendous pull of the instincts back towards the natural state. In terms of personal experience, you should not just give yourself over to desire at this point or just simply "let go"; the path of least resistance is the wrong one at this time. Rather, you need to develop a deeper will and self-discipline to overcome the instincts and to preserve your self-awareness. The patriarchal authority of the father principle—responsibility, control, discipline, material necessity, punishment, rules, worldly commitments—must be pitted against the pull of the mother principle in order to prevent the catastrophic regression. "The father," Jung notes, "is the representative of the spirit, whose function it is to oppose pure instinctuality."[3] The spiritual father principle, that is, opposes the pull of a regressive return to the prepersonal instinctuality of the maternal unconscious.

In her positive aspect, the Great Mother also represents the potential for an unconditional acceptance of life as it is, exemplified by the mother's love for her child. Whatever the child does, good or bad, the mother's love remains; everything is accepted even if is not liked or condoned. Indeed, in the embrace of the Great Mother all the opposites are reconciled, recognized as aspects of a greater unity. The realization of this encompassing unity can arise through the meeting with the goddess. The hero's journey ideally leads to a progressive union with the Great Mother in which one can arrive at a total affirmation and unconditional acceptance of life as it is, but not, however, at the expense of realized individual selfhood. This is why Campbell often tries to maintain a tension between a realized individuality and a relationship with the maternal ground of being—a tension that is even more central to Jung's view. The ultimate aim of individuation is the *hieros gamos*: the higher union of a fully developed conscious ego with the maternal ground. Needless to say, this union is very different from a regressive collapse into the arms of the Great Mother.

The elevated aspect of the Great Mother goddess furnishes one with great wisdom, the wisdom of the depths. "Being one with her," Jung notes, "means being granted a vision of deeper things, of the primordial images and primitive forces which underlie all life and are its nourishing, sustaining, creative matrix."[4] Clarissa Pinkola Estes makes a similar point, specifically with regard to the way of women's transformation, involving the recovery of a relationship with "instinctive nature," the "natural psyche," or what she calls the "Wild Woman" archetype:

> When women reassert their relationship with wildish nature, they are gifted with a permanent and internal watcher, a knower, a visionary, an oracle, an inspiratrice, an intuitive, a maker, a creator, an inventor, and a listener who guide, suggest, and urge vibrant life in the inner and outer worlds.[5]

Jung might have described such an attainment as the differentiation and integration of the animus out of the maternal unconscious, the inner depths of nature. Indeed, Marie-Louise von Franz suggests that a woman can realize her creative power and wisdom through the recognition of and critical engagement with the animus, just as the man might come into relationship with the feminine power of nature through engagement with the anima.[6]

The Evolution of the Archetypal Feminine

The Great Mother goddess is one among several forms of the archetypal feminine. She personifies the female principle as the source: Mother Earth, Mother Nature, the womb of being, the unconscious as the matrix of conscious experience. Other forms of the female principle manifest at various stages of the life cycle and at different points of the individuation process.

During the development of the ego, the ground of being is repressed, and the preconscious absorption in the ground is lost. We do not realize this is happening at the time, of course, but in retrospect it is apparent that the wholeness of experience that characterizes infancy and early childhood has come to end. Following Freud, transpersonal philosopher Michael Washburn calls this process *primal repression.*[7] Wholeness is lost, but a more concentrated consciousness begins to develop, centered on the ego. At the same time, as the ego develops and the individual person becomes ever more aware that he or she is a separate being, a compensatory drive impresses itself on consciousness: the drive for relationship, above all sexual relationships.

During puberty, according to Washburn, the life energy of the repressed ground first expresses itself as sexual drive. The initial preconscious union with the mother gives way to the separate ego's desire for sexual union and instinctual gratification, compensating, as it were, for the loss of proximity to the source, the loss of wholeness. The temporary experience of orgasmic release shatters the separate self-sense, for a brief moment, overcoming in Dionysian self-annihilation the alienation of individual consciousness. Thus orgasm promises, and unconsciously fulfills, the sought-after wholeness that was lost during the emergence of the separate ego.

On another level, a release from the separate ego can also be mediated by aesthetic rapture. Desire and the aesthetic response come together in the experience of falling in love, with the projection of the anima or animus onto another person, finding in another one's "lost" other half. The masculine and feminine principles are typically brought together on a more enduring basis, of course, in a long-term partnership such as marriage, which is the primary vehicle, according to Jungian psychologists, for working through your relationships with your own parents and the parental images of the archetypal mother and father. For psychospiritual development, the highest form of the union of masculine and feminine is the sacred marriage of a fully developed ego-consciousness with the maternal ground of being—the ultimate goal of individuation.

Marie-Louise von Franz, Jung's colleague and a leading theorist of depth psychology in her own right, explored how these transformations are depicted in the changing personifications of the anima in art and culture.[8] More undeveloped forms of the anima include erotic imagery or "primitive women" such as those in the paintings of Gauguin or the figure of Eve in the Garden of Eden. The cultivated, romantic and aesthetic forms of the anima are suggested by figures of romantic projection such as Helen of Troy or Faust's Helen, just as a spiritually-attuned anima is symbolized by the Virgin Mary and other such personages of spiritual devotion. Finally, at its most advanced stage of development, the anima might also be represented, von Franz proposes, by Athena, Greek goddess of wisdom, or Leonardo da Vinci's enigmatic *Mona Lisa*. Figures in this latter group represent more rounded characters than the one-sided spiritual purity of Mary, who is devoid of any darker, chthonic traits.

Federico Fellini's *La Dolce Vita* provides another fine example of an anima figure in the character Sylvia, the voluptuous Swedish film star who captures the attentions of the film's central character, Marcello Mastroianni, a member of the Italian paparazzi. In a memorable scene set in the Trevi Fountain, we see Sylvia frolicking in the water, playing with a white kitten on her head, and luring Marcello to dance with her. This image draws together a number of crucial aspects of the anima: its role as sensual temptress, its connection to the "waters of life" suggested by the fountain, and its archetypal or spiritual import suggested by the mythic figures adorning the fountain, with the kitten representing the innocence, purity, and playfulness of the inner child to be differentiated from the sensual and instinctual dynamism initially associated with the anima.

In personal experience, if one remains ignorant of one's feelings, or fails to heed them, the anima tends towards a cruder form of expression. The more distant one is from one's feelings, the stronger desire becomes, and the feelings then manifest on a more instinctual level—in a Dionysian manner, one might say. We can see an example of something of this kind, it seems to me, in the typical patterns of ordinary working life. By subjugating the feelings during the monotony of the typical nine-to-five working week, at the weekend when the restrictions are lifted, as it were, the violated and neglected anima demands expression, and the unexpressed feelings and desires from the week are often crudely discharged, sometimes in bouts of drunken revelry and hedonism. Such a pattern, needless to say, is not conducive to psychological maturation and spiritual growth. It tends to repeat compulsively.

An undifferentiated anima is associated with distance from one's feelings and the incapacity, therefore, to decide for oneself what one wants. Indeed, a person out of touch with the anima might find themselves utterly unable to make a decision, having abdicated the realm of feeling evaluation to the partner—a situation portrayed to caricature in many a television sitcom. Equally, we might also think here of the overly intellectual, overly rational person who, disconnected from the feeling world, is ripe for a romantic projection of some kind. Jung compared this "anima projection" to a kind of seizure, when the conscious will is overpowered and pulled in a seemingly irrational and perhaps destructive direction by the emotions.

When your relationship to the inner world of the psyche is undeveloped in this way, you are likely to project your feelings onto another person, the one who seems to be the source of all joy, meaning, and energy in your life, the one who promises fulfillment. Such projection serves an invaluable purpose in the ordinary course of human development, for without the projection of the anima or animus the young adult might be unable to free themselves from attachment to the mother and father, to forsake the familiar cozy womb of childhood in favor of participation in the wider world. The romantic projection of the anima or animus onto another person outside of the family makes possible the individual's continuing psychological development in the sphere of personal relationships.

Once the initial parental attachments are broken, and the object of the libido is transferred onto relationships outside of the family, the unconscious projection of the anima and animus has served its function. Thereafter, the anima and animus might be recognized as images of the idealized other within—the unconscious images of female and male we carry around with us. Typically, one aspires to live up to the idealized inner image of a person of one's own gender; it serves as a kind of ego-ideal. At the same time, one unconsciously seeks qualities of the other gender in one's mate—although this classical Jungian model is obviously inadequate for those relationships that fall outside the orthodox heterosexual model.

If one is not aware of the animus or anima, one is likely to fall victim to further instances of projection and romantic seizure. The underlying reason for these cases of unconscious seizure or possession seems to be to direct the individual's attention to the unconscious, to usurp the seeming control of the ego, compelling the individual along the path of individuation, albeit unconsciously.

At its deepest level, the anima, like all the archetypes, reflects the purposes of the Self, guiding the often unsuspecting individual to the fulfillment of a particular calling or life path. "Something strangely meaningful clings to her," Jung notes, "a secret knowledge or hidden wisdom" that can serve as one's guide during individuation, providing assistance that can further the realization of one's unique life path.[9] The anima is intimately connected to what is commonly understood by the expression one's *heart*—the living, pulsing emotional core within us.

Popular wisdom decrees, of course, that one should follow one's heart in love and in life. However, the heart's true desires are often buried beneath a morass of powerful, conflicting emotions. The heart's desire is not synonymous with the strongest emotion. To follow one's heart requires discernment, which is only possible through the development of the anima function. Indeed, a developed anima expresses itself as something more than mere emotion and affectivity; it is related to one's true feelings, which often lie behind more surface emotions and desires—the anima pertains to the quiet, gentle, yet unyielding choice that comes out of innocence and the authenticity of the soul, untainted by the world and a lifetime of conditioned responses. In this function, the anima represents another voice and center in the psyche, alongside the rational thinking ego.

The voice of the anima can be drowned out by the uncontrolled force of instincts. One can see something of this experience portrayed in a later scene in *La Dolce Vita*. As the film unfolds, we see Marcello, in shock following the tragic suicide of his close friend Steiner, seemingly abandon himself to his lower instincts, spending his time in hedonistic, orgiastic parties in which his behavior becomes almost bestial. At the close of the film, Marcello wearily makes his way with a group of friends from a party to the beach. Here, in the distance, he catches sight of the young waitress Paola, known to him from an earlier scene in the film. Though Paola tries to speak to Marcello, amidst the roar of waves her voice cannot be heard. Her gestures to him, barely comprehensible, meet with a reluctant shrug of the shoulders, as if he were resigned to his fate. Although drawn by Paola, Marcello chooses to remain with his group, the herd, rather than heed the voice of his anima. Symbolically, that is, with the roaring waves of instinct active in his own life, Marcello fails to respond to the cries of his anima—and therein the soul and inner child—that might lead him beyond his life of hedonistic indifference.

To realize the feminine spirit within nature, you have to engage with your desire nature, as it is through desires and feelings that the anima first appears to the adult ego. It is necessary to engage with desire in order to get the deeper life energies flowing through you. "The anima wants life," as Jung notes, and this archetype sees to it that we become ensnared in the world in pursuit of our desires and longings.[10] In mythic terms, this notion is suggested by the temptation in the Garden of Eden, in which Eve, cajoled by the serpent, leads human beings to self-conscious awareness and knowledge of the opposites through the eating of the forbidden fruit. It is only by following the way of the serpent—engaging your desires and passions—that you can come to self-knowledge and discern, in the flux of the passions, the voice of the anima which, ultimately, might lead you to discover your bliss.

Anima as Temptress

Another manifestation of the goddess is conveyed by what Campbell calls the motif of "woman as temptress." Individuation, as will be plainly evident, is not synonymous with happiness. For this reason, Jung was wary of directing people along this path unless it was absolutely essential. Many people could be happier without individuating. For others, however, individuation was unavoidable. The aim in such cases is to affirm the process so as to engage your will in what is taking place. "Free will," Jung declared, "is doing gladly and freely that which one must do."[11] It is the ability, that is, to affirm the life the Self intends.

Given the suffering involved in individuation, inevitably there are many occasions when you will feel tempted to follow another path, one that promises easier or quicker fulfillment, one that enables the gratification of the instincts and desires. The attraction to other paths is a hazard suggested by the motif of the Sirens whose enchanting melodies can lure the unwitting hero to shipwreck and disaster. Entranced by the beautiful melodies, the hero can easily stray off course, on a path to wrack and ruin. According to Campbell, the Sirens are "symbolic of the allure of the beatitude of paradise."[12] It is the paradise of the fulfillment of desire. The Sirens thus suggest the temptation of desire for blissful pleasure and fulfillment. Such a yearning serves an invaluable purpose for it can provide a motivating pull that sustains one's faith during individuation. One lives in the midst of the suffering of transformation with the promise of heavenly fulfillment in the future. The challenge, therefore, is to hold true to the promise of blissful fulfillment through the spiritualization of one's life, while refusing to consent to the apparent shortcuts to this goal and alternatives that present themselves. "Preserve me from all petty victories!" Nietzsche petitioned, for these would pale into significance at the side of the great victory that would bring the spiritual birth of the *Übermensch*.[13] "Preserve and spare me for a great destiny!"[14]

In facing this challenge, the hero Odysseus's encounter with the Sirens is instructive. By employing a deliberate strategy suggested by the goddess Circe, he is able to experience the beauty of the Sirens' melodies without meeting a tragic end. First instructing his men to put bees wax in their ears while binding him to the mast of the ship, Odysseus orders that on no account must they release him, even if he later commands them to: "If I beg you or bid you to let me loose, then you must re-doubly firm me into place with yet more bonds."[15] The men are protected from the lure of the Sirens' music by the wax, Odysseus by being bound. In psychospiritual terms, this strategy implies, I believe, that you must bind yourself to the mast of your own higher calling. That way you will be able to experience the full rush of the Dionysian rapture of desire (listening to the Sirens) without it destroying you. You need to be mindful of your mission, your purpose, and not let any desire pull you too far off track.[16]

The encounter with the feminine is an especially crucial aspect of the individuation process, one that is symbolically explored through Odysseus's encounter both with the Sirens and the goddesses, Calypso and Circe. "Fate has abandoned him," we read of Odysseus in Book 5, "to languish sorely in Lady Calypso's island, kept there by her high hand, a prisoner in her house."[17] The goddess, though she saved Odysseus from shipwreck, and "loved him and cared for him and promised . . . he should not die nor grow old all his days," condemned him to the deepest sorrow of a seven-year exile from his true life in his homeland, the life he willed, and for which his soul yearned.[18] Fearing that he would never again see his home or his beloved wife Penelope, Odysseus was to be found "sitting at the water's edge: his eyes as ever imbued with tears at this ebbing of his precious life in vain lamentations after deliverance."[19] Forced by night to sleep with the nymph goddess, during the daytime hours "he haunted the rocks and pebble beaches of the island shore, retching up his heart with crying and sighs and misery, his gaze fixed on the desolate main through a blur of tears."[20] The goddess offered Odysseus love, passion, and immortality—the fruits, that is, of absorption in the timeless pleasure of his own unconscious fantasy and emotional world, but this came at the price of his real authentic existence.

Suggesting the close association between the anima and the animal world of the instinctual power of the unconscious, the goddess Circe, in another encounter, turns Odysseus's unwitting companions into swine by tricking them into eating food laced with a magical potion. Odysseus, however, is protected by a magical herb revealed by Hermes, and is therefore immune to the goddess's potion. Demonstrating his mastery over the Circe's power, Odysseus then becomes her "bed-mate," cajoling her, as instructed by Hermes, to release his crew from their bestial form. This episode implies, though the sexual act, a union between the heroic ego and the hypnotic numinous power of the feminine unconscious, a union that is to be achieved through the development of the anima function.

Before the anima and animus are integrated during individuation, a significant quota of psychological energy and emotion often remain bound up with an internalized image of an ideal partner, or an idealized life situation or a romanticized image of what we believe life should be like. Attachment to these images prevents us from giving ourselves fully to the moment at hand—we are, in effect, kept a prisoner of our own feelings, unable to fully participate in the world. Because reality inevitably chafes against the ideal image, never quite living up to expectations of how things should be, at the mercy of the anima one might find oneself acting always under duress, struggling heroically against one's emotions, feeling perpetually dissatisfied.

It is precisely this situation that is symbolically suggested by the theme of captivity by the goddess. To individuate, one must overcome the inclination to satisfy the anima, recognizing that the impulses coming from the anima do not necessarily reflect an authentic choice, a conscious intention. One must hear the anima's demands, for it holds the key to the heart's desire, but one must not unconsciously identify with impulses arising from the anima. Although one cannot overcome the attachment to such images by an act of will, one must consistently wrestle psychological energy free from the anima by wholeheartedly committing to the reality of the living moment. As we read in *The Gospel of Thomas*, we must "turn an image into an image" such that we can see the reality of the moment for what it is, unobscured by emotional needs and projections, and deep-rooted attachments to idealized images of how things "should" be.[21]

In *The Odyssey*, episodes of physical captivity and isolation on remote islands therefore symbolically indicate that the hero (ego) remains subject to the whims of his emotional nature. These episodes imply domination by desire and victimization by an unconscious attachment to the idealized image to which we would like to make reality conform. The conscious will is effectively held captive by the anima, and is thus a victim of the feelings and desires. Often these feelings are rooted in residual childish tendencies that can color and distort our perception of the world, making us oversensitive to slights. This is what Jung sees as the negative side of the anima: moodiness, oversensitivity, affectivity.

It is well documented that Jung himself seems to have experienced a series of anima projections, becoming involving in intimate relationships with a number of his female clients and confidants. Certainly, this archetype occupied an exceptionally important place in his psychology and in his life, both as an inner psychological function and acted out through his relationships. Whatever one's judgment of the morality of Jung's lifestyle, these relationships appear to have had a crucial influence on the development of his psychological theory and, especially in the case of the relationship with Toni Wolff, provided invaluable support and insight during his confrontation with the unconscious.

Campbell, loyally devoted to his wife, the dancer Jean Erdman, encountered the feminine principle in its outer form both through his marriage and in his public life as a college professor. For many years he taught classes on literature and mythology at Sarah Lawrence, an all-girls college in New York State. Campbell said that addressing his lecture material to his female audience influenced the way he taught. The students in his classes always wanted to know the value and relevance of any myth or idea to their own lives; the material needed to be personal, applicable to everyday experiences. They engaged with a topic on the feeling level as much as the intellectual, and wanted to know how it might help them as they dealt with the practical realities of life. In response to his students' needs, Campbell seems to have developed the capacity to combine deep theoretical knowledge with a personal, direct style of communication that made complex ideas immediately accessible to people from many different walks of life. His more personal approach to the subject matter was in marked distinction to the general academic tendency to engage with material solely through the rational intellect.

By contrast, for Nietzsche, relationships with women (and also with men) were virtually non-existent. Even allowing for the fact that Nietzsche often expressed himself with irony, he provides us with plenty of examples of what can only be described as rather extreme attitudes towards gender roles and his sometimes offensive views of women. In *Thus Spoke Zarathustra*, for example, Nietzsche declares: "Man should be trained for war and woman for the recreation of the warrior; all else is folly."[22] In terms of his inner experience, too, Nietzsche's tragic heroism and pathological inflation seem to have precluded any constructive relationship with the inner feminine, which is reflected in his approach to psychological transformation. If we call to mind again Nietzsche's parable of the three metamorphoses, although the archetypal feminine principle must play a crucial role in to helping to effect the transformation from lion into child, this principle does not feature in the parable and, as far as we can tell, has no place in Nietzsche's understanding of the process of transformation.

As we have seen, the lion, representing the instinctual power of the unconscious, must be humanized, spiritualized, tamed; and this can only be done through feeling. One must transmute instinctual drive into feeling in order to probe the root motivations of the impulses behind one's desires. In dreams, the feeling function is often personified in the form of female figures. The controlling "strong man" only represses instinct; symbolically speaking, it is through the feminine principle that one is able to fully experience instinct as feeling, which enables rational consciousness to penetrate to the deeper emotions underlying the instincts. The transformation takes place at the level of the heart. It is through the heart that the "head" principle (rational ego consciousness) and the "belly" principle (the instinctual power of the archetypal unconscious) can be brought into relationship, and the conflict between reason and instinct can be healed.

Paradise Found?

Another form of distraction and temptation that arises during individuation is suggested by the idea that the hero and the traveling party happen across a spurious paradise—a motif also explored in *The Odyssey*. Odysseus and his crew visit the Land of the Lotus Eaters and are given the express instruction not to eat anything. Predictably, of course, some of the crew members disregard the warning. Eating a strange flowery food, they fall into a blissful reverie such that they have no wish to ever return home, and have to be forcibly dragged back to the boat sobbing and weeping. They are taken over by a paradisiacal rapture that is a severe danger to individuation and the continued development of consciousness. This condition amounts to a spiritual forgetfulness, a warning of the dangers of seemingly blissful pleasure to the individuation process. These seemingly paradisiacal states of being occur frequently throughout individuation. They represent the urge to give yourself away totally to some feeling, to some part of your psyche that is not your true self and center. Amidst the suffering of individuation the lure of the promise of immediate happiness can prove too great to resist.

In this episode, the disobedience of the crew suggests that the heroic ego (Odysseus) has yet to integrate all the elements of the psyche potentially at his disposal (the crew), and that certain aspects of his being are working against his intentions. Individuation and spiritual transformation, as we have seen, require that the "eye is made single," such that all parts of the psyche are subservient to the biddings of the Self. For in themselves, each drive and desire we experience will tend to pull us away from center. As individuation proceeds, however, all desires, except for those which serve the Self, ultimately prove unfulfilling, promoting an acute sense of self-loss and unreality. All drives for exclusively personal fulfillment are to be sacrificed on the altar of spiritual transformation.

Another example of this quasi-paradisiacal experience can be seen in *The Wizard of Oz*, when, in an attempt to pull Dorothy away from her mission, the Wicked Witch creates a beautiful, idyllic poppy field—the very picture of blissful tranquility on a warm summer's day. With the Emerald City in view in the distance, Dorothy is overcome with the urge to lie and rest in the field, falling into a deep sleep and thus forgetting about her mission. The poppy field here represents the gentle lull of an existence devoid of strain and struggle.

A similar experience is explored in an amusing episode of *Star Trek* from 1967 called "This Side of Paradise." In this episode, Captain Kirk and members of the crew of the Enterprise beam down onto a planet to explore an old Federation colony. Here they discover a group of people who are living in a condition of seemingly blissful paradise. One by one, under the influence of spores sprayed by mysterious flowers, each member of the landing party enters his or her own personal heaven and loses all desire to ever leave the planet, forgetting the former life and all sense of responsibility to the Enterprise or the mission. Even the arch rationalist and logician Dr. Spock is not immune to the influence of the spores; he finds himself falling deeply in love and cannot understand Kirk's resistance to his offers to join him in the colony or his captain's desire to return to the ship. Kirk, it seems, is the only one, through sheer force of character, who has any power to resist the influence of the spores.

Kirk's response in this episode provides a clue as to how to deal with these experiences when they arise. Kirk reminds himself of his original mission, recollects the importance of his commitment to the Enterprise. In these circumstances, it is essential to bring to mind some important task or mission (binding yourself to the mast) that provides a connection to another part of yourself outside of the spurious lure of paradise. Ultimately, Kirk realizes that the antidote to the spores is the experience of anger. He thus provokes Spock into a violent rage and in so doing snaps him out of the hypnotic influence of the spores. Anger is a pure and liberating emotion; it cuts through so much psychological dross and invigorates.

The delirious happy states are examples of a type of condition largely devoid of conscious self-awareness. Other conditions of this type are more traumatic in their quality. Michael Washburn describes certain experiences that occur during individuation as psychic "black holes" in which, alarmingly, conscious self-awareness seems to have all but disappeared.[23] This is a condition of "mental paralysis and darkness . . . denseness, immobility, and blankness of mind."[24] During the transition from the old ego structure to a new psychological structure, you can experience a temporary void in consciousness when you seem to have no will or no self-awareness—you experience an utter blank. These states can be the cause of acute anxiety for it seems as if your self, your personality, and your will have utterly ceased to exist. The disconnection of consciousness from instinct gives the sense that you are living in a cocooned bubble of nonexistence. In reality, however, as might become apparent in retrospect, these states are temporary conditions arising from deep-rooted fearful reactions to the changes you are experiencing, states which occur as consciousness becomes detached from the instincts and reconnects to them during the process of transformation.

Personal and Transpersonal

A final variation on the theme of temptation is well portrayed in the second *Superman* movie starring Christopher Reeve. As the film unfolds, Clark Kent's relationship with Lois Lane deepens, and, such is his love for her, he yearns to become a normal human being without carrying the immense responsibility of being Superman (his transpersonal character). As you proceed on your own life journey, you might find that there is a conflict between your transpersonal calling and your personal relationships, which usually require that you live a relatively regular life, subject to the normal human frailties, emotional responses, and concerns. Nietzsche, for example, just before he wrote *Thus Spoke Zarathustra*, had yearned for a romantic relationship with a female acquaintance, Lou Salome. He yearned to experience what it was like just to be a normal personal again, to come down from the astral philosophical heights of inspiration and the titanic struggle and loneliness of the path he was on, to live again among people, to feel that human companionship and warmth. Sadly, for Nietzsche, his wish was not to be realized.

There seems to be an inherent struggle in life to reconcile personal happiness, and fulfillment in human relationships, with a transpersonal calling. It is crucial, however, to maintain both sides of life, not to sacrifice one in favor of the other. If you live just for the personal dimension of experience, you will probably remain deeply unfulfilled, always feeling that something tremendously important is missing from your life. This situation is explored in the film *Unbreakable* starring Bruce Willis as David Dunn, a security guard who realizes that he has never suffered from an illness or injury of any kind, despite being involved in a horrific train crash in which he was the only survivor. Explaining this away as nothing more than good fortune, and refusing at first to investigate and face up to his extraordinary condition, Dunn is perpetually dissatisfied in life, until, at the film's conclusion, he realizes and accepts his invincibility, and thus becomes reconciled to his destiny as a superhero and protector of the people.

If suppressed and ignored, your transpersonal destiny might rise up against you, thwarting your every move, pursuing you relentlessly at every step, placing a tremendous strain on personal relationships, perhaps even jeopardizing your life itself. But, equally, if you live just for the transpersonal, sacrificing too much of your personal self, you can lose the balance provided by human feeling and sensitivity. "Too long a sacrifice can make a stone of the heart," as Yeats observed.[25] You might then become alienated, unable to relate to anyone. When you are dealing with the transpersonal powers of the psyche, then, it is important to maintain the personal side of your life—the love and warmth of human relationship. Without this balance, the powerful forces you will encounter during individuation can easily turn you into a monster, devoid of human emotion and sensitivity. You can become possessed. We might call to mind again here the effect of the Ring in *The Lord of the Rings* on all who come into contact with it; even the innocent, childlike Frodo is not totally immune. Recall, too, what happens to Anakin Skywalker when he forsakes his human feeling, his love, and gives vent to the rage that ultimately consumes him and leads to his metamorphosis into Darth Vader.

Part of the process of finding your center—the Self—is not identifying with any particular aspect of your psyche or any particular impulse. You are not just a spiritual person, nor just a hero, although you might experience a deluded inner voice telling you that you are. There is a powerful archetypal basis to this kind of false identification. You must always be careful to balance any supposed spirituality against the baser, more mundane reality of working and personal life, and against the more grounded parts of your character. We can see this with Jung when, in the midst of his confrontation with the unconscious, he had to continually remind himself of who he was—of his identity as a doctor with responsibilities to his patients, and as husband and father, with a wife and family, who lived at a certain address, and so forth. He had to strengthen the personal side of his existence against the transpersonal realm, which threatened at that time to overwhelm him.

If you remain true to your passion, pursuing what it is you want to do in life, this too will help spare you from the delusion that you are wholly spiritual or some kind of spiritual master. You simply need to remind yourself that you are just doing what you want, and nothing more. Then, the question of whether or not you are "spiritual" need never arise. To think of oneself as spiritually elect, as some sort of prophet, is a powerful archetypal experience. But if you identify with this, you sacrifice your self integrity and your wholeness, which includes this spiritual part but so much more too. You are always more than any particular image or idea of what you are, or any particular complex or archetype. The Self is the total psyche, and it is also the central point, from which all the archetypes can find expression in a dynamic balance.

The tendency is for every complex in the psyche—every god, if you like—to want you for itself, and to take possession of you. To counteract this, there has to be a mediated process by which all the complexes are brought into relationship with the Self, as center. One must learn to see things for what they are, in plain sight, and not become entranced by the archetypal images that can distort our experience of the world.[26] If you are attaining spiritual insights or undergoing depth experiences beyond what most people know of, it is very tempting indeed to think of yourself as some kind of spiritual guru. This is an archetypal experience—that of the *mana* personality, the personality suffused with numinous power. To identify with that power is to lose your unique individuality. You might have the potential to provide people with spiritual guidance, but you are not just a spiritual guru, you are also an ordinary person, with flaws, faults, desires, fears, complexes, relationships, other unique talents, and so forth. The result of individuation, according to Jung, is to arrive at a more or less realistic view of the world in which you have shed all false images. You have removed the beam from your own eye, to put this in biblical terms again, and are thus perhaps in a position to help others do the same.

It is worth reflecting at this point just how difficult and how rare individuation is. Few people consciously embark on this process; fewer people still could be said to become truly individuated. Yet, as Jung stressed, this is a path we are all on, in some sense, in that we are always being moved in this direction, even though we might not know it.

Atonement with the Father

Like the encounter with the mother goddess, the father archetype in myth can appear in both positive and negative forms. Here, first, is what Campbell has to say about the role of the father:

> The father is the initiating priest, through whom the young being passes on into the larger world. And just as, formerly, the mother represented the "good" and "evil," so now does he, but with this complication—that there is a new element of rivalry in the picture: the son against the father for the mastery of the universe.[27]

The idea that the son competes against the father reflects the Oedipus complex, Freud's discovery of an unconscious psychological pattern evident from infancy in which the Oedipal drive impels the son to "kill" the father and achieve union with the mother. This infantile motivation, however, reflects a multidimensional archetypal pattern that applies to the higher phases of psychospiritual development just as much as to the dynamics of childhood psychology. In terms of individuation, the father principle here reflects the old order, the established authority, the tried-and-tested truth, which the son, representing the individuating ego, must go beyond if he is to realize his own unique individuality, and—to read the Oedipus incest fantasy on a spiritual level—achieve psychospiritual union with the Great Mother.

In the following passage, Campbell draws on Freud's ideas of the superego (internalized moral conscience) and id (instinctual unconscious) to explain the psychodynamics of the father complex:

For the ogre aspect of the father is a reflex of the victim's own ego. . . . Atonement (at-one-ment) consists in no more than the abandonment of that self-generated double monster—the dragon thought to be God (superego) and the dragon thought to be Sin (repressed id). But this requires an abandonment of the attachment to ego itself, and that is what is difficult. One must have a faith that the father is merciful, and then a reliance on that mercy.[28]

These themes are explored in the dramatic culminating scene of the *Star Wars* series, in *The Return of the Jedi*, in which Luke Skywalker is forced to fight his father, Darth Vader ("son against father for the mastery of the universe"), and then finds himself subject to the full force of the dark power of the Emperor, Palpatine. Unable to resist Palpatine's assault any longer, Skywalker is on the point of death and, with nowhere left to turn, appeals in desperation and anguish to his father for help—the appeal for the father's mercy. In the dramatic events of this scene, we witness the redemption of the father, as the humanity submerged within Darth Vader movingly responds to his son's desperate plea, saving Luke by casting Palpatine down into the Death Star's reactor core to his death.

In psychological terms, this scene is symbolically related to the challenge of throwing off the dictates of the controlling superego, the internalized moral code, which is the negative aspect of the father archetype—the patriarchal senex. You must attune to the authority of the Self, the positive aspect of the father principle, rather than allow yourself to be commanded by the voice of an internalized, culturally conditioned impulse. The Self does not reflect society's moral code but one's own deep authority, or perhaps even the universe's moral code and order, which one can try to attune to. When Luke Skywalker wields the light saber in battle, he is employing the power of conscious discrimination to overcome the controlling father principle that keeps the individual captive within the demands of conventional life.

This episode points to the experience of going beyond the personal father and the personal mother, and the rejection of all substitute forms of authority, such as a religious dogma or set of rules—any "thou shalt." All such dictates and moral imperatives are cast off in favor of finding one's own inner authority, attuning to the directives and aims of the Self. This motif is conveyed most powerfully in the crucifixion, where the death of the personal human, Jesus, symbolizes the death of the personal will, which is crucified, sacrificed to the transpersonal will. The hero's journey involves a conscious allowing of the personal will and the constructed ego-personality to be "crucified" in order that you can serve the impulses and directives of the Self. This, I believe, is the psychological significance of Jesus's affirmation that "Not my will, but thine be done" (Luke 22:42).

The ego, the seat of the personal will, is understood to be but a function of the larger Self. The ego is the vehicle for the realization of the Self. As individuation proceeds, there arises ever more insistently the sense that you are not the agent of your life—thus Jung's realization that "it is not I who create myself; rather, I happen to myself." We might also call to mind the familiar words of Jesus in the Gospel of John (14:10): "The words that I speak unto you I speak not of myself: but the Father that dwelleth in me, he doeth the works" for "I and the Father are one" (John 10:30). Individuation brings a radical shift from the egoic will, conditioned by an internalized moral principle reflecting the social order (the old personal father principle), to an attunement to the will of the Self reflecting the spiritual order informing reality as a whole (the new transpersonal father principle). The old authority (often symbolized, as we have seen, by the old king who must die or be overcome, or by the strong man enforcing control with an iron will) must give way to the authority of the Self such that one learns to trust one's own inner judgment even against the conformist pressures of society or, if needs be, the entire world. In this way, the personal will is brought into alignment with a cosmic will. The Self, let us remember, represents both the center and totality of the whole psyche, and potentially is an expression of the totality of the cosmos. The realization of your own deep center is simultaneously the realization of a center through which the cosmos, or the spirit within the cosmos, can express itself.

If the hero can withstand the challenge of overcoming the dominant rule of the culturally-conditioned aspect of the father principle and attune to the spiritual father, he or she, Campbell notes, can win through to a supreme spiritual realization:

> For the son who has grown really to know the father, the agonies of the ordeal are readily borne; the world is no longer a vale of tears but a bliss-yielding, perpetual manifestation of the Presence.[29]

Such an experience is the culmination of this aspect of the hero's journey. Self-will is overcome and the radiance within and behind all forms is realized.

Apotheosis, Sophia, and the *Hieros Gamos*

The term *apotheosis* means "becoming divine"; it refers to the transformation of the human into the divine. One symbol of apotheosis is the hermaphrodite, indicating the spiritual union of male and female. During psychospiritual transformation, the female moves towards the male, as it were, and the male moves towards the female. As Jesus says in *The Gospel of Thomas*, "When you make the two One, and you make the inner as the outer, and the outer as the inner, and the above as the below, so that you make the male and the female into single One . . . then you shall enter the Kingdom."[30] This teaching describes the reconciliation of opposites, symbolized by the mystic marriage of *Sol* and *Luna*, the king and queen in alchemy. Jung calls it the *unio mystica* or the *mysterium coniunctionis*—the mystical union of spirit and nature, male and female, self and world. The opposites that were thrust apart to create the conditions for the evolution of consciousness are here brought back together. The split is healed by the dialectical exchange between the ego and the unconscious during individuation.

In Gnostic myths, the feminine half of the divine, represented by the goddess Sophia, is described as the "slumbering spirit in nature," who lies imprisoned in the "chains of physis." It is the task of consciousness—the heroic calling of the individual ego—to liberate the feminine half of the divine, Sophia, from captivity in nature and the material world. The immanent spirit in nature, which has "fallen" into the world of matter, is to be awakened and released from the instinctual sphere. Obviously, to do this you first have to engage with that realm, engage with your passions, your desires—engage with the power of nature as it manifests within. To individuate, you cannot just cultivate an observing meditative consciousness detached from your deepest drives and emotions. As we have seen, the engagement with the passions is the essence of the Romantic and Jungian approaches to life we have been considering here.

The feminine principle is to be transformed from the demonic, primitive, and threatening form of Medusa (the lower anima, as it were) to the immanent spirituality of Sophia (the higher anima). The slaying of Medusa does not, therefore, refer to the destruction of the feminine principle *per se*; rather, it symbolizes the overcoming of the gorgon's demonic power. The conflict depicted in Perseus's encounter with Medusa is between the conscious ego (symbolized by the hero) and the instinctual power of nature (Medusa). What is destroyed is the ego's domination by instincts and its unconscious identity with instinct. This destruction is necessary to come into relationship with the higher feminine principle represented by Sophia.

The release of Sophia from the "chains of *physis*" is made possible by the separation of consciousness from nature. This in turn makes possible the *hieros gamos*, the union of the "masculine" transcendent divine with the immanent "feminine" divine. In alchemical terms, King *Sol* (consciousness) is brought into harmonious relationship with Queen *Luna* (the unconscious). As we have seen, because of the one-sided dominance of ego-consciousness in the modern Western world, the *Luna* principle—the realm of feelings, the body, nature, and the earth—has remained undifferentiated and often appears as the dark, unconscious realm of the instincts and desires. However, *Luna* is also the maternal womb of being, the "belly and the womb of nature," and the "universal receptacle" from which *Sol*—the light of consciousness—emerged.[31] To bring consciousness into harmonious relationship with the maternal ground of being, the ego must descend into its own depths to confront and differentiate the undeveloped emotional realm. In this way, the two principles, *Sol* and *Luna*, can be reunited.

Wholeness, Centering, and the Opposites

As you progress on the journey of individuation, you may increasingly encounter dreams featuring the juxtaposition of pairs of opposites, such as black and white, old and young, male and female, sweet and sour , and so forth. These motifs suggest that, although the process of transformation is far from over, the painful inner division between your rational consciousness and your instincts and desires has been at least partially healed. A wedding, the conjoining of male and female opposites, is an especially apt motif of this reconciliation.

At the same time, the Self emerges as a newly discovered center and organizing principle within the psyche, counterbalancing the turbulence of the instincts. The Self is immutable, indestructible, ancient, and solid; like a mountain, the Self is unmoved by the crashing waves of desires, fears, and emotions. The emergence of the Self into the foreground of conscious experience thus brings a sense of reassurance and solidity that, despite any difficulties lying ahead, will never leave you. This new center anchors you more deeply in your being. The Self is the eternal, universal person within you—the cosmic anthropos, the "ancient one," the universal "Great Man." This center lies not within your own consciousness or your personality, for although it is indeed within you, it is also decidedly other. It is a center beyond the personality, beyond the personal will. You relate to it as a subject to an object, an "I" to an other.

The emergent wholeness of the personality is a theme suggested in the final scene of Federico Fellini's masterpiece 8½, starring Marcello Mastroianni as Italian film director Guido Anselmi. The film opens with Anselmi, seemingly on the verge of a mental breakdown, undergoing some kind of claustrophobic existential crisis while stuck in his car in a queue of traffic. As the car fills with smoke, and a panic-stricken Anselmi tries to escape, onlookers stare blankly at him with disinterest, or appear lost in the banal pleasures of life, no doubt adding to his sense of alienation and angst, and to the viewer's uneasiness.

We next witness Anselmi floating away into the sky—suggesting a kind of detachment of consciousness from the confines of his current life situation. Drifting along high in the air, he is then reeled in on a long rope, pulled back down to earth by a dark horseman on a beach. As the scene changes, Anselmi awakens in a health spa where his inner world of memories and fantasies becomes highly activated, pervading his waking reality. In the spa, while working on ideas for his latest film amidst the general chaos and confusion of his life, he juggles with the different elements of his experience, past and present, which often pull him in conflicting directions. No obvious development or progress is apparent as the film unfolds, scene by scene. At the finale of the film, however, we see the characters in Anselmi's life joining hands, dancing in a large circle, suggesting that some kind of dynamic unification and centering process has imperceptibly taken place, a process that embraces the wholeness of his life and personality.

The wholeness implied here encompasses even the supposedly negative, banal, irritating, indulgent, immoral, and chaotic aspects of life. These are to be valued, too, affirmed as essential elements of your existence. Individuation, although it might well prevent you from falling into a self-destructive life path, does not lead to saint-hood or moral perfection. The Self is an amoral wholeness, beyond good and evil, encompassing good and evil. In Christian terms, the realization of the Self is akin to learning to value and to love all aspects of your being, to serve God with your whole personality, with your vices as well as your virtues. The Self might be imagined as an altar, of sorts, to which all aspects of your life and your charac-ter, even your negative traits, may be given in service to the divine. You can learn to serve the center such that all parts of your life and your personality are affirmed and viewed in a sacred light.

Wholeness, according to Jung, is realized through a cyclical pro-cess of psychological integration. Over the course of time, the differ-ent aspects of your personality come to the fore and find expression in your life, then recede into the background, in an alternating pat-tern. Gradually, and often indirectly, these aspects become better related to the Self as the unknown center of the personality. "There is no linear evolution," Jung reflected, looking back on his life; "there is only a circumambulation of the self."[32] During this circling process, each complex and each archetype and drive will ideally find its proper place in relation to Self, the central organizing archetype of the psyche. It is through this process that "thine eye is made sin-gle," to put it in Christian terminology, as the multiplicity of the psyche becomes synthesized into a complex unity, organized around the Self.

Both the inner union of the opposites and the realization of this new center within the psyche are suggested by the symbolism of geometrically designed sacred drawings known as *mandalas*. These symbolic drawings, Jung suggests, are depictions of the state of the Self, representing the fourfold nature of the psyche organized around a central point.

As the traumatic period of Jung's psychospiritual transformation drew to a close around 1920, he made many such mandala drawings, portraying the movement towards a realization of the wholeness of the Self. His individuation process reached a point of culmination in dream from 1927 of the English city of Liverpool, the "pool of life" as Jung understood its meaning, which appeared as a mandala-like arrangement:

> When we reached the plateau, we found a broad square dimly illuminated by street lights, into which many streets converged. The various quarters of the city were arranged radially around the square. In the centre was a round pool, and in the middle of it a small island . . . blazed with sunlight. On it stood a single tree, a magnolia, in a shower of reddish blossoms.[33]

The dream confirmed for Jung his insight into the psychological centering process that takes place during individuation, and it also provided the foundation for his own individual myth:

> This dream brought with it a sense of finality. I saw that here the goal had been revealed. One could not go beyond the centre. The centre is the goal, and everything is directed towards that centre. Through this dream I understood that the self is the principle and archetype of orientation and meaning. . . . Out of it emerged the first inkling of my personal myth.[34]

In mythic terms, the center, symbolically portrayed, is the treasure that the hero discovers in the depths. The discovery of the Self is the "ultimate boon," variously symbolized as the attainment of everlasting life, the discovery of the fountain of youth, the drinking of ambrosia or the elixir of life, the attainment of the Golden Fleece, the discovery of the Holy Grail, or the alchemical creation of the Philosopher's Stone. The Self is the eternal, universal human, described by Jung as the archetype of the "God-image" within each of us. To discover the Self might thus be construed as realizing the divine will within.

On the path of the mystic, by attaining this ultimate boon death itself is transcended. For it was the promise of Jesus that the person who can realize the Christ within, realize the Kingdom of Heaven, will not taste death.[35] Such a person will be in touch with the eternal wellspring of life that never dies and will thus have transcended the limits of personal identity. He or she will have tasted the *ambrosia* of the gods, accessed the eternal as it manifests in the realm of space and time. Similarly, the Holy Grail, to call upon another of Joseph Campbell's favorite symbols, is to be attained only by the person who has lived his or her own life, not followed the way of another. It is the culmination and the fruit of individuation, the realization of one's unique individual selfhood, one's unique life destiny.

CHAPTER 9

The Return Journey: The World Transformed

*Every culture-hero has achieved a synthesis between
consciousness and the creative unconscious. He has found
within himself the fruitful center, the point of renewal and rebirth
. . . upon which the continued existence of the world depends.*
—Erich Neumann

Thus far, we have explored the first two phases, those of separation and transformation. The third phase is that of return. Having broken away from society, turned within, descended into the underworld of the psyche, passed through a transformative initiation, and won through to a victory over the unconscious, the hero then has to return to the daylight world with the boon that was retrieved from the depths. He or she has to teach what has been learned, to share the insights from the experience. Psychologically, during this phase one is charged with the challenge of incorporating the energy released from the unconscious into the fabric of one's life. One must learn to express it, to use it in service of the Self.

The Path of the Return

Many of the themes introduced in the stage of departure and separation are present throughout the hero's adventure. Typically, however, the motif of return does not receive as much emphasis in books and films as the other stages of the hero's adventure. Often there is some kind of decisive victory and then, in an instant, the hero and his or her entourage are shown back in the homeland, basking in glory and content in the arms of a beloved; the deed and the adventure are done; order is restored; the world is renewed. The return is not typically explored in any great depth. Yet, as we will see, it is a crucial phase of the adventure, with its own peculiar challenges and demands.

One form of the return phase is the *magic flight*, portrayed as the hero taking flight from pursuers and guardians of the treasure. This motif refers particularly to a situation in which there has been a *boon theft*, as Campbell terms it, such as Prometheus stealing fire from the gods or Jason stealing the magical Golden Fleece. Understood psychologically, the theft suggests there has been a violation of nature by human consciousness. Nature has been robbed of its powers, its secrets, which provokes a violent counterbalancing reaction on the part of the unconscious.

Jung said that individuation involves a "violation of the merely natural man."[1] For nature to be realized as spirit by human consciousness, the natural instinctual mode of being has to be violated. The development of ego-consciousness entails a loss of natural innocence; the unconscious wholeness of the psyche is destroyed. Individuation, we noted, is a running against nature even as it is, paradoxically, a natural process. The magic flight in myth suggests the reaction of the powers of nature to this violation.

These reflections are perhaps also relevant to our current collective situation. For on the evolutionary journey that has brought forth the development of human consciousness and civilization, perhaps we are now ourselves suffering something of the fate of a Prometheus. Having wrested powers from nature with the might of science and technological innovation, and having stepped beyond the containing matrix of Christianity and forsaken the metaphysical and psychological security this provided, it seems that we are now being forced to face, or take flight from, the reactive powers of nature, and the unconscious. Have we flown too high, like Icarus? Have we become too distant from the Earth, from nature, from our instinctual foundations? Are we facing a catastrophic *enantiodromia*? The symptoms we see all around us—the ecological crisis, the mass extinction of species, global terrorism, the global financial crisis, and much more—suggest such an interpretation is not to be readily discounted.

Another theme of the return phase, an alternative to the magic flight, is that of *rescue from without*. The hero is liberated, brought back to the daylight world, through some kind of external intervention rather than through an act of will. The return is not initiated by taking flight from avenging forces within; rather, it is enforced from the outside. Often, it is the practical necessities of living—the need to earn money, have a place to live, and care for your family, for example—that pulls your attention away from the inner life, back from the underworld, into the daylight world. When the time is right, these external pressures can serve an invaluable function in helping to restore a balance to life after a period of inner reorientation. They can force you to get back to a more extraverted, normal way of living, turning away from the fantastic inner world of mythic images, intense emotions, and high drama, which naturally has a powerful hypnotic allure. Ultimately, the rescue does not happen just once but many times, as one moves through an alternating pattern of engaging the unconscious and activity in the world.

Crossing the Return Threshold

To leave behind this amazing, if traumatic, adventure and return to the often humdrum, mundane reality of everyday life is the challenge of the crossing of the return threshold. Eventually the hero returns from the adventure or initiation: Jonah is spewed forth by the whale; Odysseus arrives home after his long voyage; Frodo and Sam go back to the Shire; Jesus returns to the Father; the Buddha returns to the world after his enlightenment to help others achieve liberation; Ofelia is reunited with her spiritual family after many lifetimes of separation; Dorothy wills herself back to the farm in Kansas ("there's no place like home").

"The first problem of the returning hero," according to Campbell, "is to accept as real, after an experience of the soul-satisfying vision of fulfilment, the passing joys and sorrows, banalities and noisy obscenities of life. Why re-enter such a world?"[2] The challenge is to repeatedly release one's hold on the blissful attainment that one has found and commit oneself to the everyday reality of the world.

During a period of convalescence following an accident in his later life, night after night in hospital Jung experienced a series of fantastic cosmological visions through which he gained deep insight into the nature of reality and the meaning of his own existence. But when morning came the visions passed, and much to his disappointment he was amidst the all-too-ordinary world, recovering in a hospital bed. In the sobering light of day, he was left to contemplate a reality that, in comparison to his fantastic nighttime experiences, now seemed to him two-dimensional, flat, banal, and lifeless, like a cardboard cut-out model. How could he ever again take this world as real and commit himself to life?

This dilemma is similar to the challenge facing the returning hero after a sojourn in the underworld or in the cosmic heights of spiritual realization, during the pulsating excitement and intensity of the hero's adventure. It is similar, too, to the situation facing soldiers returning from war. As Campbell stressed, war, for all its horrors, gives an intensity to life that is not usually present. It is a "terrible beauty," as Yeats put it, bringing to end the "casual comedy" of peacetime existence.[3] The soldier at war feels truly alive, because life at war is lived on the edge of death. In these extreme conditions, everything becomes precious, every moment experienced intensely, every small pleasure savored. Pierre Teilhard de Chardin gave a similar analysis. He realized from his own experience serving on the front line in the First World War that the soldiers in trenches were able to tap into a zest for life, as he called it; they were able to draw forth more of their power, and experience a greater intensity of feeling. Suddenly, energies that are not normally available to us are, in times of war, vividly present, and one gets a sense of how life could be experienced if these energies were also accessible in ordinary life. "Build your houses on the slopes of Vesuvius," Nietzsche instructed, for that way danger would be ever-present and stir within one a sharpened sense of being alive.[4] One would live in the face of death, not run or hide from it behind the superficial comforts and numbing delusions of worldly life. In *The Power of Myth*, Campbell tells the story of Native American Indians riding off into battle saying to each other "what a wonderful day to die!"[5] What a contrast, he observed, from how we are conditioned to respond to the prospect of death. There is no sense in the Indian warriors of holding back in fearful self-protection. There is a total pouring forth of one's energy and attention into the deed ahead. It is an act of total life affirmation in the face of death.

The crux of the crossing of the return threshold, then, is the challenge of leaving behind a more intense, intoxicating, enchanted mode of experience to return to the often mundane reality of the everyday world. In his or her dealings with the everyday world, the hero acquires, often through painful experience, a sense of detachment even from the most powerful and profound states of consciousness. The returning hero naturally wishes to cling to the excitement and adventure, to know only spiritual uplift and the life of great and important deeds. But the wholeness of the psyche demands an embrace of the littleness and pettiness of life too. Again, one is not just a hero; one is other things besides: a husband or wife, a father or mother, a son or daughter, with a profession, with personal commitments and ambitions, and so forth. The return to the ordinary world can have a crushing effect on the ego, serving to annihilate further the individual self-will and any false sense of egoic identity. If one comes back from the marvelous adventure of self-discovery and self-overcoming with any psychological inflation, any exalted sense of one's own worth, this must be abandoned. One needs a pragmatic, matter-of-fact attitude. Any delusory sense that one is in some way spiritually superior is punctured by living in the everyday world, amidst the orthodox community. The mystic has to undergo a full psychospiritual death, which means dying to any sense that he or she might be special. "Knowledge puffeth up" according to an ancient alchemical dictum; psychological inflation can result from a depth encounter with the unconscious. Ultimately, however, individuation leads one, as Jung put it, towards a more or less realistic view of the world. All false images and illusions about one's life are to be shed; all forms of unconscious identification with the archetypes are to be recognized and overcome. The realization of the Self lies beyond one's psychological attachment to all such images.

The crossing of the return threshold is the counterpart to the crossing of the first threshold. The latter marks the decisive point of entrance into the underworld, the movement of consciousness away from the daylight world, away from extraverted activity, to the inner world and the depths of the unconscious. During the return crossing, the ego, even as it continues to undergo profound transformation through a dialectical encounter with the unconscious, has to direct its will and its attention to tasks at hand in the world.

Communication: Sharing the Boon

A further challenge facing the hero during the return journey, according to Campbell, and one that is especially relevant to creative mythology, is that of communicating the discovered truth to the wider community by finding a way to make it relevant to the established knowledge and consensus reality of the place and period in history. The boon, gold, the treasure—that which is brought back out of the depths—can sometimes, Campbell warns, just turn to ashes if the culture is not ready to receive the message. The messenger might be subject to quizzical stares, meaningful smiles, or even ridicule and persecution. One need look no further than Jesus's persecution by the Roman State, or Copernicus and Freud, both ridiculed for their theories from certain quarters when first presented. In *The Gay Science* and *Thus Spoke Zarathustra*, Nietzsche's "the Madman," announcing the death of God in the marketplace, suffers the scorn of "the herd":

> They do not understand me: I am not the mouth for these ears.
>
> Perhaps I have lived too long in the mountains, listened too much to the trees and the streams: now I speak to them as to goatherds.
>
> Unmoved is my soul and bright as the mountains in the morning. But they think me cold and a mocker with fearful jokes.
>
> And now they look at me and laugh: And laughing, they still hate me. There is ice in their laughter.[6]

There can be a tragic ending to the grand adventure. The spirit of the times can react with cold ignorance against the man or woman attuned to the spirit of the depths.

One is charged at this stage, then, with the labor of communicating one's insights to the world, with finding a way to enable the world to hear and comprehend one's revealed truth. Communication requires a constant passing back and forth between the inner depths and the outer world. The return threshold-crossing does not mark the end of the ego's encounter with the unconscious; rather, there is an ongoing process of continual transformation and deepening insight into life. Indeed, individuation, Jung believed, never really reaches an endpoint. It is an ideal to be constantly strived for.

One of the main responsibilities of the return and communication phase is drawing on one's own insights and experiences to help others. Campbell placed high value on the Bodhisattva vow that, upon attaining enlightenment, the Bodhisattva chooses to forsake ultimate release from the sorrows of existence, to forsake *nirvana*, and returns to help others achieve their own spiritual liberation from the self-propagating cycle of births and deaths. It is the Bodhisattva's aim to help people find liberation from the pain and suffering of existence. One of Campbell's favorite expressions was "joyful participation in the sorrows of the world," which well conveys the Bodhisattva's attitude.[7]

Nietzsche and Jung, as we have seen, were both affected by what they saw as the increasing remoteness of Church teachings to the challenges of the life of the modern individual. Their own experiences took them far beyond the understanding of the spirit presented in orthodox Christianity. Both men were thus impelled to formulate their own life philosophies and myths, addressing their writing to an emerging stratum of individuals who were coming into contact with the transformative power and mystery of the unconscious psyche. In this way, their individual life experience took on a profound collective import.

Jung went to great lengths to communicate his own insights both to the wider scientifically informed community and to a Christian audience. Realizing that he no longer lived within the Christian myth, he devoted himself to the discovery and formulation of his own personal myth, centered on his model of individuation.[8] Yet he did not abandon Christianity, for he recognized its central place in the Western psyche, and the profound spiritual significance of its symbolism.

Indeed, although individuation is a solitary, individual path, this is not to say that it cannot take place within one of the established religious traditions. But if this is to happen, it is essential that the religious teachings be interpreted psychologically, in terms of their relevance for psychological transformation. The meaning of the symbols has to be "amplified" or elaborated anew so that the religious teachings remain vital and relevant. Such a renewal and expansion of meaning is exactly what Jung tried to do for Christianity through his explorations of the individuation process, Gnosticism, and the psychospiritual significance of alchemy. This was the primary labor of the communication phase of Jung's life journey.

One consequence of the individual's struggle to communicate his or her insights and experiences, then, can be just this kind of contribution to the evolution of the established traditions themselves. The case of Pierre Teilhard de Chardin illustrates the point. Teilhard remained with the Jesuit tradition of his upbringing even as he worked as a paleontologist and pioneering evolutionary theorist. Although many of his scientific and evolutionary theories contradicted orthodox religious teachings and were censored by the Jesuit authorities, Teilhard did not simply walk away from the Jesuit order, but tried to find a way to integrate his intellectual insights with his passionate faith in Christ and his Christian heritage. Teilhard realized, like Jung, that the problem arises when the teachings of a religion become rigid doctrine, no longer a source of ongoing revelation, and the spiritual message is lost. By neglecting to considering anew the meaning of its symbols, the religion ceases to grow and evolve. It is a peculiarity of our age that a tremendous religious syncretism is taking place. All the different religions are being exposed to ideas from other traditions and cultures, which is helping to revitalize them. The individual, bringing diverse insights together in search of his or her own life meaning and personal myth, is the vehicle for any such revitalization.

Hospitality to the Gods

Heroism in myth is to do with sacrifice; in psychological terms, one sacrifices the former egoic identity that a new, deeper identity might be born. The ultimate act of the heroic journey is the death and rebirth of the hero into a new life. Although fundamental to the process of individuation, the hero archetype is itself just one archetype among many in the psyche. It, too, must serve the center and totality of the psyche, the larger Self. The phase of heroic struggle during individuation does not continue indefinitely. Indeed, Jung makes the point that heroism overdone can become a cramp. Everything then becomes a titanic struggle, everything an adventure to be conquered, an obstacle to be overcome, a battle to be won.

While the principle of ego consciousness remains dominant, there is the grave danger of psychotic inflation through identification with the Self and with the creative power of the unconscious. Then, as Jung points out, Nietzsche's heroic *Übermensch* represents "the over-weening pride, the hybris, of individual consciousness."[9] To successfully relate to the powers of the unconscious, there must be a transformation from an attitude of heroic will and conquest to a reverent receptivity to the archetypal powers of the unconscious. "The psyche," Jungian analyst Roger Brooke observes,

> cannot unfold and realize itself to an egoic attitude of heroic mastery. For both Jung and Heidegger, Nietzsche stands at the pinnacle of egoic (Jung) or anthropocentric (Heidegger) life, and as such epitomizes nihilism. Thus the guiding metaphor of Jung's life and work . . . is not Faust (or Nietzsche) but Philemon, the humble hermit, who gave hospitality to the gods in our ungodly age.[10]

Brooke adds, quoting Heidegger, that "Man is not the lord of beings. Man is the shepherd of Being."[11] The ego, to draw upon the language of New Testament parable, is like a tenant preparing the house (of being) for the return of the owner (the Self). It is not itself the owner or master of the house.

This shift to an attitude of hospitality to the gods, of reverence rather than heroic struggle, is only fully possible after the tyrant-ogre part of the ego has been destroyed and the instincts subdued. The struggle usually comes first, later to be followed by a reverent acceptance in which the archetypes are invited into one's life; the gods, stripped of their power of archetypal compulsion, are free to dance across the field of being rather than bang against the walls of an isolated autocratic ego. This condition reflects a more relational, participatory engagement with the unconscious, one that is essential for individuation to unfold.

Campbell uses Nietzsche's image of "the cosmic dancer" to convey the idea of a person who is able to move backwards and forwards between the daylight world of consciousness and the inner depths of nature—the unconscious—and thus bridge the two. In the return phase of the hero's journey, one must become the "master of two worlds," the initiate who can dance lightly between the depths within and the sphere of action without, bridging consciousness and the unconscious. The ego, having been transformed, can thus serve as a vehicle for the expression of the Self in the world.

In terms of personal experience, as one enters more fully into this transformation the visceral intensity of desire subsides, to be replaced by a way of being that one might describe as earnest play, purposeful play. By this stage, to a large extent consciousness has come to terms with, or reconciled itself to, the instinctual power of nature. The instincts, now controlled and brought into relationship with consciousness, are made subservient to the Self; discharged of their excess of energy, they have their place within the individual's life but they no longer dominate and possess consciousness. The individual becomes an emissary of the divine in the world, giving expression to the creative power of the inner depths of nature.

Freedom and the Transcendence of Self-will

The final section of the journey Campbell calls the *freedom to live*. It is often supposed that the course of psychological development leads towards ever greater freedom. As individuation proceeds, however, your individual freedom, in one form, has to be given up. Your freedom, thereafter, depends on how you respond to the creative impulses emerging from your depths, which do not originate from your own conscious volition. "A creative person has little power over his own life," Jung notes: "He is not free. He is captive and driven by his daimon."[12] Individuation is the process by which you become reconciled to this loss of freedom. The part of you that desires to be free is made subservient to your wholeness, to the authority of the Self. You might come to realize, in fact, that there is no real freedom outside of the Self, outside of the Logos—the cosmic order that governs all things, or, in Christian terms, the Word and the Will of God.

The freedom implied here thus refers not to personal freedom, not to freedom at the level of the ego, but to a condition of psychological freedom in service to the Self. It marks a state of liberation from incapacitating psychological resistances, which thus permits a wholehearted affirmation of life as it is. Individuation also brings a freedom from the limiting influences of the external world. The more one is able to attune to one's own inner authority, the less one is adversely affected by external influences. The ways of living and the erroneous attitudes and opinions of the collective world fall away. Old, culturally conditioned life patterns fall away. And the mode of self that functioned within these collective patterns passes away too. One is free to be the person one always was *in potentia*. The effort to *be* someone, to adapt oneself to the demands of the collective, is no longer required. Indeed, the strain of trying to be someone, of trying to live in a certain way, is utterly destroyed. One's efforts henceforth are directed to the expression of one's creative daemon, and to the fulfillment of the life pattern of the Self. One has transcended socio-cultural patterns, and realized the freedom of one's inherent nature.

Such a freedom, however, is not a static endpoint or a state of unchanging peace, but a condition of dynamic tension between consciousness and the unconscious, a creative tension rooted in the Self. Jesus thus describes the Kingdom of Heaven as a "movement with a repose."[13] It is a condition of being able to experience the full power of life energy with equanimity and balance.

For Jung, we noted, the dynamic tension between ego-consciousness and the unconscious is never fully resolved, indeed it is a pre-condition, Jung believes, of self-conscious awareness. Campbell, influenced by the mystical philosophy of the East, is willing to go further than Jung in his assessment of the meaning of the endpoint of the hero's journey:

> The meaning is very clear; it is the meaning of all religious practice. The individual, through prolonged psychological disciplines, gives up completely all attachment to personal limitations, idiosyncrasies, hopes and fears, no longer resists the self-annihilation that is the prerequisite to rebirth in the realization of truth, and so becomes ripe, at last, for the great at-onement. His personal ambitions become totally dissolved, he no longer tries to live but willingly relaxes to whatever may come to pass in him: he becomes, that is to say, an anonymity. The Law lives in him with his unreserved consent.[14]

For Campbell, self-will is utterly extinguished, and the individual becomes a living embodiment of divine law. One might call to mind again here Yoda's instruction to Luke Skywalker in *The Return of the Jedi* in response to the aspiring Jedi's strained efforts at mastery. "Do or do not," Yoda declares. "There is no try." Personal will, trying, effort, are to be totally vanquished such that there remains just a spontaneous expression of the divine through the Self in the human being. We return, then, to the notion of creative play, and freedom from the ego's resistance to life as it actually is. Consciousness, stripped of self will, allows a playful response to life to emerge. The transformed human spirit, as Roberto Asssagioli notes, thus acquires "an acute, formidable power: it is capable of wuwei, action without action, which nothing can resist."[15]

The transformation taking place during psychospiritual death-rebirth comes a little at a time, first in glimpses, then for longer periods, as the old ego gradually undergoes a complete death—a painful, demoralizing and ultimately annihilating experience. In the final act, at the end of the transformative journey, the hero is to be sacrificed to the greater identity and wholeness of the psyche. That is to say, the ego experiences a final death, and the individual is reborn as the Self. The final phases of this ultimate ego death can only be experienced as a crushing obliteration of psychological resistance, which mystics refer to as the "dark night of the soul."[16] The dark night, Assagioli explains, is "a crucible in which all the human elements that still go to make it [the soul] up are melded together" characterized by "an inner state of suffering and privation" that can last for many years.[17] It is a "mysterious stage" of

> . . . "passive purification" in which the mystic's consciousness undergoes a new, more radical negative experience and in which the death of his old personality, or "Adam," actually takes place—a necessary condition for his resurrection in Christ. It is in this mystical death, I believe, that human suffering reaches its highest level: it is an inexpressible torment, a real conscious agony.[18]

The trials of dark night, however, are to be followed by the illumination and liberation of a new dawn, bringing a cessation of suffering and a "glorious spiritual resurrection."[19] Stripped of self-will, on the mystical path the spiritual hero enters into a condition of absolute unification with the spirit.

The individual is also reconciled to the world. In becoming oneself, in realizing the Self, the defensive separation from the world is healed. The individuation process is conceived by Jung as "a journey from the isolation and alienation of separate ego consciousness to binding indissoluble communion with the world at large."[20] Indeed, the fulfillment of the tasks and duties of one's own life adventure, the assumption of the great burden of the realization of the Self, might enable one, like the mythic Atlas, to take upon one's shoulders the weight of the destiny of the whole planet. Individuation thus brings the unique satisfaction that comes from influencing at a deep level the transformation of the historical-evolutionary unfolding of human civilization. To undertake one's own individuation is simultaneously to participate in the transformation of the entire planetary consciousness.

The effect of the successful adventure of the hero, Campbell suggests, is the reactivation and release of life energy. The hero taps into the wellsprings of life in the unconscious, overcomes deep-rooted psychological resistances, thereby releasing psychological energy that had been locked away in unconscious complexes. Libido that was bound up with compulsive desires or impulses is liberated, ultimately to be used by the ego in the service of the Self. In this way, the hero renews and rejuvenates the wasteland, serving as a vessel for the creative expression of spirit in the world.

The Re-enchantment of the World

At the anticipated end of the hero's spiritual journey, the heroic struggle subsides, having served its purpose. In psychological terms, the power locked up in instinct has been confronted, integrated, overcome; the latent power of one's destiny has been realized in actuality, in the events of life. The adventure thus draws to a close and the kingdom is unified, the life-resistant aspects of the psyche having been banished or transformed, and the destructive aspects accepted and affirmed, subsumed within the new wholeness. In *Star Wars*, upon his death the redeemed Darth Vader takes his place with Yoda and Ben Kenobi. Through the encounter with the dark side, the unity and wholeness of existence is recovered. The dark power, seemingly lost to the Jedi Order, is redeemed through the heroism of Luke Skywalker.

The experience of rebirth or resurrection is the fulfillment of the archetypal pattern of the hero. Through the completion of the death-rebirth process, ego-consciousness bows to the Great Reality that brought it forth, and the divine aspect of one's being is thus exalted. A surrender takes place, and with it, perhaps, a poignant homecoming of consciousness to the soul and to the world. Seen through the eyes of the soul, the world might be recognized and remembered as it once was, before it was tainted and obscured by the thousand-and-one things. To the triumphant spiritual hero, the enchanted world of childhood is known again: pristine, mysterious, familiar, thunderous, alive, wondrous, murmuring, promising, bubbling. An innocence, a simplicity, which once seemed gone and never to return, reveals itself anew, now wedded to learned wisdom, hard-earned self-knowledge, a concentrated consciousness, and resolute will. After the dark night of the soul, Assagioli explains, "the world itself is transformed," and the mystic "feels the powerful heartbeat of the supreme unity in all things and in all beings."[21]

For all the unavoidable suffering it entails, individuation brings with it the experience of deep life meaning that can sustain one through even the most arduous trials and tribulations. By accessing a flow of life energy unavailable to normal ego consciousness, one can attain a fullness, intensity, and depth to experience that are ordinarily lacking. Experiencing the full power of one's life passion, swept along by the excitement of one's life adventure, the way of individuation gives to life a perpetually unknown and emerging quality, restoring to experience a springtime freshness and uniqueness—a condition prophesied and promised in the words of Christ: "I will give you what no eye has seen, no ear has heard, and what no hand has touched, and what has not arisen in the heart of man."[22]

Campbell's description of the journey's fulfillment, borrowed from Grimm's fairytales, strikes a suitably poetic chord: "When the Prince of Eternity kissed the Princess of the World, her resistance was allayed: 'She opened her eyes, awoke, and looked at him in friendship. Together they came down the stairs, and the king awoke and the queen and the entire courtly estate, and all looked at each other with big eyes.'"[23] In this royal union lies the ideal consequence of the epic voyage of the hero through the wonderland of the unconscious: the mystic marriage of the opposites, the liberation of the slumbering spirit of nature, and the intersection of the eternal and the temporal in the *unio mystica*, which, according to Jung, is tantamount to a union of the individual with "the eternal Ground of all empirical being."[24] Here, in the Romantic vision of the fulfillment of the spiritual odyssey of the modern self, individuation approaches its final end of triumphant rejuvenation and the joyous affirmation of life. "Where spring-like joy and expectation reign," Jung observes, "spirit can embrace nature and nature spirit."[25]

Acknowledgments

Much of the material included in this book was originally based on a graduate course exploring the psychological significance of the mythic pattern of the hero's journey through the work of Joseph Campbell, which I taught at the California Institute of Integral Studies, San Francisco, in summer 2010. I wish to express my thanks to my students whose astute questions and comments helped to shape my approach to this project and to draw out specific aspects of the text you see before you. I am especially grateful to Chad Harris and Jessica Garfield-Kabbara for their assistance in the classroom and for providing me with audio recordings of the lectures. The book has also been enriched by my involvement in the Jungian and Archetypal Studies Specialization of the Depth Psychology Program at the Pacifica Graduate Institute, California.

I am grateful for the friendship and expertise of Tim Read and Mark Chaloner, whose vision and enterprise resulted in the formation of Muswell Hill Press in 2011 with the express aim of publishing a new collection of books in the field of transpersonal psychology. I am also indebted to David and Margaret Davies whose ongoing support made it possible for me to devote time to writing during late 2010 and 2011. Above all, I would like to express my gratitude to my wife, Kathryn, for encouraging me to put my ideas from the course into book form and for providing invaluable editorial assistance in the preparation of the manuscript for publication. I feel fortunate indeed that our lives and creative pursuits have unfolded together for so many years.

KLG
August 2012

Notes

Preface

1. *Jung, Face to Face Interview* (with John Freeman), BBC Television, October 22nd 1959. A transcription of this interview may be found in Jung, *C. G. Jung Speaking: Interviews and Encounters*, 380–393.

Chapter 1
Joseph Campbell and the Place of Myth in Modern Culture

1. For information on Campbell's life and work, I refer you to the excellent biography *A Fire in the Mind: The Life of Joseph Campbell* by Stephen Larsen and Robin Larsen. See also Campbell, *The Hero's Journey: Joseph Campbell on His Life and Work*; and Campbell, *Reflections on the Art of Living: A Joseph Campbell Companion.*
2. For treatments of the different approaches to myth and definitions of myth, see Dundes, *Sacred Narrative* and Segal, *Myth: A Very Short Introduction.*
3. Campbell, *Creative Mythology*, 5.
4. Campbell, *Hero with a Thousand Faces*, 1–2.
5. A number of these points are discussed in William Bascom's essay "The Forms of Folklore: Prose Narratives," in Dundes, *Sacred Narrative*, 5–29.
6. Campbell, *Creative Mythology*, 6.
7. Jung, *Memories, Dreams, Reflections*, 373.
8. In the late nineteenth and early twentieth centuries, many scholars subscribed to the Enlightenment view of myth. Bethe, writing in 1904, described myth as "primitive philosophy," serving an explanatory function; Gomme, in 1908, decreed myth to be a primitive form of explanation; Janet Bacon reiterated that myth

has an explanatory function; and, most notably, James G. Frazer declared that myths are "mistaken explanations of phenomena." See Bascom "Forms of Folklore," in Dundes, *Sacred Narrative*, 23–28.

9. Mann, "Freud and the Future," 371.

10. The terms *total demythologization* and *partial demythologization* are employed by Lauri Honko in "The Problem of Defining Myth" in Dundes, *Sacred Narrative*, 42–43.

11. Campbell, *Hero with a Thousand Faces*, 2.

12. Murray, *Myth and Mythmaking*, 22.

13. Campbell, *Creative Mythology*, 4.

14. Campbell, *Mythic Dimension*, 220.

15. Campbell, *Mythic Dimension*, 220.

16. Blake, "Auguries of Innocence."

17. Campbell, *Creative Mythology*, 4.

18. For an exploration of the cosmological dimensions of myth and archetypal psychology, see Le Grice, *Archetypal Cosmos*.

19. Campbell, *Creative Mythology*, 4–5.

20. See Campbell, *Flight of the Wild Gander*, 55.

21. Campbell, *Occidental Mythology*, 521.

22. While the Christian church maintains that the Bible is the revealed Word of God, the emergence of science meant that many details in the Bible presented as—or assumed to be—historical fact were shown to be false. Campbell used science to take issue with the literalism of orthodox Christianity. He quipped, as did Jung, that space explorers had failed to discover Heaven in the sky, nor was there any evidence yet that it was possible to be conceived of a virgin. The literalism of orthodox Christianity obviously put it at odds with the emerging science in the modern era. The more science gained in strength, the more an increasingly scientifically aware population started to doubt the claims of religion. Faith (coming from the Judeo-Christian stream of Western culture) and reason (from the other, Greco-Roman stream) were at odds with each other, and reason was to win out—at least in the academic and scientific strata of the population. People were asked to believe in things that they knew intellectually could not be true creating ever greater dissonance in the modern psyche.

23. Contemporary spirituality, as I see it, refers to the phenomenon of individuals seeking their own spiritual experiences rather than following a religious doctrine or a set of beliefs based on other people's spiritual experiences, which took place hundreds or thousands of years ago. In this sense, spirituality is coming to replace orthodox religion for many people. Myth, in the way that Campbell understood it, is part of the new era of spirituality, part of the quest for deeper meaning and an individual spiritual path. The disintegration of the religious traditions in the West has forced people to go in search of their own spiritual experiences, which obviously would not have happened if these people could have remained happily within the context of orthodox Christianity.

24. Jung interviewed by John Freeman, *Face to Face Interview* (BBC television, October 22nd 1959) reproduced in *C. G. Jung Speaking*, 383. See also Jung's letter to *The Listener* (January 21st 1960), replying to comments made after the airing of his interview, in which he responds to and clarifies the meaning of his attitude to belief in God. http://uncertaintist.files.wordpress. com/2012/04/jung-on-god.pdf (accessed July 23rd 2012).

Chapter 2
Mythology: East and West

1. Campbell, *Occidental Mythology*, 7.
2. Campbell, *Occidental Mythology*, 3.
3. Campbell uses this term in *The Power of Myth* interviews with Bill Moyers and throughout his work.
4. A focus on individual emancipation from karma and the cycle of death-rebirth is evident in Buddhism, of course. However, this path does not entail the realization of the individual personality as in the West.
5. See Campbell, *Creative Mythology*, 33, 79.
6. Campbell, *Occidental Mythology*, 24.
7. Campbell, *Occidental Mythology*, 24.
8. Many of these inconsistencies are highlighted by Robert Segal in *Joseph Campbell: An Introduction*.
9. Campbell distinguishes between the biblical myth of the Fall and the Persian myth of the Fall as set forward in Zoroastrianism.

In the former, Campbell points out, evil proceeds from within human nature—the Fall results from an act of human disobedience. In the latter, evil is a cosmic principle that is antecedent to the Fall and any human involvement. "The biblical view, placing the Fall within the frame of human history as an offense against its god, cuts out the wider reach of a challenge to the character of that god, denigrates the character of man, and fosters, furthermore, an increasingly untenable insistence on the historicity of its myth" (*Occidental Mythology*, 208).

10. Campbell, *Creative Mythology*, 393.
11. "According to our Holy Bible," Campbell observed, "God and his world are not to be identified with each other. God, as Creator, made the world, but is not in any sense the world itself or any object in it. . . . There can therefore be no question, in either Jewish, Christian, or Islamic orthodoxy, of seeking God and finding God either in the world or in oneself" (*Occidental Mythology*, 108).
12. Campbell, *Creative Mythology*, 394.
13. Campbell points out that the central features of the biblical description of the events taking place in Eden are variations on themes found in primitive mythology, but in these, earlier instances, there is no equivalent to the Fall into sin. See Campbell, *Occidental Mythology*, 105.
14. Campbell and Moyers, *Power of Myth*, 66.
15. Campbell and Moyers, *Power of Myth*, 29.
16. Campbell, *Occidental Mythology*, 258.
17. Cited in Cornford, *From Religion to Philosophy*, 127.
18. For Tarnas's discussion of disenchantment, see *Cosmos and Psyche*, 16–25.
19. Cornford, *From Religion to Philosophy*, 255–261. A countertrend or complement to this development, which emerged out of the Greek tradition, was described by Campbell as "a shift of loyalty from the impersonal to the personal," a shift that placed increasing emphasis on the values of human individuals rather than impersonal cycles of nature or group values. In Campbell's view, this development was "comparable to an evolutionary psychological mutation." See Campbell, *Occidental Mythology*, 236.

20. Eliade, *Sacred and the Profane*, 110.
21. According to Eliade: "For religious man of the archaic cultures, the world is renewed annually; in other words with each new year it recovers its original sanctity" (*Sacred and the Profane*, 75).
22. Eliade defines the eternal return as "the eternal repetition of the fundamental rhythm of the cosmos" (*Sacred and the Profane*, 108).
23. "The Ten Commandments," Exodus 20:3 and 20:4, *The Holy Bible: New International Version*.
24. Eliade, *Cosmos and History*, 102–103.
25. Jung, *Memories, Dreams, Reflections*, 284.
26. The contrast between hero myths in the West and the East is instructive. In Japanese mythology, for example, the heroic adventure, if there is one, ultimately leads nowhere; Japanese myths are pervaded with a sense of unreality, as if, within the narrative, nothing significant had happened at all. The Western insistence upon meaning or moral purpose is not evident in many Eastern myths. From an Eastern perspective, the Western belief that everything matters, the affirmation of the reality and value of history, and the insistence that the individual life is of the utmost importance is relativized by the insight that the separate individual does not really exist in any substantial form and, indeed, that the historical process is something of an illusion. Contemplating both traditions might yield an awareness of a greater wholeness within which both perspectives have their place. Western heroic individualism might be balanced by the Eastern recognition of emptiness; just as the Western affirmation of the reality of the world and corporeal existence might be balanced by the Eastern recognition of reality as illusion. Meaning and meaninglessness, reality and unreality, existence and non-existence might each themselves be realized as complementary poles within a wholeness embracing all opposites, and beyond all such categorizations.

    I am grateful to Hiroko Shiota for drawing my attention to Japanese myths through the work of Jungian scholar Hayao Kawai.
27. Barrett, *Irrational Man*, 205.
28. Tarnas, *Passion of the Western Mind*, 439.

29. Plato, *Apology*, 38a.
30. Freud, *New Introductory Lectures on Psycho-Analysis*, 100.
31. Tarnas, *Passion of the Western Mind*, 280.
32. Jung, "Spiritual Problem of Modern Man" in *Civilization in Transition*, 75.

Chapter 3
The Death of God and the Übermensch

1. Jung, *Psychology and Religion,* 102.
2. Eliade, *Sacred and the Profane*, 202.
3. Weber, "Science as a Vocation," in *From Max Weber*, 154.
4. Jung, "Analytical Psychology and the *Weltanschauung*," in *Structure and Dynamics of the Psyche*, 380. As Richard Tarnas argues in *The Passion of The Western Mind*, Nietzsche embodied and expressed in his life and work the full implications of the withdrawal of all meaning from the world and from any hypothesized transcendent realm. Nietzsche's radical nihilism, Tarnas suggests, emerges from the full realization of the implications of the Copernican and Darwinian revolutions in science, and of the Cartesian and Kantian ontological and epistemological distinctions between the human self and the world. Nietzsche felt charged to complete the Enlightenment project of the emancipation of the modern individual self from the shackles of past dogma and false beliefs. To achieve this end, one final obstacle remained: to destroy the belief in God and with it the basis of an outmoded Christian morality—a challenge that until then had been inconceivable.

   Nietzsche's pronouncement that "God is dead" reflected and anticipated an emerging skepticism in the wider culture about the relationship between human beings and a transcendent divine, a relationship that had for centuries provided a reassuring metaphysical support for human life. Confronting this new reality, Nietzsche stared into the existential abyss that the collapse of all metaphysical and cosmological meaning had exposed, and, transferring the locus of all meaning to within the human self, discovered, in the depth of his own darkness, the life-affirming vision of the *Übermensch*. For further analysis of the cosmological and metaphysical implications of Nietzsche's proclamation of the "death of God," see Joseph Kearns, "The Shape of Nihilism: A Cosmological Exegesis of Nietzsche's 'The Madman'."

5. See Nietzsche, "On the Genealogy of Morals," in *Basic Writings of Nietzsche*.

6. Solomon and Higgins, *Short History of Philosophy*, 234.

7. Campbell, too, was post-Christian, informed by Nietzsche's proclamation of the "death of God." In Campbell's hands, though, Nietzsche's radical anti-morality is not so extreme, yet he follows Nietzsche in a commitment to aspire for excellence and to a fullness of being. Although Nietzsche's fierce antagonism to Christianity had resonances with Campbell's own experience, Campbell was able to see Nietzsche's ideas from within the larger perspective afforded him by his study of Eastern religion and philosophy, which maintain that good and evil are not absolute ethical categories but complementary opposites. With this in mind, and also following the Greek philosopher Heraclitus, Campbell emphasized that all acts have both good and evil consequences. The best we can do, he advised, is to lean toward the good. Ultimately, spiritual realization takes us beyond all opposites, including good and evil. See Campbell and Moyers, *Power of Myth*.

8. See Nietzsche, "The Case of Wagner," in *Basic Writings of Nietzsche*, 619–620.

9. Nietzsche experienced extremes of suffering himself, both psychological and physical, and yet his will was driving him on relentlessly through the suffering, and deeper into it. One can imagine how that would have translated into a life philosophy—indeed, it perhaps helps to account for his more vehement assertions and the sometimes polemical tone of his writing.

10. Nietzsche, *Thus Spoke Zarathustra*, 43.

11. Nietzsche, *Thus Spoke Zarathustra*, 104.

12. Nietzsche, *Thus Spoke Zarathustra*, 42.

13. See Jung, *Alchemical Studies*, Book IV.

14. Nietzsche, *Thus Spoke Zarathustra*, trans. Thomas Common (cited in Campbell, *Occidental Mythology*). For a variant form of this expression, see Hollingdale's translation of *Thus Spoke Zarathustra*, 71.

15. See Jung, *Two Essays on Analytical Psychology*, 155.

16. Jung, "Spiritual Problem of Modern Man." In *Civilization in Transition*, 196–197.

17. Ross, *Gospel of Thomas*, logion 108, 65.
18. Campbell makes this point in the *Power of Myth* interview with Bill Moyers.
19. Ross, *Gospel of Thomas*, logion 77, 53.
20. In the 1980s and 1990s, an eclectic range of individual forms of spirituality emerged. A "spiritual revolution" of sorts was taking place as more and more people were leaving behind the established religions in search of new sources of meaning and spiritual sustenance (See Hanegraaff, *New Age Religion and Western Culture*; Heelas and Woodhead, *Spiritual Revolution*; and Tacey, *Spirituality Revolution*). Campbell was a key figure in this development, communicating the insights of mythology, Eastern thought, and Jungian psychology to a large audience. In 1987 Campbell's PBS interviews with Bill Moyers were recorded at George Lucas's Skywalker Ranch and the Museum of Natural History in New York, divided into six one-hour episodes. The broadcast of these interviews brought Campbell international posthumous acclaim. As is well known, Campbell's ideas were also conveyed to a global audience through Lucas's rendering of the motifs and stages of the hero myth through the *Star Wars* films, some of which are explored later in this book. Campbell's *The Hero with a Thousand Faces* was also especially influential on Hollywood screenwriter Christopher Vogler's *The Writer's Journey: Mythic Structures for Writers*.
21. A variation on a point Campbell makes in *Inner Reaches of Outer Space*, 39.

Chapter 4
Creative Mythology and Individuation

1. Campbell, *Creative Mythology*, 4.
2. Campbell, *Creative Mythology*, 3–4.
3. Campbell, *Creative Mythology*, 3.
4. Jung, *Spirit in Man, Art and Literature*, 89–90.
5. Jung, *Spirit in Man, Art and Literature*, 89–90.
6. Jung, *Spirit in Man, Art and Literature*, 90.
7. See Campbell, *Flight of the Wild Gander*, 36.
8. Mann, "Freud and the Future," in Murray, *Myth and Mythmaking*.

9. There was a powerful aesthetic influence on Campbell during his stay in Paris in the 1920s. At that time, the French capital was the hotbed of culture, particular of modern art. The painting of the first decades of the twentieth century was a high period in the art world, blessed with a number of towering geniuses: Picasso, Matisse, Cezanne, Klee, Kandinsky, Rouault, and many others. This period saw the bursting forth of many new movements: Cubism, Fauvism, Dadaism, Surrealism, and Primitivism, each going far beyond conventional forms of representation. In Paris, then, for Campbell to see firsthand, were artists as mythmakers, giving form to their own experiences and visions of the world, communicating to others through the medium of their art, breaking away from tradition, finding and developing their own styles. These qualities Campbell later described as fundamental to creative mythology.

10. Boeck and Sabartes, *Pablo Picasso*, 269.

11. A similar process is described in the symbolism of alchemy, which provided Jung with a source of external corroboration of his own model of individuation. According to Jung, alchemy symbolically portrays a movement through the following stages: (1) the *unio naturalis*, the condition of an original unconscious wholeness; (2) the *unio mentalis*, which involves a separation of rational consciousness from the passions and bodily sphere of the instincts; (3) the reconnection of the separated *unio mentalis* with the body; and (4) the *unio mystica* or *mysterium coniunctionis*, which is tantamount, Jung believed, to a reunion of consciousness with the empirical ground of all being. For Jung's treatment of this topic, see especially *Mysterium Coniunctionis*.

12. The immediate personal circumstances of Campbell's life as he was growing up were shaped by Roman Catholicism, against which he later struggled to emancipate himself, much in the manner of Stephen Dedalus, the hero of James Joyce's *A Portrait of the Artist as a Young Man*, which Campbell valued so highly as a guide to the challenge we each might face to win through to our spiritual autonomy. Reading Campbell now, it is apparent that he retained an ambivalence towards organized Christian religion throughout his life—a legacy of his own early struggles, no doubt. Yet in this experience we can see the seeds of Campbell's belief in the necessity for each individual

to embark on his or her own path, leaving behind the old traditions, the old religions, in search of authentic individual experience. Cultivating an aesthetic sensibility is one way this can be done; building one's life orientation around one's own spiritual insights and experiences is another.

13. Campbell, *Creative Mythology*, 85–86.

14. Nietzsche, *Thus Spoke Zarathustra*, 55.

15. Nietzsche, *Thus Spoke Zarathustra*, 55.

16. For conceptual clarity, here and throughout I am using the term *Self* (beginning with a capital letter) to differentiate Jung's concept of the center and wholeness of the total psyche from the ordinary usage of the term *self* (beginning with a lowercase letter) to mean individual personhood. The English translations of Jung's *Collected Works* and *Memories, Dreams, Reflections* do not follow this practice.

17. Aphorism attributed to Pablo Picasso. For a variation on this quote see Penrose, *Picasso: His Life and Work*, 307.

18. Lee, *Bruce Lee: Artist of Life*, 18.

19. Lee, *Bruce Lee: Artist of Life*, 194.

20. Myth is not *exclusively* psychological for Campbell, but it is *primarily* psychological. For Campbell, however, the psychological interpretation of myth is often rooted in human biology: the gods, he said, represent the energies of the body, personifications of desire systems that are in conflict with each other. One of the critiques that could be leveled at Campbell, therefore, is that of biological reductionism in that, following Freud, he sometimes appears to reduce the gods and goddesses to nothing but symbols of biological-instinctual energies. And, following Jung, Campbell could also be accused of psychologism, reducing myth and religion to nothing but psychology. But these critiques must be balanced against the pervasive spirituality inherent in Campbell's work; his books and lectures are suffused with spiritual insights; he is a champion of spiritual experience. Recalling the first function of myth, Campbell would say that myth has a metaphysical import, although, like Freud and Jung, Campbell was working within a world view that construed the psyche as radically separate from the cosmos and categorically different to matter. His tacit epistemological framework, like that of Freud and Jung, was Kantian.

21. Campbell, *Hero with a Thousand Faces*, 2.
22. Jung, *Archetypes and the Collective Unconscious*, 35.
23. Jung, *Two Essays on Analytical Psychology*, 158.
24. In his later work (such as *The Power of Myth* and *The Way of Myth*), Campbell focuses less on the processes of inner psychological transformation than he did in *The Hero with a Thousand Faces*, and champions the hero myth in a more general sense. Not only, in these later works, is the hero myth the model for inner, mystical transformation, but for any life authentically lived.
25. See Swimme, *Hidden Heart of the Cosmos*, 85–86.
26. Another figure who went through this kind of experience was Brother Klaus (also known as Brother Nicholas of Flue) who, as Jung describes, stared into the dark face of the divine but was able to emerge from this experience intact due to his firm grounding in Christian religious dogma. See Jung *Archetypes and the Collective Unconscious*, 11.
27. See Hollingdale's introduction to *Thus Spoke Zarathustra*, 28–29.
28. Jung, *Archetypes and the Collective Unconscious*, 172.
29. Edinger, *Ego and Archetype*, 131.
30. Jung, *Memories, Dreams, Reflections*, 49.

Chapter 5
The Hero's Adventure: Call and Refusal

1. Campbell, *Hero with a Thousand Faces*, 104.
2. Campbell, *Creative Mythology*, 378.
3. Hegel, *Introduction to the Philosophy of History*, 33.
4. Eliot, *Selected Poems*, 64.
5. Campbell, *Hero with a Thousand Faces*, 211.
6. In an article for the BBC website, Krystina Nellis points out that, in 2012, for the first time, three of the year's top ten films have a female protagonist: *The Hunger Games, Snow White and the Huntsman,* and Disney's *Brave.* Dan Jolin of *Empire* magazine suggests this might reflect a gradual trend redressing the balance in favor of casting women in the role of hero, going some way to rectifying the longstanding bias towards depicting heroes as male. See Nellis, "Hollywood Heroines: Here to Stay?"

7. Jung, *Symbols of Transformation*, 186.

8. Estes, *Women Who Run with the Wolves*, 2.

9. Campbell, *Hero with a Thousand Faces*, 12.

10. Campbell, *Hero with a Thousand Faces*, 12.

11. Campbell (with Bill Moyers), *Power of Myth* interview.

12. Nietzsche, *Ecce Homo*, section 5, in *Basic Writings of Nietzsche*, 786.

13. For Jung, the term *libido* means psychological energy, life energy. For Freud, it is defined more narrowly as sexual energy.

14. Jung, *Mysterium Coniunctionis*, 546.

15. Campbell, *Hero with a Thousand Faces*, 42–43.

16. Campbell, *Hero with a Thousand Faces*, 42–43.

17. Campbell, *Hero with a Thousand Faces*, 43.

18. Dante, *Divine Comedy*, 47.

19. Cited in Assagioli, *Transpersonal Development*, 145.

20. Cited in Assagioli, *Transpersonal Development*, 146.

21. Cited in Assagioli, *Transpersonal Development*, 146.

22. Assagioli, *Transpersonal Development*, 147.

23. Assagioli, *Transpersonal Development*, 147.

24. Tolkien, *Lord of the Rings*, 75 (three preceding quotes).

25. Tolkien, *Lord of the Rings*, 76.

26. Tolkien, *Lord of the Rings*, 77.

27. Homer, *Odyssey*, 9.

28. See Campbell, *Power of Myth*, 158.

29. Jung explores the phenomenon of synchronicity in "Synchronicity: An Acausal Connecting Principle," in *The Structure and Dynamics of the Psyche*, 417–518.

30. On an inward level, Jung felt the presence of a greater destiny in his life from a very early age. Through a number of powerful childhood dreams and visions he was called to an encounter with the "spirit of the depths." See Le Grice, "The Dark Spirit in Nature: C. G. Jung and the Spiritual Transformation of Our Time."

31. Jung, *Memories, Dreams, Reflections*, 130.

32. Campbell turned his back on a traditional academic career at this point, preferring the freedom of the life of an independent thinker to that of the academic scholar with its "publish or perish" mentality. He believed that embarking on a Ph.D. program just at the point in life when the world of ideas is opening up could be damaging, stifling creative impulses, forcing the

individual into an academic straightjacket. Consequently, even though he was later to take up a position as professor at Sarah Lawrence college in New York State, Campbell's life philosophy was somewhat anti-intellectual. Indeed, his admiration for the straight-talking sportsman contrasted with his contempt for the over-educated, over-deliberating scholar, lacking conviction and authority, lacking his or her own voice. See, for example, Campbell, *Way of Myth*, 86.

33. Campbell himself confessed to not really having a spiritual path to speak of. He recounts an amusing discussion with Alan Watts on this matter. Impressed by the wide-ranging spiritual insights that continually poured forth from Campbell, Watts inquired just what Campbell's form of "yoga" was—what was the spiritual practice that led him to these profound insights? Much to Watts's astonishment, Campbell's said that his yoga was nothing other than underlining sentences! He simply read one book after another, making notes, and reflecting deeply on the material he studied. See, for example, Campbell, *Way of Myth*, 82. This episode is also recounted in *The Power of Myth* interviews with Bill Moyers.

Although Campbell did experience some psychological difficulties during his five-year retreat from the world in the late 1920s and early 1930s, he did not have a psychological break like Nietzsche's or like Jung's confrontation with the unconscious. Yet Campbell clearly had a profound grasp of the same terrain explored by Nietzsche and Jung. He was able to draw on the insights of Nietzsche, Freud, and especially Jung, apply depth psychological ideas to the mythological history of the world, and relate it in a very direct way to the personal problems and challenges of contemporary life.

34. See Hillman, *The Soul's Code: In Search of Character and Vocation.*

35. Jung, "Men, Women and God." In *C. G. Jung Speaking: Interviews and Encounters*, 242.

36. Jung, *Psychology and Religion: West and East*, par. 391. Campbell also takes up this theme in *Creative Mythology*, the fourth volume of *The Masks of God* series, in his exploration of the understanding of the nature of fate within different traditions.

37. Commenting on Goethe, Nietzsche writes: "A spirit thus eman-cipated stands in the midst of the universe with a joyful and trusting fatalism, in the faith that only what is separate and individual may be rejected, that in the totality everything is redeemed and affirmed—he no longer denies" (*Twilight of the Idols*, 114).
38. Campbell, *Hero with a Thousand Faces*, 49.
39. Campbell, *Hero with a Thousand Faces*, 49.
40. See Campbell, *Way of Myth*, 9, 146–147.
41. Ross, *Gospel of Thomas*, logion 16, 19.
42. Ross, *Gospel of Thomas*, logion 16, 19.
43. Nietzsche, *Thus Spoke Zarathustra*, 86.
44. Campbell, *Hero with a Thousand Faces*, 53.
45. Campbell, *Hero with a Thousand Faces*, 53.
46. Campbell, *Hero with a Thousand Faces*, 196.
47. Nietzsche, *Thus Spoke Zarathustra*, 77.
48. Ross, *Gospel of Thomas* (logion 35), 30.
49. A comment made by Campbell in *Reflections on the Art of Living*.
50. Lambdin (translator), *Gospel of Thomas*, logion 70 (http://www.sacred-texts.com/chr/thomas.htm).
51. Dostoevsky, *Notes from Underground*, 17.
52. See Jung, *Two Essays on Analytical Psychology*, 184.
53. Steinbeck, *Grapes of Wrath*, 33.
54. Steinbeck, *Grapes of Wrath*, 35.
55. Steinbeck, *Grapes of Wrath*, 35.
56. Nietzsche, *Thus Spoke Zarathustra*, 75.
57. Nietzsche, *Thus Spoke Zarathustra*, 77.
58. Nietzsche, *Thus Spoke Zarathustra*, 76.
59. Nietzsche, *Gay Science*, 283.
60. Patterson and Robinson (translators), *Gospel of Thomas*, logion 49 (http://www.gnosis.org/naghamm/gth_pat_rob.htm)

Chapter 6
Beyond the Threshold and Through the Opposites

1. Jung, *Archetypes and the Collective Unconscious*, 221.
2. Nietzsche, *Thus Spoke Zarathustra*, 111.

3. A comment made by Campbell in *The Power of Myth* interview. In 1924, Campbell took a trip to Europe with his family on which he experienced a number of serendipitous encounters with people and ideas. Chief among these events was his meeting with Jiddu Krishnamurti on the transatlantic crossing. Krishnamurti introduced Campbell to the treasures of Eastern philosophy and religion, which were to be so influential on Campbell's subsequent thought and work, particularly in his association with Heinrich Zimmer, the great Indologist, whose unfinished works on Indian religion Campbell edited after Zimmer's passing.

4. Dante, *Divine Comedy*, 47–48.

5. Assagioli, *Transpersonal Development*, 123.

6. Hendrix, from the album *Are You Experienced?*

7. Jung, *Archetypes and the Collective Unconscious*, 121.

8. Campbell, *Hero with a Thousand Faces*, 303.

9. Nietzsche, "Beyond Good and Evil," aphorism 146 in *Basic Writings of Nietzsche*, 279.

10. Jung, *Memories, Dreams, Reflections*, 224.

11. See Grof, *Psychology of the Future.*

Chapter 7
Dual Threats: The Empire of the Ego and the Beast Within

1. Jung, *Mysterium Coniunctionis*, 362.

2. Compare logion 98 in Ross, *Gospel of Thomas*, 60.

3. Watts explores the notion of the double bind in *The Taboo Against Knowing Who You Are.* He explores similar themes in *The Meaning of Happiness.*

4. Ross, *Gospel of Thomas*, logion 6, 13; and logion 14, 18.

5. The axiom for which Campbell is best known is "follow your bliss" (*Way of Myth*, 146)—an exhortation to live one's life by pursuing one's deepest passion. Campbell's understanding of the meaning of this axiom seems to come from two main sources. The first is the Hindu metaphysical concept of *Sat-Chit-Ananda,* or being-consciousness-bliss, as it is sometimes translated. Campbell observes that at any given moment you might not know where your being is or even where your con-

sciousness is, but you will have an idea of where your bliss, your deepest happiness, lies. If you follow your bliss, he reasons, it will lead you to your source, your center, and bring your being and consciousness to the same place. The second source is Nietzsche's idea of *amor fati*, the love of one's fate, by which Nietzsche had in mind the cultivation of an affirmative, yea-saying approach to life, the joyous affirmation of every aspect of one's life experience. Bliss, thus understood, is not just happiness, for it includes pain and suffering too. It is an experience that embraces both agony and ecstasy. Only by affirming suffering can you come through to bliss and discover your deeper purpose and find fulfillment.

6. Ross, *Gospel of Thomas*, logion 97, 60.
7. Jung, *Two Essays on Analytical Psychology*, 169–170.
8. For Jung's discussion of this topic, see *Two Essays on Analytical Psychology*, 30–35.
9. Compare Jung: "There could be no greater mistake than for a Westerner to take up the practice of Chinese yoga, for that would merely strengthen his will and consciousness against the unconscious and bring about the very effect to be avoided. The neurosis would then simply be intensified" ("Commentary on 'The Secret of the Golden Flower'" in *Alchemical Studies*, par. 16, 14). For an analysis of Jung's relationship to Eastern philosophy and religion, see Clarke, *Jung and Eastern Thought*.
10. A comment made by Campbell in *The Power of Myth* interview with Bill Moyers.
11. Based on a comment made by Campbell in *The Power of Myth* interview with Bill Moyers.
12. Jung, *Memories, Dreams, Reflections*, 306. I do not wish to criticize Buddhist approaches here, merely to point out that this type of spiritual path might lead in a different direction to individuation.
13. See Jung, *Aion*, 70.
14. Jung, *Memories, Dreams, Reflections*, 200–201.
15. Jung, *Memories, Dreams, Reflections*, 201.
16. Jung, *Memories, Dreams, Reflections*, 203.
17. Nietzsche, *Thus Spoke Zarathustra*, 39.

18. Goethe, *Faust Part II*.
19. For Jung's discussion of the dark spirit in nature, which he describes as the "spirit of the depths," see Jung, *The Red Book*.
20. Jung, *Mysterium Coniunctionis*, 521.
21. Jung, *Mysterium Coniunctionis*, 272.
22. Jung, *Mysterium Coniunctionis*, 272.
23. The *prima materia*, also known as the arcane substance, is the literally the "first matter," symbolizing one's essential nature to which one must return in order to be transformed. Jung describes the *prima materia* as the mother of the *lapis*—the Philosopher's Stone. See Jung, *Mysterium Coniunctionis*, 18–19.
24. Jung, *Mysterium Coniunctionis*, 283.
25. Jung, *Mysterium Coniunctionis*, 283.
26. Jung, *Mysterium Coniunctionis*, 277. Jung defines the *aqua permanens* as "a ubiquitous and all-pervading essence, an anima mundi and the 'greatest treasure,' the innermost and most secret numinosum of man" (*Mysterium Coniunctionis*, 278).
27. Jung, *Psychology and Alchemy*, 340.
28. Jung, *Mysterium Coniunctionis*, 90.
29. According to Edward Edinger: "The fire for the process comes from the frustration of these instinctual desires themselves. Such an ordeal of frustrated desire is a characteristic feature of the developmental process" (*Anatomy of the Psyche*, 22).
30. Jung: *Psychology and Alchemy,* 90.
31. Tolkien, *Lord of the Rings*, 419.
32. Tolkien, *Lord of the Rings*, 418–419.
33. Tolkien, *Lord of the Rings*, 419.
34. Tolkien, *Lord of the Rings*, 419.
35. Tolkien, *Lord of the Rings*, 420.
36. Ross, *Gospel of Thomas*, logion 7, 13.
37. Campbell and Moyers, *Power of Myth*, 202.
38. See Neumann, *Origins and History of Consciousness*, 214. As we have seen, the Medusa theme is also conveyed in the figure of the god Pan, and his connected to the blind panic-terror or dread that can be triggered when consciousness first stares into the abyss of the unconscious.
39. Ross, *Gospel of Thomas*, logion 67, 49.
40. Nietzsche, *Thus Spoke Zarathustra*, 111.

41. For an explanation of the perinatal domain of the psyche, see Grof, *Psychology of the Future*, 29–56.
42. Nietzsche, *Thus Spoke Zarathustra*, 111.

Chapter 8
The Encounter with the Goddess and the Sacred Marriage

1. This is a point made by John Beebe in Jung and Segaller, *The Wisdom of the Dream, vol. 3: The World of Dreams.*
2. Jung, *Archetypes and the Collective Unconscious*, 29.
3. Jung, *Symbols of Transformation*, 260–261.
4. Jung, *Symbols of Transformation*, 413
5. Estes, *Women Who Run with the Wolves*, 6.
6. von Franz, "Process of Individuation," in *Man and His Symbols*, 193–195.
7. See Washburn, *Ego and Dynamic Ground*, 17–26.
8. von Franz, "Process of Individuation," in *Man and His Symbols*, 184–186.
9. Jung, *Archetypes and the Collective Unconscious*, 30.
10. Jung, *Archetypes and the Collective Unconscious*, 28.
11. Jung quoted in Jensen, *C. G. Jung, Emma Jung, Toni Wolff: A Collection of Remembrances*, 119.
12. Campbell, *Occidental Mythology*, 172.
13. Nietzsche, *Thus Spoke Zarathustra*, 231.
14. Nietzsche, *Thus Spoke Zarathustra*, 231.
15. Homer, *Odyssey*, 173.
16. The mast can also be seen as a crucifix symbol, suggesting the crucifixion of one's desire nature. See, for example, Neumann, *Great Mother* (plates), 120.
17. Homer, *Odyssey*, 69.
18. Homer, *Odyssey*, 72–73.
19. Homer, *Odyssey*, 73.
20. Homer, *Odyssey*, 73.
21. Ross, *Gospel of Thomas*, logion 22, 24.
22. Nietzsche, *Thus Spoke Zarathustra*, 91. For further examples, see "Of Old and Young Women," *Thus Spoke Zarathustra*, 91–93.
23. Washburn, *Ego and Dynamic Ground,* 188–196.
24. Washburn, *Ego and Dynamic Ground,* 196.

25. Yeats, "Easter, 1916" in *Collected Poems of W. B. Yeats*, 153.
26. Ross, *Gospel of Thomas*, logion 22, 24.
27. Campbell, *Hero with a Thousand Faces*, 115.
28. Campbell, *Hero with a Thousand Faces*, 107–110.
29. Campbell, *Hero with a Thousand Faces*, 126.
30. Ross, *Gospel of Thomas*, logion 22, 24.
31. Jung, *Mysterium Coniunctionis*, 129.
32. Jung, *Memories, Dreams, Reflections*, 222.
33. Jung, *Memories, Dreams, Reflections*, 223–224.
34. Jung, *Memories, Dreams, Reflections*, 224.
35. See Ross, *Gospel of Thomas*, logion 19, 21.

Chapter 9
The Return Journey: The World Transformed

1. Jung, *Mysterium Coniunctionis*, 471.
2. Campbell, *Hero with a Thousand Faces*, 189.
3. Yeats, "Easter 1916" in *The Collected Poems of W. B. Yeats*, 152–154.
4. Nietzsche, *Gay Science*, 228.
5. Campbell and Moyers, *Power of Myth*, 188.
6. Nietzsche, *Thus Spoke Zarathustra*, 47.
7. Campbell, *Way of Myth*, 123, 141.
8. See Jung, *Memories, Dreams, Reflections*, 195.
9. Jung, *Psychology and Alchemy*, 479.
10. Brooke, *Jung and Phenomenology*, 90.
11. Heidegger, *Being and Time*, 221 (quoted in Brooke, *Jung and Phenomenology*, 90).
12. Jung, *Memories, Dreams, Reflections*, 390.
13. Ross, *Gospel of Thomas*, logion 50, 38.
14. Campbell, *Hero with a Thousand Faces*, 204–205.
15. Assagioli, *Transpersonal Development*, 114.
16. Although in common usage the term *dark night of the soul* is now often employed to describe any period of existential crisis when one feels cut off from the divine or a source of greater life meaning, according to Assagioli the term should be reserved for the final agonizing stages of purification and transformation on the spiritual journey.

17. Assagioli, *Transpersonal Development*, 114; 153–154.
18. Assagioli, *Transpersonal Development*, 136.
19. Assagioli, *Transpersonal Development*, 127.
20. Jung, *Two Essays on Analytical Psychology*, 178.
21. Assagioli, *Transpersonal Development*, 113.
22. Ross, *Gospel of Thomas,* logion 17, 20.
23. Campbell, *Hero with a Thousand Faces*, 209.
24. Jung, *Mysterium Coniunctionis*, 534.
25. Jung, *Mysterium Coniunctionis*, 490.

Bibliography

Abrams, M. H. *Natural Supernaturalism: Tradition and Revolution in Romantic Literature.* 1971. Repr. New York: W. W. Norton & Co., 1973.

Assagioli, Roberto. *Transpersonal Development: The Dimension Beyond Psychosynthesis.* London: The Aquarian Press, 1991.

Aurobindo Ghose, Sri. *The Life Divine.* Pondicherry, India: Sri Aurobindo Ashram Press, 1970.

Bair, Deidre. *Jung: A Biography.* London: Little, Brown and Company, 2003.

Barrett, William. *Irrational Man: A Study in Existential Philosophy.* 1958. Repr., New York: Anchor Books, 1990.

Bascom, William. "The Forms of Folklore: Prose Narrative." 1965. In *Sacred Narrative: Readings in the Theory of Myth.* Edited by Alan Dundes. Berkeley: University of California Press, 1984.

Boeck, Wilhelm, and Jaime Sabartes. *Pablo Picasso.* Harry N. Abrams, 1961.

Blake, William. "The Auguries of Innocence." http://www.artofeurope.com/ blake/bla3.htm.

Brooke, Roger. *Jung and Phenomenology.* 1991. Repr., London: Routledge, 1993.

Campbell, Joseph. *The Flight of the Wild Gander.* Chicago: Gateway, 1972.

———. *The Hero with a Thousand Faces.* 3rd edition. Novato, CA: New World Library, 2008.

———. *The Hero's Journey: Joseph Campbell on His Life and Work.* Edited by Phil Cousineau. San Francisco: HarperSanFrancisco, 1991.

———. *The Inner Reaches of Outer Space: Metaphor as Myth and Religion.* Novato, CA: New World Library, 2002.

———. *The Masks of God, Vol. III: Occidental Mythology.* 1964. Repr., New York and London: Penguin Arkana, 1991.

————. *The Masks of God, Vol. IV: Creative Mythology.* 1968. Repr., New York and London: Penguin Arkana, 1991.

————. *The Mythic Dimension: Selected Essays 1959–1987.* Edited by Anthony Van Couvering. Novato, CA: New World Library, 1997/2007.

————. *Myths to Live By: Mythology for Our Time.* London: Souvenir Press, 1973.

————. *Reflections on the Art of Living: A Joseph Campbell Companion.* Selected and edited by Diane K. Osbon. New York: HarperCollins, 1991.

————. *Thou Art That: Transforming Religious Metaphor.* Novato, CA: New World Library, 2001.

Campbell, Joseph, and Bill Moyers. *Joseph Campbell and the Power of Myth with Bill Moyers.* New York: Mystic Fire Video, 1988.

————. *The Power of Myth.* 1988. Repr., New York: Anchor Books, 1991.

Campbell, Joseph, and Frazer Boa. *The Way of Myth: Talking with Joseph Campbell.* Boston, MA: Shambhala Publications, 1989.

Chauduri, Haridas. *The Evolution of Integral Consciousness.* Wheaton, IL: Quest Books, 1978.

Clarke, John J. *Jung and Eastern Thought: A Dialogue with the Orient.* London: Routledge, 1994.

Corbett, Lionel. *The Religious Function of the Psyche.* London: Routledge, 1996.

Cornford, F. M. *From Religion to Philosophy: A Study in the Origins of Western Speculation.* New York: Harper & Row, 1957.

Dante Aligheri. *The Divine Comedy.* Translated by C. H. Sisson. Oxford: Oxford University Press, 1998.

Dostoevsky, Fyodor. *Notes from Underground.* Translated by Richard Pevear and Larissa Volokhonsky. Repr., London: Vintage Books, 1993.

Dundes, Alan, ed. *Sacred Narrative: Readings in the Theory of Myth.* Berkeley: University of California Press, 1984.

Edinger, Edward. *Anatomy of the Psyche: Alchemical Symbolism in Psychotherapy.* Peru, IL: Open Court, 1991.

————. *The Creation of Consciousness: Jung's Myth for Modern Man.* Toronto: Inner City Books, 1984.

———. *Ego and Archetype: Individuation and the Religious Function of the Psyche.* 1973. Repr., Peru, IL: Open Court, 1992.

Eliade, Mircea. *Cosmos and History: The Myth of the Eternal Return.* New York: Harper & Row, 1959.

———. *The Sacred and the Profane: The Nature of Religion.* Translated by Willard R. Trask. New York: Harvest Books, 1968.

Eliot, T. S. "The Waste Land." In *Selected Poems.* London: Faber and Faber, 1954.

Estes, Clarissa Pinkola. *Women Who Run with the Wolves: Myths and Stories of the Wild Woman Archetype.* New York: Ballantine Books, 1995.

Frazer, James G. "The Fall of Man." 1918/1923. In *Sacred Narrative: Readings in the Theory of Myth.* Edited by Alan Dundes. Berkeley: University of California Press, 1984.

Freud, Sigmund. *Civilization and its Discontents.* 1930. Repr., NewYork: W. W. Norton & Co., 1989.

———. *New Introductory Lectures on Psycho-Analysis.* Standard edition. 1933. Translated by James Strachey. Repr., New York: W. W. Norton & Co., 1965.

Frey-Rohn, Liliane. *From Freud to Jung: A Comparative Study of the Psychology of the Unconscious.* Translated by Fred Engreen and Evelyn Engreen. New York: Delta, 1974.

Gebser, Jean. *The Ever-Present Origin.* Translated by Noel Barstad and Algis Mickunas. Athens, OH: Ohio University Press, 1984.

Goethe, J. W. von. *Faust Parts One and Two.* Translated by David Luke. Oxford: Oxford University Press (Two Volumes), 1999.

Grof, Stanislav. *The Cosmic Game: Explorations of the Frontiers of Human Consciousness.* Albany: State University of New York Press, 1998.

———. *Psychology of the Future: Lessons from Modern Consciousness Research.* Albany, NY: State University of New York Press, 2000.

Hanegraaff, Wouter. *New Age Religion and Western Culture: Esotericism in the Mirror of Secular Thought.* Albany, NY: State University of New York Press, 1998.

Heelas, Paul, and Linda Woodhead. *The Spiritual Revolution: Why Religion is Giving Way to Spirituality.* Oxford: Blackwell Publishing, 2005.

Hegel, G. F. W. *An Introduction to the Philosophy of History.* Translated by Leo Rauch. Indianapolis, IN: Hacket Publishing, 1988.

Heidegger, Martin. *Being and Time.* 1927. Translated by J Macquarrie and E. Robinson. Oxford: Basil Blackwell, 1962.

Hesse, Hermann. *Steppenwolf.* 1929. Revised edition. Translated by Basil Creighton. London: Penguin, 1965.

Henderson, Joseph. *Shadow and Self: Selected Papers in Analytical Psychology.* Wilmette, IL: Chiron Publications, 1990.

Hillman, James. *The Soul's Code: In Search of Character and Calling.* New York: Warner Books, 1996.

Hölderlin, Friedrich. *Selected Poems and Fragments.* Translated by Michael Hamburger. Repr., London: Penguin Classics, 1998.

Homer. *The Odyssey.* Translated by T. E. Lawrence. Repr., Ware, Herts.: Wordsworth Editions Limited, 1992.

Honko, Laurie. "The Problem of Defining Myth." 1972. In *Sacred Narrative: Readings in the Theory of Myth.* Edited by Alan Dundes. Berkeley: University of California Press, 1984.

Huxley, Aldous. *The Doors of Perception and Heaven and Hell.* 1954. Repr., New York: Harper Perennial, 1990.

———. *Huxley and God: Essays.* Edited by Jacqueline Hazard Bridgeman. Repr., New York: HarperSanFrancisco, 1992.

———. *The Perennial Philosophy.* 1946. Repr., London: Fontana Books, 1959.

Jaffe, Aniela. *The Myth of Meaning in the Work of C. G. Jung.* Zurich: Daimon Verlag, 1986.

James, William. *The Varieties of Religious Experience.* 1902. Edited by Martin E. Marty. New York: Penguin, 1985.

Jensen, Ferbe, ed. *C. G. Jung, Emma Jung, Toni Wolff: A Collection of Remembrances.* San Francisco: The Analytic Psychology Club of San Francisco Inc., 1982.

Joyce, James. *A Portrait of the Artist as a Young Man.* Ware, Herts, UK: Wordsworth Editions Limited, 1992.

Jung, Carl Gustav. *The Collected Works of C. G Jung.* 19 vols. Translated by R. F. C. Hull Princeton: Princeton University Press and London: Routledge & Kegan Paul, 1953–1979.

———. *Aion: Researches into the Phenomenology of the Self.* 2nd ed. *The Collected Works of C. G. Jung,* vol. 9, part II. Translated by R. F. C. Hull. Princeton: Princeton University Press, 1969.

————. *Alchemical Studies*. Vol. 13 of *The Collected Works of C. G. Jung*. Translated by R. F. C. Hull. Princeton: Princeton University Press, 1968.

————. "Analytical Psychology and the Weltanschauung." 1928/ 1931. In *The Structure and Dynamics of the Psyche*. Vol. 8 of *The Collected Works of C. G. Jung*. Translated by R. F. C. Hull. London: Routledge & Kegan Paul, 1960.

————. *Answer to Job. The Problem of Evil: Its Psychological and Religious Origins*. 1960. Translated by R. F. C. Hull. Repr., Cleveland, OH: Meridian Books, 1970.

————. "Archetypes of the Collective Unconscious." 1934/1954. In *The Archetypes and the Collective Unconscious*. 2nd ed. *The Collected Works of C. G. Jung*, vol. 9, part I. Translated by R. F. C. Hull. Princeton: Princeton University Press, 1968.

————. *The Archetypes and the Collective Unconscious*. 2nd ed. *The Collected Works of C. G. Jung*, vol. 9, part I. Translated by R. F. C. Hull. Princeton: Princeton University Press, 1968.

————. *C. G. Jung Speaking: Interviews and Encounters*. Edited by William McGuire and R. F. C. Hull. London: Pan Books Ltd., 1980.

————. *Civilization in Transition*. 2nd ed. Vol. 10 of *The Collected Works of C. G. Jung*. Translated by R. F. C. Hull. Princeton: Princeton University Press, 1970.

————. "Commentary on 'The Secret of the Golden Flower'." In *Alchemical Studies*. Vol. 13 of *The Collected Works of C. G. Jung*. Translated by R. F. C. Hull. Princeton: Princeton University Press, 1968.

————. *Man and His Symbols*. Edited by C. G. Jung and Marie-Louise von Franz. 1964. Repr., London: Aldus Books Ltd., 1979.

————. *Memories, Dreams, Reflections*. 1963. Edited by Aniele Jaffe. Translated by Richard Wilson and Clara Wilson. Repr., London: Flamingo, 1983.

————. *Mysterium Coniunctionis*. 2nd ed. 1955–1956. Vol. 14 of *The Collected Works of C. G. Jung*. Translated by R. F. C. Hull. Repr., Princeton: Princeton University Press, 1989.

————. *Nietzsche's Zarathustra: Notes on the Seminar Given in 1934–9*. Edited by James Jarrett. 2 Vols. Princeton, Princeton University Press, 1988.

———. "The Phenomenology of the Spirit in Fairytales." 1945/1948. In *The Archetypes and the Collective Unconscious.* 2nd ed. *The Collected Works of C. G. Jung*, vol. 9, part I. Translated by R. F. C. Hull. Princeton: Princeton University Press, 1968.

———. *Psychology and Alchemy*, 2nd ed. Vol. 12 of *The Collected Works of C. G. Jung.* Translated by R. F. C. Hull. Princeton: Princeton University Press, 1968.

———. *Psychology and Religion: West and East.* Vol. 11 of *The Collected Works of C. G. Jung.* Translated by R. F. C. Hull. London: Routledge & Kegan Paul, 1958.

———. "The Psychology of the Child Archetype." 1940. In *The Archetypes and the Collective Unconscious.* 2nd ed. *The Collected Works of C. G. Jung*, vol. 9, part I. Translated by R. F. C. Hull. Princeton: Princeton University Press, 1968.

———. *The Red Book.* Edited and Introduced by Sonu Shamdasani. Translated by Mark Kyburz, John Peck, and Sonu Shamdasani. New York: W. W. Norton & Co., 2009.

———. "Synchronicity: An Acausal Connecting Principle." 1955. In *The Structure and Dynamics of the Psyche.* Vol. 8 of *The Collected Works of C. G. Jung.* Translated by R. F. C. Hull. London: Routledge & Kegan Paul, 1960.

———. *The Spirit in Man, Art, and Literature.* 1966. Vol. 15 of *The Collected Works of C. G. Jung.* Translated by R. F. C. Hull. Repr., Princeton: Princeton University Press, 1971.

———. "The Spiritual Problem of Modern Man." 1928/1931. In *Civilization in Transition.* 2nd edition. Volume 10 of *The Collected Works of C. G. Jung.* Translated by R. F. C. Hull. Princeton: Princeton University Press, 1989.

———. *The Structure and Dynamics of the Psyche.* Vol. 8 of *The Collected Works of C. G. Jung.* Translated by R. F. C. Hull. London: Routledge & Kegan Paul, 1960.

———. *Symbols of Transformation.* 2nd ed. 1967. Vol. 5 of *The Collected Works of C. G. Jung.* Translated by R. F. C. Hull. Repr., Princeton: Princeton University Press, 1976.

———. *Two Essays on Analytical Psychology.* 2nd ed. 1966. Vol.7 of *The Collected Works of C. G. Jung.* Translated by R. F. C. Hull. Repr., London: Routledge, 1990.

———. *The Undiscovered Self.* 1958. Repr., New York: Signet, 2006.

Jung, Carl Gustav, and John Freeman. *Face to Face Interview: Professor Jung.* London: BBC Television, 1959.

Jung, Carl Gustav, and Karl Kerényi. *Science of Mythology: Essays on the Myth of the Divine Child and the Mysteries of Eleusis.* Revised edition. Repr., London: Routledge, 2002.

Jung, C. G., and Stephen Segaller. *The Wisdom of the Dream, vol. 3: The World of Dreams.* Homevision/RM Associates, 2000.

Kaufmann, Walter, ed. and trans. *Existentialism: From Dostoevsky to Sartre.* New York: Plume, 1975.

Kearns, Joseph. "The Shape of Nihilism: A Cosmological Exegesis of Nietzsche's 'The Madman'." In *Beyond a Disenchanted Cosmology. Archai: The Journal of Archeypal Cosmology.* Issue 3 (Fall 2011). Edited by Keiron Le Grice, Grant Maxwell, and Bill Streett. San Francisco: Archai Press, 2011.

King, Ursula. *Spirit of Fire: The Life and Vision of Teilhard de Chardin.* Maryknoll, NY: Orbis, 1996.

Lambdin, Thomas O., B. P. Grenfell, A. S. Hunt, and Bentley Layton, trans. *The Gospel of Thomas.* http://www.sacred-texts.com/chr/thomas.htm. (accessed August 1, 2012).

Larsen, Stephen, and Robin Larsen. *A Fire in the Mind: The Life of Joseph Campbell.* New York: Bantam Doubleday, 1993.

Le Grice, Keiron. *The Archetypal Cosmos: Rediscovering the Gods in Myth, Science and Astrology.* Edinburgh: Floris Books, 2010.

———. "The Dark Spirit in Nature: C. G. Jung and the Spiritual Transformation of Our Time." In *Beyond a Disenchanted Cosmology. Archai: The Journal of Archetypal Cosmology.* Issue 3 (Fall 2011). Edited by Keiron Le Grice, Grant Maxwell, and Bill Streett. San Francisco: Archai Press, 2011.

Lee, Bruce. *Bruce Lee: Artist of Life.* Compiled and edited by John Little. Boston, MA: Tuttle Publishing, 2001.

Malinowski, Bronislaw. "The Role of Myth in Life." In *Sacred Narrative: Readings in the Theory of Myth.* Edited by Alan Dundes. Berkeley: University of California Press, 1984.

Mann, Thomas. "Freud and the Future." 1937. In *Myth and Mythmaking.* Edited by Henry A. Murray. New York: George Braziller, 1960.

Metzner, Ralph. *The Unfolding Self: Varieties of Transformative Experience.* Novato, CA: Origin Press, 1998.

Murray, Henry A., ed. *Myth and Mythmaking*. New York: George Braziller, 1960.

———. "The Possible Nature of a 'Mythology' to Come." In *Myth and Mythmaking*. Edited by Henry A. Murray. New York: George Braziller, 1960.

Nellis, Krystina. "Hollywood Heroines: Here to Stay?" BBC News Website. August 14 2012. http://www.bbc.co.uk/news/entertainment-arts-19061388.

Neumann, Erich. *The Great Mother: An Analysis of the Archetype*. 1955/1963. Second edition. Translated by Ralph Manheim. Princeton: Princeton University Press, 1991.

———.*The Origins and History of Consciousness*. 1954. Translated by R. F. C. Hull. Princeton: Princeton University Press, 1995.

Nietzsche, Friedrich. *Basic Writings of Nietzsche*. Translated by Walter Kaufmann. New York: The Modern Library, 2000.

———. "Beyond Good and Evil." In *Basic Writings of Nietzsche*. Translated by Walter Kaufmann. New York: The Modern Library, 2000.

———. *The Birth of Tragedy: Out of the Spirit of Music*. Translated by Shaun Whiteside. Edited by Michael Tanner. London: Penguin Books, 1993.

———. "The Case of Wagner." In *Basic Writings of Nietzsche*. Translated by Walter Kaufmann. New York: The Modern Library, 2000.

———. "Ecce Homo." In *Basic Writings of Nietzsche*. Translated by Walter Kaufmann. New York: The Modern Library, 2000.

———. *The Gay Science: With a Prelude in Rhymes and an Appendix of Songs*. Translated by Walter Kaufmann. New York: Vintage Books, 1974.

———. "On the Genealogy of Morals." In *Basic Writings of Nietzsche*. Translated by Walter Kaufmann. New York: The Modern Library, 2000.

———. *Thus Spoke Zarathustra*. Translated by R. J. Hollingdale. New York: Penguin, 1968.

———. *Thus Spoke Zarathustra*. Translated by Thomas Common. Forgotten Books, 2008. http://www.forgottenbooks.org (accessed August 1, 2012).

————. *The Twilight of the Idols and The Anti-Christ*. 1990. Translated by Michael Tanner. Repr., London: Penguin, 2003.

Otto, Rudolf. *The Idea of the Holy*. 1923. Repr., London: Oxford University Press, 1958.

Patterson, Stephen J., and James M. Robinson, trans. *The Gospel of Thomas*. The Gnostic Society Library/The Nag Hammadi Library. http://www.gnosis.org/naghamm/gth_pat_rob.htm (accessed August 1, 2012).

Penrose, Roland. *Picasso: His Life and Work*. 3rd edition. Berkeley, CA: University of California, 1981.

Perera, Sylvia Brinton. *Descent to the Goddess: A Way of Initiation for Women*. Toronto: Inner City Books, 1981.

Plato. "Apology." In *Five Dialogues: Euthyphro, Apology, Crito, Meno, Phaedo*. 2nd edition. Trans. G. M. A. Grube. Indianapolis, IN: Hacket Publishing Company, Inc., 2002.

————. *Timaeus and Critias*. Translated by Desmond Lee. London: Penguin Books, 1977.

Rogerson, J. W. "Slippery Words: Myth." 1978–1979. In *Sacred Narrative: Readings in the Theory of Myth*. Edited by Alan Dundes. Berkeley: University of California Press, 1984.

Ross, Hugh McGregor, trans. *The Gospel of Thomas*. London: Watkins Publishing, 2002.

Samuels, Andrew. *Jung and the Post-Jungians*. London: Routledge, 1986.

Sartre, Jean-Paul. *Being and Nothingness: An Essay on Ontology*. 1943. Translated by Hazel E. Barnes. Repr., Abingdon, Oxon: Routledge, 2005.

Schopenhauer, Arthur. *The World as Will and as Representation*. Translated by E. F. J. Payne. Mineola, NY: Dover Publications, 1966.

Segal, Robert A. *Joseph Campbell: An Introduction*. 1987. Repr., New York: Meridian, 1990.

————. "Joseph Campbell's Theory of Myth." In *Sacred Narrative: Readings in the Theory of Myth*. Edited by Alan Dundes. Berkeley: University of California Press, 1984.

————. *Myth: A Very Short Introduction*. Oxford: Oxford University Press, 2004.

Shamdasani, Sonu. *Jung and the Making of Modern Psychology: The Dream of a Science.* Cambridge: Cambridge University Press, 2003.

Solomon, Robert C. and Kathleen M. Higgins. *A Short History of Philosophy.* New York: Oxford University Press, 1996.

Spengler, Oswald. *The Decline of the West.* London: George Allen & Unwin, 1926.

Steinbeck, John. *Cannery Row.* 1945. Repr., London: Mandarin, 1995.

———. *The Grapes of Wrath.* 1939. New York: Penguin, 2002.

Swimme, Brian. *The Hidden Heart of the Cosmos: Humanity and the New Story.* Maryknoll, NY: Orbis Books, 1996.

Tacey, David. *Spirituality Revolution: The Emergence of Contemporary Spirituality.* Hove, Sussex: Brunner-Routledge, 2004.

Tarnas, Richard. *Cosmos and Psyche: Intimations of a New World View.* New York: Viking, 2006.

———. *The Passion of the Western Mind: Understanding the Ideas That Have Shaped Our World View.* 1991. Repr., London: Pimlico, 1993.

Teilhard de Chardin, Pierre. *The Phenomenon of Man.* New York: Harper & Row, 1965.

Tolkien, J. R. R. *The Lord of the Rings.* London: Guild Publishing, 1980.

Toynbee, Arnold J. *A Study of History*, Vol 1. 1946. Abridgement of Volumes I–VI by D. C. Somervell. Oxford: Oxford University Press, 1987.

———. *A Study of History*, Vol 2. 1957. Abridgement of Volumes VII–X by D. C. Somervell. Oxford: Oxford University Press, 1987.

van Gennep, Arnold. *The Rites of Passage.* Reprint edition. Chicago: University of Chicago Press, 1961.

Vogler, Christopher. *The Writer's Journey: Mythic Structure for Writers.* Third edition. Studio City, CA: Michael Wiese Productions, 2007.

von Franz, Marie-Louise. *Archetypal Patterns in Fairytales.* Toronto: Inner City Books, 1997.

———. "The Process of Individuation." In *Man and His Symbols.* Edited by C. G. Jung and Marie-Louise von Franz. 1964. Repr., London: Aldus Books Ltd., 1979.

Washburn, Michael. *The Ego and the Dynamic Ground: A Transpersonal Theory of Human Development*. 2nd edition. Albany: State University of New York Press, 1995.

Watts, Alan. *The Meaning of Happiness. The Quest for Freedom of the Spirit in Modern Psychology and the Wisdom of the East*. 2nd edition. New York: Harper & Row, 1970.

———. *The Taboo Against Knowing Who You Are*. 1966. Repr., New York: Vintage Books, 1989.

———. *The Two Hands of God: The Myths of Polarity*. 1963. Repr., London: Rider & Company, 1978.

Weber, Max. "Science as a Vocation." 1919. In *From Max Weber: Essays on Sociology*. Translated and edited by H. H. Gerth and C. Wright Mills. Repr., New York: Oxford University Press, 1946.

Whitmont, Edward. *Return of the Goddess*. New York: Crossroad Publishing Company, 1982.

Wilber, Ken. *Sex, Ecology, Spirituality: The Spirit of Evolution*. Boston: Shambhala Publications, 2000.

Woodman, Marion. *The Pregnant Virgin: A Process of Psychological Transformation*. Toronto: Inner City Books, 1985.

Yeats, William Butler. "Easter, 1916." In *The Collected Poems of W. B. Yeats*. Ware, Herts, UK: Wordsworth Editions Limited, 1994.

Motion Pictures and Television Series

Avildsen, John G., director, *The Karate Kid*. Culver City, CA: Columbia Pictures, 1984.

Chaffey, Dan, director. *Jason and the Argonauts*. Culver City, CA: Columbia Pictures, 1963.

Darabont, Frank, director. *The Shawshank Redemption*. Burbank, CA: Warner Bros. Pictures, 1994.

Davis, Desmond, director. *Clash of the Titans*. Beverly Hills, CA: Metro-Goldwyn-Mayer, 1981.

Del Toro, Guillermo, director. *Pan's Labyrinth [El Laberinto del Fauno]*. New York: Picturehouse, 2006.

Disney, Walt, producer. *Fantasia*. Burbank, CA: Walt Disney Productions, 1940.

———. *Pinocchio*. Burbank, CA: Walt Disney Productions, 1940.

Donner, Richard, and Richard Lester, directors. *Superman II*. Burbank, CA: Warner Bros. Pictures, 1980.

Fellini, Federico, director. *8 ½*. Culver City, CA: Columbia Pictures, 1963.

———. *La Dolce Vita*. New York: Koch-Lorber Films, 1960.

Fleming, Victor, director. *The Wizard of Oz*. Beverly Hills, CA: Metro-Goldwyn-Mayer, 1939.

Hodges, Mike, director. *Flash Gordon*. Universal City, CA: Universal Studios, 1980.

Jackson, Peter, director. *The Fellowship of the Ring*. Part 1 of *The Lord of the Rings* trilogy. Los Angeles: New Line Cinema, 2001.

Lachowski, Andy, and Larry Lachowksi, directors. *The Matrix*. Burbank, CA: Warner Bros. Pictures, 1999.

Lucas, George, director. *Star Wars*. Episodes I–VI. San Francisco: Lucasfilm, 1977, 1980, 1983, 2002, 2005, 2008.

Senensky, Ralph, director. "This Side of Paradise." *Star Trek* (Original Series). Created and produced by Gene Roddenberry. Los Angeles: Desilu Productions, 1967.

Shyamalan, M. Night, director. *Unbreakable*. Burbank, CA: Touchstone Pictures, 2000.

Music LPs

The Doors. *The Doors*. Burbank, CA: Elektra Records, 1967.

The Jimi Hendrix Experience. *Are You Experienced?* London: Track Records, 1967.

Index

Made in the USA
Columbia, SC
10 October 2017